PRODUCING SPOILERS

PRODUCING SPOILERS

Peacemaking and the Production
of Enmity in a Secular Age

Joyce Dalsheim

OXFORD
UNIVERSITY PRESS

OXFORD
UNIVERSITY PRESS

Oxford University Press is a department of the University of Oxford.
It furthers the University's objective of excellence in research, scholarship,
and education by publishing worldwide.

Oxford   New York
Auckland   Cape Town   Dar es Salaam   Hong Kong   Karachi
Kuala Lumpur   Madrid   Melbourne   Mexico City   Nairobi
New Delhi   Shanghai   Taipei   Toronto

With offices in
Argentina   Austria   Brazil   Chile   Czech Republic   France   Greece
Guatemala   Hungary   Italy   Japan   Poland   Portugal   Singapore
South Korea   Switzerland   Thailand   Turkey   Ukraine   Vietnam

Oxford is a registered trade mark of Oxford University Press
in the UK and certain other countries.

Published in the United States of America by
Oxford University Press
198 Madison Avenue, New York, NY 10016

© Oxford University Press 2014

Library of Congress Cataloging-in-Publication Data
Dalsheim, Joyce, 1961–
Producing spoilers : peacemaking and the production of enmity
in a secular age / Joyce Dalsheim.
p.   cm.
Includes bibliographical references and index.
ISBN 978–0–19–994442–2 (cloth : alk. paper)   1. Peace-building—Religious
aspects. 2. Peace-building—Middle East. 3. Radicalism—Religious
aspects. 4. Radicalism—Middle East. 5. Enemies—Middle East. 6. Religion
and politics. 7. Religion and politics—Middle East. 8. Arab-Israeli
conflict—1993—Peace. 9. Judaism and politics—Israel. I. Title.
BL65.P4D35 2014
303.6'6—dc23
2013049364

1   3   5   7   9   8   6   4   2

Printed in the United States of America on acid-free paper

For Edan and Ziev, who deserve much more than a dedication.

CONTENTS

ACKNOWLEDGMENTS: TO BE AT HOME IN THE WORLD

"[T]he unwillingness to see phenomena . . . without applying categories to them. . . . It is just this that constitutes theoretical helplessness."

—Hannah Arendt (2013/1970:79)

"[T]he rabbis themselves . . . treated language as that part of the world given by God to humanity in order to make sense of the world. For that reason . . . the rabbis were bound to stretch language to its utmost, to make it reveal as many of its potential meanings as possible."

—Jonathan Boyarin (1996:64–65, referring to D. Boyarin's analysis)

This book is an attempt to see beyond categories, to stretch language in ways that might broaden the potential meanings of difficult ideas like peacemaking and enmity. Stretching language and thought is one way to escape theoretical helplessness. But it may not be a comforting or comfortable endeavor either for the reader or for the writer. It can require a particular kind of endurance and produce a sense of exhaustion for both (Povinelli 2012). That's just the way it works. But exhausting or not, such stretching is part of the process of trying to understand. And understanding, Hannah Arendt explains, "as distinguished from having correct information and scientific knowledge, is a complicated process which never produces unequivocal results. It is an unending activity by which, in constant change and variation, we come to terms with and reconcile ourselves to reality, that is, try to be at home in the world" (Arendt 1994/1954:307–308).

She went on to say that it is common to "want to cut this process short in order to educate others and elevate public opinion." These words seem especially pertinent in times of economic crisis, when budgets are slashed and funding that might support certain kinds of thinking in the humanities and social sciences is increasingly difficult to find. Funding always seems to be available to research war, weaponry, or, these days, terrorism. And funding often turns to, and returns to us, particular kinds of thinking that explore the complications of keeping systems of political and institutional inequality intact.

But we might think of such funding decisions as Arendtian short-cuts. These kinds of short-cuts worried her because she thought that the "result of all such attempts is indoctrination. . . . Indoctrination is dangerous because it springs primarily from a perversion, not of knowledge, but of understanding. The result of understanding is meaning which we originate in the very process of living insofar as we try to reconcile ourselves to what we do and what we suffer" (Arendt 1994/1954:309). Trying to be at home in the world in this way, stretching our thoughts in the service of understanding, can and probably should lead to intense debate, which is what I encountered all along the way as I discussed and presented and published pieces of this book. Here I would like to thank the people who helped me by joining and furthering these debates in so many different ways.

I would like to begin by thanking Ursula Le Guin and Salman Rushdie, whose work I was reading as I wrote, because really good creative writing plays an under-recognized role in opening up a space for thinking and understanding. I would like to thank Talal Asad for his thinking and teaching and for demonstrating modes of inquiry that stretch the meanings of language and challenge us to rethink much of what we've come to take for granted.

I wrote in the pre-dawn hours, while the world was sleeping, before class and in the evenings afterward, on airplanes and in coffee shops, at the dining room table whose chairs supported sagging piles of library books, in the passenger's seat of our car on long family trips, and during precious stolen weekends away from home in Wilmington and in Black Mountain. I am especially indebted to Ron Collman and his family, as well as to Amy Diamond for providing me with spaces away from home in which to think and write. The time for this book came directly out of the time I should have spent with my family. For my distraction and neglect I want to apologize to Rafi, Edan, and Ziev. And for their (usually) patient tolerance of that distraction and neglect and those endless piles of books scattered about every horizontal surface of the house, I want to thank them. To my parents, Olga and Steve, who also always deserve more attention than I ever seem to have time for, I apologize. But I would also like to thank them for often acting as research assistants and for always being there for me. To Alisa, for always being there for them, thank you!

Many thanks go to Gregory Starrett, who first suggested, shortly after I published my first book, that the tangled connections between the two articles I was then working on, and the flurry of ideas they were forcing me to confront, might be an indication that the task merited more sustained treatment in the form of another book. I encourage my family to blame him for the sacrifices they have endured over the last two years. Although Gregg has provided endless wisdom and support for this project, he wishes to minimize his contributions, and has told me that he would much rather be renowned around the world, above all else, for his profoundly admirable humility.

I am very grateful to countless colleagues for reading or listening to versions of this work, providing encouragement or arguing strenuously and with strong principle against it, and especially grateful to those who cared enough to ask difficult questions: Gil Anidjar, Mohammed Bamyeh, Zvi Bekerman, Louise Bethlehem, Nurit Bird-David, Jonathan Boyarin, Glen Bowman, Rebecca Bryant, Virginia Dominguez, Charlie Kurzman and the Carolina Center for the Study of the Middle East and Muslim Civilizations, and Valerie Hoffman for organizing the New Middle East Conference. Thanks belong to Amalia Sa'ar for inviting me to Haifa, and to Hillel Cohen, Assaf Harel, Loren Lybarger, Yehuda Shenhav, Jackie Smith, and Rebecca Stein for insightful conversations.

Two parts of this book were published in different form in *Theory, Culture and Society*, and in *Social Analysis*. I am grateful to the editors and anonymous reviewers for their careful readings and sometimes furiously critical feedback. Thanks go to my editor Cynthia Read at Oxford for all her support and to the anonymous reviewers of this manuscript. I am also grateful to the audiences, co-presenters, and discussants at numerous meetings of the American Anthropological Association and the Middle East Studies Association (MESA). In particular, I am indebted to Andrew Shryrock for his incisive comments as discussant on our MESA panel, and to Virginia Dominguez for attending my talks at Urbana-Champaign and in Chicago and for asking the kinds of difficult questions that seemed to be on so many peoples' minds; questions that force one to think a little deeper and address important concerns. I am indebted to a very long list of other people as well, some of whom—like, perhaps, some of those named above—find this work so troubling that they prefer not to be associated with it.

In times of economic drought, public institutions like mine are particularly hard-hit. So, I am very grateful to UNC Charlotte for awarding me a Faculty Research Grant that will help further my research. Thanks go in particular to Dean Nancy Gutierrez of the College of Liberal Arts and Sciences for insisting that thinking matters and providing a space in which to do so.

Most importantly, perhaps, I also owe a deep debt of gratitude to the founding and sustaining members of the highly innovative Screen Porch Institute (SPI), where unconventional thinking is encouraged and ideas are nurtured. Finally, for his unconditional and unending support of the SPI, and for long, thoughtful walks, I would like to thank Rusty.

INTRODUCTION

Everybody loves a good story (or at least so we're told). Whether it ends happily or tragically matters less, as long as the story is compelling and makes you want to keep on reading or listening. As long as there is a plot that leads from beginning to end, whether in a newspaper or in a novel, we crave the narrative. Narrativity helps make sense of the world, drawing together all sorts of information to give meaning to practices and events that might otherwise not make sense. Narrative closure provides a sort of satisfaction; now we have the answer, we know what ought to be done.

But the world isn't like that, and neither is this book. Many readers will crave a narrative that defines the conflict in Israel and Palestine, one that names its heroes and villains and points in the direction of a just and peaceful resolution. There are already countless books that instruct on who is right and who is wrong, who stole the land and to whom it belongs, but this is not one of them. This book does not offer an answer to the conflict. It is precisely *not* another narrative that teaches a particular truth about who is right and wrong. Instead, it suggests that the "who" in this case is a "what," and provides some insight on how we got into this mess in which there appears to be a single, intractable conflict.

That "what" is, at least partially, the rigid framework of nations and nationalism that has proven to be so resilient to scholarly deconstruction that, two decades after Benedict Anderson first published *Imagined Communities*, we find we can still not quite find a way to heed the call to "think ourselves beyond the nation," as Arjun Appadurai (1993) has urged. In this sense, parts of this book may seem very familiar. To experts on nationalism and "the Israeli-Palestinian conflict" in particular, some chapters and sections will contain information you've heard and read before. I re-present it here both for the benefit of non-experts and in an attempt to make the familiar strange, in the hope that we might think again in a different way about things we're convinced we already know. Those readers well versed in the anthropology of Israel/Palestine may find that parts of this book resonate uncannily with Jonathan Boyarin's *Palestine and Jewish History*. In some ways, I think this is a continuation of that project (although I don't know if Jonathan would agree). Both projects try to demonstrate the always ongoing, fragile, and tentative work of producing separate national collectives in Israel/Palestine as well as the frustrating, endless project of *tikkun olam* that critical scholarship aspires to partake in.

My purpose here is not to provide a new recipe for solving this or other conflict situations; I leave that to the peace scholars and policymakers. I ask readers to resist the desire for either narrative or theoretical closure and instead to clear some space to ponder what lies outside the categories through which we generally arrange people and their projects. Readers will find all sorts of examples of how we might be able to push our thinking beyond the recipes of conventional contemporary peacemaking. (Some readers will be amused by some of these stories and repelled by others, and vice versa.) These examples are set before you not to distinguish between good and evil, but to illuminate other sides of the familiar tales often told about this place, its peoples, and their conflicts. They emphasize connections, commonalities, and strategies that cross the boundaries of ethnic, religious, or political divisions and might spark the imagination. In suggesting similarities among ideas and practices that are often thought to be at odds, these stories reframe what we take to be surprising and might leave some readers feeling frustrated or confused. If so, I hope readers might consider those sensations as they would the kind of confusion or frustration Rushdie's *Midnight's Children* evokes (and only wish I had a tiny fraction of Rushdie's talent).

This book is an attempt to think beneath hegemony and counter-hegemony, and beneath and outside categories of Israeli and Palestinian. This is not a new endeavor, but it is a difficult one requiring every bit as much practice as that which has led to the development and hardening of those categories themselves. This thinking beneath or thinking outside can be done in many ways, not all of which seek to undermine or to dissolve this categorical distinction, but simply to see it as part of a broader conceptual system and to take note of how adjusting or changing other terms within that system alters the substance and significance of the distinction itself.

In following the call to "think beyond the nation," I first provide a conceptual framework that I am calling "scattered hegemonies/ scattered heterotopias." Second, I outline a way of thinking about the nation as a set of relationships between the ideas of people, territory, and sovereignty, and focus on sovereignties rather than identities. Because many scholars—including me—have focused on identity and its deconstruction as a way of seeing something else and making room for subaltern voices and visions, here I ask who can be counted as subaltern and under what conditions. I am hoping to contribute not only to thinking about Israel/Palestine but also to the broader processes of ethical engagement involved in living together well. And so, while this book is about Israel/Palestine, it is not only about Israel/Palestine.

Critical theorists sometimes provide a moral to their stories. Some have suggested, for example, that democracy as a practical political arrangement is flawed and just needs to be better. Or that "democratic sensibility" (Asad 2011) needs to be cultivated, yet is undermined by democracy as a state political system. I provide no such comfort, no conclusion or moral to the story, but remain with a set of unsettling juxtapositions instead. In his recent book *The Moral Imagination*, John Paul Lederach illustrates some ways in which the work of a peacemaker cannot really follow a linear narrative path (although he does not use these words) because peacebuilding, like life itself, does not happen in just the ways we've planned. Lederach is a leading scholar of faith-based peacemaking. His work is a deeply ethical, spiritually motivated project of making the world a better place through active intervention in conflict situations. Based on extensive experience working for peace around the globe, he offers "the moral imagination" as a guiding tool for peacemakers. The moral imagination involves, among other things, paying attention to that which makes people's lives meaningful, drawing on their knowledge and sensibilities to think creatively, imaginatively, and artistically, taking advantage of opportunities that arise serendipitously in ways that can facilitate a more lasting and encompassing peace. The anthropologist in me is worried about which knowledges and sensibilities peacemakers choose to draw upon and which meanings will be discarded or minimalized. And so I discuss a range of local knowledges, sensibilities, and practices found among people in Israel/Palestine that some peacemakers might not notice, and that some might find inappropriate, unappealing, or just irrelevant. But it is precisely these minor or outside examples that have something important to teach us. Although I am not proposing a solution to conflict, it is in the spirit of peacebuilding that I offer this book. I don't know if Lederach would consider this an endeavor of the moral imagination, but I hope so.

The first part of the book (Chapters 1 through 3) is about the "campfire," a hegemonic moral order in which liberal peacemaking takes place. Those readers already familiar with liberal peacemaking and its poststructural critique might choose to skip parts of Chapter 1. Experts on nationalism and its deconstruction might find they are already familiar with parts of Chapter 1 as well. Experts on the case of Israel/Palestine can skip the first part of Chapter 2 and begin reading at the subheading "Storytelling, Dialogue, and Peacemaking."

The book begins by looking at how the foundations of contemporary peacemaking are produced and reproduced at the same time as peacemaking produces enemies. It investigates the importance of recognition to the parties in conflict, asking who is being recognized, as what, and what such recognition accomplishes. Peace processes involve mutual recognition of the parties to conflict and of the narratives enemy factions tell about the conflict, its causes, and the suffering of the parties involved. However, as Franz Fanon taught us, recognition itself is not necessarily liberating, and in this case does not necessarily move beyond positions of enmity. In Chapter 2, I illustrate how such recognition can also work to continue to produce identities in conflict. This chapter is primarily concerned with how national groups are reproduced through peacemaking work, taking into account the efforts of grassroots activists to deconstruct national identity and find common interests across presumed enemy lines.

Chapter 3 considers history, alternative histories, and alternatives to history in the process of making peace. Not all versions of the past can be included in peacemaking efforts, either at the diplomatic or at the grassroots level, and narrations always rely on exclusion to achieve a sense of coherence. This chapter considers the stories, especially the religious stories, that are often left out or marginalized in mainstream peacebuilding narratives. It considers why certain versions of the past are difficult to include as part of secular peace processes and suggests moving beyond the idea of *adding more* stories or providing alternative pasts. Instead, this chapter looks at the idea of alternatives *to* conventional histories in the form of moral tales about the past told by Palestinian and Jewish communities in the contentious city of Hebron. These communities are usually considered to be among the most impassioned enemies but they may be finding ways to move beyond historical narratives that frame them as necessary antagonists.

The second part of the book (Chapters 4 through 7) offers another conceptualization. It begins with alternatives to history (because historicism is trapped within the flames of the campfire) and pulls together the stories in this book and provides additional ones that are meant to push our thinking even further. Readers who are sure that we (critical scholars who sit around our own campfire) have already managed to think beyond the nation and its secular concepts of temporality and historicism are encouraged to consider once more the ways in which these ideas trap us, even when we try very hard to avoid them. But those who just can't stand thinking about it again may want to begin reading at Chapter 4. (In any case, all readers are invited to approach this book from front to back, back to front, or middle and outward—or, like me, you might start by reading the footnotes [endnotes, in this case], my favorite part of any scholarly work.)

Chapter 4 considers how certain taken-for-granted assumptions, in particular the naturalness of nations and a particular narrative of progress, interfere with even the most progressive scholars and activists seeking peace and social justice; indeed, sometimes they even seem to undermine their own goals. Ideas of progressive temporality are deeply embedded in our modern secular age. These ideas, often unwittingly, enter into and potentially undermine the possibility of imagining and enacting a more peaceful future and seeking social justice. Chapter 4 looks at how the idea of anachronism is variously deployed in the space of Israel/Palestine, conditioning the ways in which ethnic, national, and religious groups are either hated or pitied as a result of this thinking. This part of the book sheds light on a conundrum about who or what belongs to the past, and how thinking in such terms can contribute to the production of moral collectives and to the production of enmity.

The book then considers some of the beliefs and practices that get pushed to the margins, beyond the blinding light of the campfire. Chapter 5 looks at local solutions arrived at among Israelis and Palestinians who find ways to cooperate that might also be considered collaborating with the enemy. These local forms of working together are examples of the ways in which people are thinking and acting beyond the national order of things. While scholars have called for such "thinking beyond the nation," they have tended to promote a deconstruction of national identity toward achieving that goal. Here people retain their collective identities as well as their attachment to territory, but imagine and act according to alternative ideas about sovereignty. Finally, I suggest it is worthwhile to consider these unusual acts not as unusual, but as the other side of scattered hegemony, to recognize the patterns emerging in these other spaces that we tend to ignore.

Chapters 6 and 7, the last two chapters of the book, compare some of the ideas and practices of the Rabbi introduced at the opening of the book to ideas recently proposed by a secular Palestinian intellectual to show how these patterns are emerging beyond the campfire, a pattern that reveals subtle changes in everyday practices that point toward other ways of living together beyond the seemingly intractable conflict that characterizes Israel/Palestine today.

PRODUCING SPOILERS

Peace and Justice
in a Secular Age

PRELUDE

Once upon a time there was a rabbi. He was a very wise and learned rabbi, yet so many of the people around him said he was crazy. Some of the people in his own community threw rocks at his house. "He's not just crazy," they would say, "he's dangerous!" This rabbi lived in an Israeli settlement in the West Bank, yet advocated and practiced coexistence with Palestinians. He was passionate about the Holy Land, but not concerned about owning it. He believed Jews should be able to live anywhere in the Land of Israel, but he was less interested in Jewish political control over that land. Because he held these two beliefs together, people from across the range of social, religious, and political beliefs in Israel marginalized him and thought he was strange. He seemed to be living beyond what could be imagined about the nature of territorial nationalism and human sovereignty.

Stories of "crazy" rabbis are the stuff of *meises*, tales that are told in order to convey a message indirectly. Like fables, they are tales with moral messages, often told by other rabbis who have been asked for their advice. Maybe the story of this rabbi should be considered a *bubbe meise*, the kind of story that grandmothers might tell, stories that are often discounted as nonsense when, in fact, a great deal can be learned from listening to them very carefully.[1]

This rabbi is a very real character who lives at the edge of seemingly contradictory moral orders, an edge that marks the boundaries of the acceptable. I have concealed his identity here because I met him while carrying out ethnographic fieldwork among Israeli settlers, and have concealed the identities of all the subjects of that research project (Dalsheim 2011). Beyond simple methodological and ethical issues of research and representation, naming this rabbi seems once again to mark him as exceptional; this could mean exceptionally insightful, but it has often been an easy way of disregarding what he might represent. To think of his ways of being and believing as an exception can mean they are representative of nothing other than his individual eccentricity, and this, I submit, is both untrue and not the point. There are others who share these ways of being and believing—sometimes partially and often fluctuating, as with all sets of beliefs and practices. But more importantly, his marginalization as eccentric and as not representative of broader beliefs, practices, and trends marks the borders of a powerful moral order.[2]

The moral order that produces the Rabbi as outside its bounds, and therefore as crazy, is a complicated one. For its adherents, it promises both freedom and justice, but it does so within a framework in which those values are only guaranteed by the division of the world into nation-states in which well-defined populations exercise political sovereignty over territory.[3] The Rabbi values boundaries that define human difference, but rejects both human sovereignty and the importance of territorial borders. The Rabbi values the difference, for example, between being Jewish or gentile, as Jewishness is a central part of his own identity. And, although he rejects the notion of human sovereignty, he lives every day as though he has agency, making the kinds of decisions necessary to repair the world or make it a dwelling place for the Lord (*tikkun olam*) as required by God. After all, although only He is ultimately sovereign, the Lord sets choices before human beings, requiring them to make decisions and asking that they choose righteousness.

As we will see later, the moral order that produces the Rabbi as outside its bounds can trap even those who may not wish to fully adhere to it. People who accept the idea of human sovereignty and territorial borders, but who reject the naturalness of human difference, find that when they try to solve the problem of conflict in Israel/Palestine by talking about territorial compromise, they have no way to do so except by reinscribing the very differences they would like to overcome. Their moral order demands that *recognizing the humanity* of people in situations of conflict requires recognizing them as members of ethnic/national groups: Israelis and Palestinians. I will say a great deal more about matters of recognition in the next chapter. For now, I return to the contemporary moral order in which what some political scientists call "liberal peacemaking" or "democratic peace" takes place (Newman, Paris, and Richmond 2009).

This moral order can be understood in terms of what Charles Taylor (2007) calls a secular age, the contemporary moment in which tolerance for differences is valued and different ways of being and believing are understood as collective identities or traditions to be respected.[4] The secular age, or (Western) modernity (Taylor 2002), is characterized by a conception of the moral order that has become so self-evident it is sometimes difficult to see. It is even more difficult to imagine that this might be only *one* among many possible ways of ordering society. This moral order is founded on a belief in the autonomy of the individual and, according to Taylor, is characterized by other features, including the market economy, the public sphere, and sovereignty in the form of self-governing peoples. I am especially interested in the contemporary investment in self-governing, the notion of democracy as rule of the people by the people, which is dependent on the idea of human sovereignty. In other words, self-rule requires both a collective self to be ruled and a collective with the capacity, the power, and the authority to govern and to control, to make rules and enforce them. It seems to me that much in mainstream efforts at peacemaking turns on the possibility of such sovereignty, while many peacemakers might also argue that such a thing is elusive at best in the contemporary world, if not altogether impossible.

In this book I argue that within this hegemonic moral order peacemakers may unintentionally undermine their own goals through recognition and peacebuilding activities that reinscribe enemy groups[5] in the process of producing a moral community.[6] Gil Anidjar (2003), echoing the words of Jacques Derrida, has asked if the enemy is the cause of conflict or its product.[7] This book considers some of the ways in which peacemaking itself works to *produce* enmity. Before delving deeper, first allow me to set the stage for the stories that will unfold here.

SOVEREIGNTY/NATION

[Moses] conceived and executed the astonishing project of creating a nation out of a swarm of wretched fugitives, without arts, arms, talents, virtues or courage, who were wandering as a horde of strangers over the face of the earth without a single inch of ground to call their own. Out of this wandering and servile horde Moses had the audacity to create a body politic, a free people . . . he gave them that durable set of institutions, proof against time, fortune and conquerors, which five thousand years have not been able to destroy or even alter . . . To prevent his people from melting away among foreign peoples, he gave them customs and usages incompatible with those of other nations; he over-burdened them with peculiar rites and ceremonies; he inconvenienced them in a thousand ways in order to keep them constantly on the alert and to make them forever strangers among men.

—Rousseau, in Gilroy (2005:155–156)

Paul Gilroy quotes Jean-Jacques Rousseau describing a very early "project of creating a nation," marking what might be thought of as the beginning of analysis and debate on the origins and nature of nations. Scholars have been deliberating for decades whether nations are primordial groups or modern constructs. Ernest Gellner (1981, 1983) argues that nations are in fact modern. Benedict Anderson goes further, arguing that nationalism "invents nations where they do not exist" (1983:6) and demonstrating the processes through which nations come into being as imagined communities. One might argue, according to this definition, that Moses was a very early inventor of the nation. The nation, Anderson wrote, "is an imagined political community—and imagined to be both inherently limited and sovereign. It is imagined because the members of even the smallest nation will never know most of their fellow-members, meet them, or even hear of them, yet in the minds of each lives the image of their communion" (1983:6). Earlier than Anderson, Eugen Weber (1976) described the processes through which "the French" were produced as a national collective. Modernization was key. Building roads that connect people, instituting public education, determining a single language, all worked to produce a collective out of disparate groups. It seems that whether the social groups in question are ancient or modern, most scholars agree that national groups are social and historical constructs.[8] Later scholarship not only continued to question the naturalness of nations, but also analyzed nationalism as inherently racist and cruel. And yet, despite all this scholarship, many of us continue to think of (or without meaning to, just reproduce as if inevitable) nations as naturally occurring groups, and to tell stories about nation-states as the obvious political actors within the order of our world.

Stories that coincide with this order are those we tell ourselves around what I will call "the campfire." I borrow the metaphor of the campfire from an essay by Ursula Le Guin (1980). The stories we tell accomplish all sorts of things. They remind us of who we are and how we arrived at this time and place. They remind us of the order of things, what we consider valuable, what is wrong and what is right. And in so doing, these stories provide comfort that helps us to sleep, or that keeps us alive, as in the case of that most famous storyteller, Scheherazade.

It was a dark and stormy night
and Brigham Young and Brigham Old
sat around the campfire.
Tell us a story, old man!
And this is the story he told:

It was a dark and stormy night
and Brigham Young and Brigham Old
sat around the campfire.
Tell us a story, old man!
And this is the story he told:
. . .

It was a dark and stormy night
and Brigham al-Rashid sat around the campfire with his wife
who was telling him a story in order to keep her head on
her shoulders,
and this is the story she told:
The *histoire* is the what
and the *discours* is the how
but what I want to know, Brigham,
is *le pourquoi*.
Why are we sitting here around the campfire?

Tell me a story, great-aunt,
so that I can sleep.
Tell me a story, Scheherazade,
so that you can live.
Tell me a story, my soul, . . .
for the word's the beginning of being
if not the middle or the end.

"A beginning is that which is not itself necessarily after anything else, and which has naturally something else after it; an
end, that which is naturally after something else, either as its

necessary or usual consequent, and with nothing else after it; and a middle, that which is by nature after one thing and has also another after it." (Aristotle)

But sequence grows difficult in the ignorance of what comes after the necessary or at least the usual consequent of living, that is, dying,

and also when the soul is confused by not unreasonable doubts of what comes after the next thing that happens, whatever that might be.

It gets dark and stormy when you look away from the campfire.
—Le Guin (1980:187–195)

It gets dark and stormy when we look away from the campfire, from the place of comfort and warmth that we know well. Around the campfire, we tell and retell stories that keep us together and that remind us of the order of things. This book asks that we look away from the campfire, away from our places of comfort, because looking away can help us to think.[9]

Around the metaphorical campfire, we tell stories that arrange people and actions in ways that help us make sense of our world. We drink tea and negotiate peace there, but our well-lit surroundings are deceptive. We are drawn to the light over and over without always realizing the partiality of what is illuminated, the limits imposed on our thinking and on the possibilities we might consider for peaceful futures. The Israeli/Palestinian campfire illuminates a particular range of social and political positions, a kind of map that helps us navigate the sociopolitical terrain. This conflict is situated within a broader normative framework in which the orderly and successful "West" is seen in stark contrast to radical religious groups or terrorist organizations that seek to disrupt or destroy it. Within this framework, Israel is seen as part of the West, which is conceptualized as the rational, secular, modern source of liberalism and liberal peacebuilding.[10]

Liberal peacemaking is born of the Enlightenment idea that democratic states are not only the most legitimate form of sovereignty, but also the best means for maintaining peace. But liberal peace is dependent more on maintaining order than on achieving justice (Mullin 2010:540). Within this framework, Israel is seen as a rational state actor, while the Palestinians have long been considered threatening. The Palestinians as represented by the Palestinian Liberation Organization (PLO) were long considered terrorists. But since 1991 the PLO, a secular nationalist organization established in 1964, has been recognized as the legitimate representative of the Palestinian people, the group with whom negotiations should take place. Now the Islamist group Hamas, elected to rule the Gaza Strip in 2006, continues to be seen as threatening to the West and to Israel in particular. Hamas, an acronym for the Islamic Resistance Movement, was founded in 1987 during the first Palestinian uprising (*Intifada*) as an offshoot of the Muslim Brotherhood in Egypt. When Hamas won the elections in Gaza, they ousted the Fatah party, founded by Yasser Arafat as the largest political faction of the PLO, resulting in an internal conflict between Hamas and Fatah, who struggle to claim the role of sole legitimate representative of the Palestinian people.

While Fatah has been recognized as a negotiating partner for Israel, Hamas continues to be marginalized. It is not only their religiosity but also their extremist version of Islam that places them outside of peace. They are considered intolerant and therefore not worthy of toleration, irrational fanatics who cannot be partners in rational peacemaking.

Around the campfire of liberal peacemaking, religiously motivated Jewish settlers are also seen as extremists, radical religionists, or fundamentalists (Lustick 1988; Silberstein 1993; Sivan 1995), although in a different way from Hamas. These settlers are a thorn in the side of peace-seeking Israelis, but are supported by the Israeli government and protected by the Israeli armed forces. They are often conceptualized by other Israelis as outliers, exceptions that are not representative of Israel or of Judaism. I use the term "religiously motivated" in reference to those Jewish settlers who maintain that it is their responsibility to fulfill the will of God in bringing a Jewish presence to the biblical land of Israel. Such people are often referred to as "Jewish Fundamentalists" (Aran 1991; Lustick 1988; Sivan 1995), the "radical right wing," or as members of Gush Emunim, as the settler movement was once called (see Dalsheim and Harel 2009). These settlers are predominantly religiously motivated nationalists who make their homes on Palestinian land conquered by Israel in the June 1967 war, and who believe deeply in the value of Jewish presence in the biblical Land of Israel. They believe that peace will come when justice has been done, and justice means returning all the Land of Israel to its rightful owners, the People of Israel to whom God promised it. To facilitate the coming of the Messiah, the Jewish people must live on the Land of Israel and lead their lives according to the commandments in the Torah.

Around the campfire of Israeli-Palestinian peace negotiations, we find the left wing and the right wing of politics. Religious and secular groups are also there. We are familiar with the moderate and extreme positions we see represented. They are all more or less clearly marked, giving us a sense of predictability, if not peace. The campfire of liberal peacemaking is set in a world of nations and states, where people rule over their own territory. The moderates around the campfire propose compromise. They are Israelis and Palestinians who each see themselves as nations with the right to sovereignty in their territory, but who are willing to negotiate over some of that territory for the sake of peace. Currently, the moderates are those who accept a two-state solution to the conflict.

The majority of Israelis and Palestinians believe that dividing the territory into two states is the best possible compromise, and yet they do not implement (or have not yet implemented) this solution. Sometimes, they claim they cannot arrive at a solution because there is no partner on the other side. For Israelis, this can mean that the Palestinians are split between the Fatah and Hamas parties, so they do not have a single representative who can negotiate a settlement for all Palestinians. For Palestinians, this can mean that Israel has not acted in good faith, which would mean ending the expansion of Israeli settlements in occupied territories. As long as Israel continues to build, taking more and more territory that might have become part of a Palestinian state, they cannot be partners to peace. Sometimes, both Israelis and Palestinians claim they cannot arrive at a solution because extremists on both sides act as "spoilers" to peace processes.

Those extremists are unwilling to compromise. They are ideologues who want it all for themselves. They are willing to use violence or to act against the law. They dehumanize their enemies and seek to triumph against them. Around this campfire, religious radicals are extremists. Among both Israelis and Palestinians, religiously motivated extremists are the ones who interfere with peacemaking. Islamists are spoilers who refuse to recognize the state of Israel and who carry out acts of violence that bring peacemaking efforts to a halt. Religiously motivated Jewish settlers are spoilers who attack Palestinians and steal more and more land, making territorial compromise seem impossible.

THE OUTSIDE OF PEACE/WITHIN THE GLOW OF THE CAMPFIRE

What do Islamists and radical religious Jewish settlers have to do with the international peace process, other than providing an alibi for its failure? High-level diplomatic negotiators and grassroots peace activists blame religious extremists for spoiling rational negotiation and have often been concerned with neutralizing, co-opting, or marginalizing them. It might be more useful, however, to explore the problem of stalled peacemaking by looking at spoilers not as its cause, but as a symptom of systemic malfunctions within the concept of the nation-state itself, and the secular constructs of historicism that support it. In other words, spoilers mark the boundaries of the acceptable, the reasonable, the rational. Falling outside of peace and peacemaking, they allow us to see the moral community produced through their exception and provide an opportunity to ask a series of questions about that moral order and its possibilities and limits for making peace.

Since the demise of the Oslo peace process,[11] it seems clear that for many Israelis and members of the international community, Hamas is best described as an uncompromising group. Many Palestinians are equally unhappy with Hamas, explaining that the acts of violence they commit are not the Islamic way. Islam is the religion of peace. But at the same time, it seems that for many Palestinians Hamas are not the only ones standing in the way of achieving peace, increased freedom, or social justice (Allen 2013). While most Palestinians see the Israelis as the primary cause of Palestinian suffering, the Palestinian leadership in the West Bank is also blamed for cooperating with the Israeli occupation forces. Palestinian leaders in positions of authority coordinate with Israel on all kinds of practical matters, but for many Palestinians these leaders are not bringing Palestinian independence. Instead, they are doing Israel's dirty work. Some might argue that it is now Fatah, the party of Yasser Arafat, who are actually the spoilers. Many have long been suspicious of Fatah. The leadership was in exile in Tunisia during the 1980s, and when they returned they seemed like outsiders (R. Khalidi 1997), behaving in ways that were not consistent with local norms. The Fatah leadership also seemed to be profiting personally from their positions in the party while ordinary Palestinians continued to suffer.

Religiously motivated Jewish settlers are also seen as extremists who combine religious beliefs with nationalism in dangerous ways.[12] They engage in acts of violence against Palestinians, most recently in the form of "price tag" retaliations (see Harel 2012). In these cases, when the Israeli government implements a decision with which settlers disagree, such as the demolition of settler homes built on illegally obtained Palestinian property, the settlers do not necessarily respond violently against other Israelis or members of their government. Instead, they attack Palestinians, raising the political "price" of government action against them.

CONCEPTUAL THREAT

How is it possible that such small minorities can stand in the way of peace negotiations that appear to be in the interests of the vast majority of Israelis and Palestinians, and popular with most of the rest of the community of nations? Within the contemporary episteme of nation-state politics, peacemaking is founded on fixed borders, stable national groups, and elite sovereignty (which sometimes poses as "popular" insofar as it is claimed to arise from "the people"). Groups whose ideas or actions challenge any of those foundations are produced as "spoilers." That is, by falling outside the system (as anachronistic, or ineligible to produce acceptable violence, or rejecting either the definition of national group or the notion that national sovereignty is the only possible guarantee of personal survival), their actions themselves, rather than the framework in which those actions take place, appear as responsible for ruining peace. Within this framework, rational processes of negotiation are the ritual means through which that order of fixed goods—people, land, and sovereignty—is maintained.

The production of these small groups as alibis[13] for the failure of official peace negotiations makes conflict appear intractable, revealing both how that order makes the conflict possible in the first place, and how it limits its potential solutions.

> September 2, 2010
> Fox News
>
> Middle East peace talks got under way Thursday for the first time in nearly two years with a violent reminder sent by the Palestinian terror group Hamas that it will try to torpedo any agreement struck in Washington between Israelis and the Palestinian Authority.
>
> Hamas refuses to recognize Israel's right to exist despite that acknowledgment by the Palestinian Authority more than a decade ago.

As a result, the PA, led by President Mahmoud Abbas and his Fatah Party, run the West Bank while Hamas has its thumb on Gaza. Joining the two territories into one state is one of the Palestinians' objectives of peace talks.

Ignoring Hamas, however, is tricky business. The group flexed its muscles with back-to-back attacks this week on Israelis in the West Bank. Those kinds of attacks position it to spoil any meeting of the minds. (http://www.foxnews.com/ politics/2010/09/02/hamas-looms-spoiler-middle-east-peace-talks/#ixzz2JO27s520)

The EU also, along with a number of states and organizations, has classified Hamas as a terrorist organisation. Following the electoral victory of 2006, the international community sought to isolate Hamas even further and a strategy of hard negative conditionality has seen the infliction of punishment (sanctions) and withdrawal of benefits (aid and diplomatic relations) in a bid to elicit a disavowal of terrorism . . . . Hamas is perceived as a 'spoiler' in negotiations, dedicated to rejecting any peace with Israel. (Austin et al. 2011:32)

Hamas is a player in the peace process in the sense that they spoil the game when they engage in violent acts that undermine the process from which they are excluded. In any case, such is the story told about them around the campfire. In 2005 Israel unilaterally withdrew from Palestinian territory in the Gaza Strip, leaving Gaza under Palestinian control. Although Israel still controls the borders, some would argue that withdrawing its military and its settlers from Palestinian areas is sufficient, precisely what Palestinians have been struggling to achieve. The end of Israeli military occupation should be considered a step toward independence and statehood for Palestinians. Many Israelis hoped the withdrawal from Gaza would set a precedent. Palestinians would turn their attention to internal matters, to building their economy and establishing their own rule.[14] Good neighborly relations would be built between

Israel and the Palestinians, and Israel might decide it was in its best interest to relinquish additional territory and end the occupation altogether. But Israel's withdrawal from Gaza did not lead to peace between neighbors.

In 2007, Hamas took power in the Gaza Strip and ever since has been actively carrying out a military campaign against Israel. They fire rockets over the border into southern Israel. Israel retaliates, and the cycle repeats itself. For Israelis, the moral of this story is that it is dangerous to relinquish territory. The end of Israeli occupation of the Gaza Strip resulted in rising extremism and the threat of violence. Some of the Israelis seated around the campfire do not trust Palestinians. They say that when given the opportunity to rule themselves in their own territory, Palestinians choose war against Israel as a first priority. Given the case of Gaza and Hamas, it will be even more difficult than before to restart peace negotiations. Hamas is a spoiler of peace processes, then, but what exactly does Hamas spoil?

Beyond their acts of violence against Israelis, groups like Hamas are threatening because they do not accept the foundational assumptions of contemporary peacemaking. The ethos of Hamas is not based on achieving peace through negotiations. According to Hamas, "God will give victory over Israel when Palestinian Muslims return to Islam; Islam is the only true way for the salvation of humanity" (Abu-Nimer 2003:166). If salvation is dependent upon religious practices, what good are political negotiations?

The deeper threat posed by radical religious spoilers, then, may have less to do with their acts of violence than with the threat their beliefs and practices pose to the very foundations of "liberal peace" (Mullin 2010) that provide the normative framework for peacemaking. Peacemaking within this liberal framework is based on a moral and political order that Hamas, other Islamists, and radical Jewish settlers transgress.

The order of sovereign democratic nation-states is premised on the idea that individuals enter into a contract in which they receive freedom and security while granting the sole right to violence to the state. This order is supposed to create international stability because a general consensus is required to go to war, and most people will be reluctant to do so. This idea emerges from Immanuel Kant's writing on "Perpetual Peace" in the eighteenth century. Kant wrote that "if the consent of the citizens is required in order to decide that war should be declared, . . . nothing is more natural than that they would be very cautious in commencing such a poor game, decreeing for themselves all the calamities of war" (1903/1795:122). Not only would the citizens have to fight, they would also bear the costs of the war and of reconstruction afterward. The citizens, Kant writes, "having painfully to repair the devastation war leaves behind, and, to fill up the measure of evils, load themselves with a heavy national debt that would embitter peace itself and that can never be liquidated on account of constant wars in the future" (1903/1795: 121–123). Clearly, he suggests, since rational citizens would be loath to enter into a state of war for all it would cost them in life and livelihood, peace should be the expected norm in a world of democratic nation-states.

This is one of the primary reasons justifying Western powers' attempts at state-building around the world. In the case of conflict resolution, peace is expected to last when parties to conflict take their place in the world order of nation-states, where they will have sovereignty over their own territory and act in their own interests. Thus, order, and specifically the order of nation-states, is foundational to liberal peace processes—perhaps order more than justice.

The narrative of the state foundational to liberal peacemaking "is that the modern state system is a European construct . . . which put an end to the religious conflicts of the late 16th and 17th centuries in Europe" (Mullin 2010:531). According to this narrative, it was the elimination of God from the realm of politics that paved the way for modern sovereignty. This was a secular sovereignty based on a set of principles including individualism and personal pursuits of liberty and happiness that ultimately became foundational both to free markets and to the international order of nation-states. But free markets do not necessarily make us free. While liberal peacemaking sees participation in the international marketplace as part of creating stable states, free markets do not result in equitable distribution of resources and wealth or create an equal playing field. In fact, they lead to great gaps in wealth, which makes some people much more free to act than others (Scott 2012). Such conditions may lead to future conflicts. But liberal peacemaking projects have been further criticized for imposing top-down solutions that suit the international order of nation-states and the global capitalist economy. Such projects, critics claim, are unsustainable because they fail to fully account for the local contexts that lead to conflict or to consider issues that are especially important to local people involved in conflict. Indeed, some critics suggest that liberal peacemaking in many cases is little more than a form of neo-colonialism (Paris 2010). Such peacemaking efforts can lead to enemy-making between the conflict-ridden society and those powers in the international community who brokered the peace. The liberal foundations of contemporary peacemaking actually lead to the production and reproduction of enmity. It reinscribes national groups as enemies and creates spoilers—both in the sense of shaping them as groups and in the sense of placing them in the position of blame for the conflict—who are outside the liberal order and therefore mark the outsides of peace.

Organizations such as Hamas challenge the national order of things. They do not support nationalism inasmuch as it undermines their broader allegiance to the supranational community of Muslims. This is the story they tell about themselves. One of their founding principles was that they should *not* make territorial compromises.

> The Islamic Resistance Movement believes that the land of Palestine is an Islamic Waqf consecrated for future Muslim generations until Judgment Day. It, or any part of it, should not be squandered: it, or any part of it, should not be given up. (http://www.mideastweb.org/hamas.htm)

Instead of national sovereignty, they place their faith in the sovereignty of God. In their eyes the secular state can never actually be a sovereign entity, a role reserved only for God.

> The Islamic Resistance Movement is one of the wings of Muslim Brotherhood in Palestine. [The] Muslim Brotherhood Movement is a universal organization which constitutes the largest Islamic movement in modern times. It is characterised by its deep understanding, accurate comprehension and its complete embrace of all Islamic concepts of all aspects of life, culture, creed, politics, economics, education, society, justice and judgment, the spreading of Islam, education, art, information, science of the occult and conversion to Islam. (http://www.mideastweb.org/hamas.htm)

Individuals and governments should strive to implement His will; that is the limit of their sovereignty. This is quite different from the narrative that limits such sovereignty to a particular geographical territory, populated by a particular people/nation. But it is not only *different* from this narrative; it is premised on a divergent set of assumptions, an episteme that denies the very foundations of the international order of nation-states.[15] One might argue, therefore, that organizations like Hamas are threatening not only because they carry out acts of violence aimed at disrupting conventional diplomacy and peacemaking, but because they threaten to spoil the very epistemic foundations of normative international relations. This threat marginalizes and excludes them from conventional peace processes because this order forms the field in which the conflict is played out and in which peace must be made.

SETTLEMENT

> Settlement activities embody the core of the policy of colonial military occupation of the land of the Palestinian people and

all of the brutality, aggression and racial discrimination against our people that that policy entails. The policy constitutes a breach of international humanitarian law and United Nations resolutions. It is the primary cause of the failure of the peace process, the collapse of dozens of opportunities and the burial of the great hopes that arose from the signing of the Declaration of Principles in 1993 between the Palestine Liberation Organization and Israel to achieve a just peace that would begin a new era for our region.

—Mahmoud Abbas (UN 2011; http://unispal.un.org/UNISPAL.NSF/0/
93AFB927919E10588525793500537B16)

According to Palestinian president Mahmoud Abbas,[16] Israeli settlement in the Occupied Territories is the primary obstacle to peace. Members of the international community as well as many Israelis agree and are particularly concerned about religious settlers because their religious beliefs prevent them from considering territorial compromise. Settler policies and politics have increasingly influenced Israeli governments. Moreover, the extensive security infrastructure erected by the Israeli state in order to protect these settlers disrupts the normal flow of goods and people through what might eventually become a Palestinian state, preventing the development of an environment in which Palestinians can shape their own future.

Religiously motivated settlers threaten the possibility of a peace agreement that would create two states for two nations. This is the story told about them around the campfire. They oppose territorial compromise because the Land of Israel was promised by God to the Jewish people. It is their rightful inheritance and not something to be bargained away. "The Land of Israel for the People of Israel according to the Torah of Israel," they say (Dalsheim 2011; Lustick 1988). It is not only their right, but their obligation to settle the Land, their duty to God to fulfill His promise. According to Rabbi Tzvi Yehuda Kook, son of Rabbi Abraham Isaac Kook, together the spiritual founders of the religious settler movement, "The state of

Israel was created and established by the council of nations by order of the Sovereign Lord of the Universe so that the clear commandment in the Torah 'that they shall inherit and settle the Land' would be fulfilled" (in Lustick 1988:35). Some of the more radical settlers also engage in direct violence against Palestinians. They are spoilers of peace who uproot Palestinian olive groves, shoot Palestinians, harass their children on the way to school, and destroy or steal their property. In extreme cases, they carry out violent acts of terrorism like the 1994 massacre in Hebron, when a settler, Baruch Goldstein, opened fire in a mosque, killing 29 Palestinians.

Some religious settlers condemned that act, but others thought the shooter was not only heroic but was also sanctifying God's name. According to a pamphlet called *Baruch Hagever* (Gorenberg 2000) circulated among religious settlers, Goldstein had sacrificed himself for the good of the Jewish people (Sprinzak 1999:259–260). His act had actually saved Jewish lives and in so doing had sanctified the name of the Lord.

And so, within the campfire of liberal peace discourse, we can make peace with those seated close to the fire. Peace agreements can be reached among the moderates within a framework of nation-states. Extremists must be held in check; their influence must be defused so that peace can be achieved. Members of radical religious groups, either Muslim or Jewish, must be neutralized. They are the worst of enemies to each other, to members of the other national group, and to peace itself.

This conclusion excludes whatever falls beyond the light of the campfire, whatever fails to match familiar patterns. Beyond the campfire are other stories that don't fit comfortably within the normative categories of liberal peace discourse. These are stories, like that of the "crazy" rabbi at the opening of this chapter, that cross boundaries or unsettle assumptions about divisions between social, political, and geographical differences, stories at the edge of contradictory moral orders.

Chapter 2

Matters of Recognition

You know, it would be no great tragedy if Israelis no longer existed.
—College Professor (2012)

One can easily imagine a Palestinian, or perhaps some European radical of the Left or Right, making such a remark. In fact it might be an understatement coming from a Palestinian. No great tragedy? No, indeed. If there were no longer Israelis, that might be a reason to celebrate. It would mean the end of occupation, the end of the Palestinian struggle. But the comment above was not made by a Palestinian, or by a terrorist, or by a hater of the Jews. The speaker was an Orthodox Jew, an intellectual, a renowned scholar of Jewish life.

No great tragedy? Well maybe not for him, I thought. He is not an Israeli, although he does have Israeli friends and relatives. So I pushed him on this idea. "If it would be no great tragedy if Israelis no longer existed, what about Palestinians?" I asked. Also not necessarily a bad thing, he replied. Thinking that for this devout Jew, who rose each morning to participate in a *minyan* at his synagogue to pray, Jewishness would be much more meaningful to him personally, I pushed him again. "What about Jews?" I asked. Again, he said, after a short pause, no great tragedy if there were no more Jews.

Of course, when he said "no longer existed," this scholar, strolling along a wooded path with me on a warm summer afternoon, casually dressed in slacks and sneakers, and as usual with his black *kippah* on his head, did not mean genocide, death, or destruction. He was talking about collective identity as something we perpetually have to create and recreate; about how invested people become in their sense of who they are and how hard they work to maintain those identities. He was talking about how the content of identity (what it means to be American or French, for example) can shift over time and how we have to work to make sure our children and grandchildren will remain committed to their peoples. And even how, sometimes, we have to change our ideas about who we are—like changing religious doctrine to allow more congregants to feel they belong—to make sure our collective stays strong. In the context of the Israeli-Palestinian conflict, he was thinking not only about how groups are created, but about how enemies are produced through social and political processes, because we were talking about my ideas for this book.

* * *

Is the enemy the cause of conflict or its effect, or product?

—Gil Anidjar (2003)

This chapter is about how recognizing collective identity in the process of conflict resolution can work to produce or reproduce enmity, and about how the complex notion of "recognition," which emanates from a desire to implement equality, to do justice, and to build peace, also has the potential to undermine these goals. We might all think at some point that it would be no great tragedy if a particular collective no longer existed, realizing that so many people are so invested in such identifications that these identities have become what people fight and die to defend. In other words, without collective identity, and in the case of Israel/Palestine specifically national identity, there might be no enemies. Or at least not particular kinds of enemies defined as national or confessional or ethnic groups. And without these enemies there would be no conflict. Hence, no great tragedy if these enemy groups no longer existed. While this, of course, is an oversimplification, the kind of thinking that lies behind these words suggests that no one would have to die in order for a national group to cease to exist, while in fact many people have suffered and died in the name of nationalism itself. Of course, people who identify as Israeli or Palestinian might have very different opinions on the subject. Having suffered for the cause can intensify one's commitment to the nation.

Palestinians and Israelis have worked long and hard to have their collectives recognized as national groups. In fact, each has declared statehood based on these identities.

Tel Aviv, May 14, 1948

On the day the British Mandate over Palestine expired, the Jewish People's Council gathered at the Tel Aviv Museum and approved the following proclamation, declaring the establishment of the State of Israel:

> The Land of Israel (*Eretz-Israel*) was the birthplace of the Jewish people. Here their spiritual, religious and political identity was shaped. Here they first attained to statehood, created cultural values of national and universal significance and gave to the world the eternal Book of Books.
>
> After being forcibly exiled from their land, the people kept faith with it throughout their Dispersion and never ceased to pray and hope for their return to it and for the restoration in it of their political freedom.
>
> Impelled by this historic and traditional attachment, Jews strove in every successive generation to re-establish themselves in their ancient homeland. . . .[1]

Algiers, November 15, 1988

Forty years later, the Palestinian declaration of independence was adopted by the Palestinian National Council, the legislative body of the Palestine Liberation Organization (PLO). On November 15, 1988, Yasser Arafat, the Chairman of the PLO, unilaterally declared the establishment of the state of Palestine:

> Palestine, the land of the three monotheistic faiths, is where the Palestinian Arab people was born, on which it grew, developed and excelled. The Palestinian people was never separated from or diminished in its integral bonds with Palestine. Thus the Palestinian Arab people ensured for itself an everlasting union between itself, its land and its history.
>
> Resolute throughout that history, the Palestinian Arab people forged its national identity, rising to unimagined levels in its defense, as invasion, the design of others, and the appeal special to Palestine's ancient and luminous place on that eminence where powers and civilisations are joined. All this intervened thereby to deprive the people of its political independence. Yet the undying connection between Palestine and its people secured for the land its character, and for the people its national genius.[2]

The land that these two declarations claim as the birthplace of their peoples is the same land. But declarations of independence, as performative statements, are bound by certain conditions[3] that determine whether or not they are able to effect the state of affairs they announce (Austin 1962). In the case of Israel and Palestine, these declarations seem to have had very different results in the larger world. But their underlying similarity is that both serve to explain to the people thereby constituted what they are up to, and why they are waging their particular struggles.

In the Israeli case, the world's superpowers began to respond quickly with diplomatic recognition of the new state. In fact, the

Israeli Ministry of Foreign Affairs website constructs the authority of its narrative of the birth of the modern Israeli nation by linking to the following text on the website of the Harry S. Truman Presidential Library:

> At midnight on May 14, 1948, the Provisional Government of Israel proclaimed the new State of Israel. On that same date the United States, in the person of President Truman, recognized the provisional Jewish government as de facto authority of the new Jewish state (de jure recognition was extended on January 31). . . . On May 15, 1948, the Arab states issued their response statement and Arab armies invaded Israel and the first Arab-Israeli war began.[4]

In 1917 Chaim Weizmann, scientist, statesman, and Zionist, persuaded the British government to issue a statement favoring the establishment of a Jewish national home in Palestine. The statement, which became known as the Balfour Declaration, was, in part, a form of compensation to the Jews for their support of the British against the Turks during World War I. After the war, the League of Nations ratified the declaration and in 1922 appointed Britain to rule in Palestine.

This course of events caused Jews to be optimistic about the eventual establishment of a homeland. Their optimism inspired the immigration to Palestine of Jews from many countries, particularly from Germany when Nazi persecution of Jews began. The arrival of these immigrants in the 1930s awakened Arab fears that Palestine would become a national homeland for Jews. By 1936 guerrilla fighting had broken out between the Jews and Arabs. Unable to maintain peace, Britain issued a white paper in 1939 that restricted Jewish immigration into Palestine. The Jews, feeling betrayed, bitterly opposed the policy and looked to the United States for support.

While President Franklin D. Roosevelt appeared to be sympathetic to the Jewish cause, his assurances to the Arabs that the United States would not intervene without consulting both parties caused public uncertainty about his position. When President Harry S. Truman took office, he made clear that his sympathies were with the Jews and accepted the Balfour Declaration, explaining that it was in keeping with former President Woodrow Wilson's principle of "self-determination." Truman initiated several studies of the Palestine situation that supported his belief that, as a result of the Holocaust, Jews were oppressed and also in need of a homeland.[5]

Arab countries did not recognize the newly declared Jewish homeland as the United States did. They recognized it as a state to fight against; or, perhaps, by fighting against it recognized it as another kind of state: a state of theft, of aggression, of invasion.[6]

Sixty years after its establishment Israel launched a political campaign (http://www.recognizeisrael.com/) to persuade countries that had not yet recognized the Israeli state to establish full diplomatic ties. The government of Israel continues to insist that recognition of its right to exist as a state (a fundamental existential recognition rather than the *de facto* or even *de jure* diplomatic recognition of a particular government, which is contingent and can be withdrawn) must be a precondition for peace negotiations.

The struggle for recognition continues for both Israelis and Palestinians. Palestinians have been calling for recognition of their existence both as a people and as a nation deserving the right to self-determination. On November 16, 1988, the new state of Palestine declared by the Palestinian National Council was recognized by Algeria, and a day later by Turkish Cyprus. Currently, according to the Negotiation Affairs Department of the PLO (http://www.nad-plo.org/etemplate.php?id=5), 122 nations recognize the state of Palestine.

Palestinians, though, have no text from an American presidential library on which they can establish the authority of their own narrative. Writing in 1979, Edward Said noted that "those nations most intimately concerned with the Palestinians challenge . . . the very existence of Palestinian identity" (1992/1979:169, 170).[7] Even today, the widespread recognition of that identity has not resulted in the achievement of a Palestinian state. Instead we see an "administration" of Palestinians by Palestinians.[8]

Said called for recognition of the Palestinian struggle as a specifically national one (Said 1992/1979:10). He noted the variation among the Arabs of Palestine—demographically, economically, and politically—and yet consistently claimed, along with other spokespeople, that Palestinians are united against Zionism and struggle for sovereign nationhood. The people who struggle against Zionism, in other words, are the Palestinians, a nation constituted through the struggle itself. In *Zionism from the Standpoint of its Victims*, Said called for recognition of the Palestinians as a people, of their plight as refugees, and of their suffering, displacement, and dispossession by Zionism in ways that resonate with the Israeli Declaration of Independence and its own discourse of exile and dispossession.

This claim to nationhood in response to Jewish national claims to the land—to the Zionist immigration or colonization of Palestine beginning in the late 1800s—has also provided the grounds to delegitimize the idea of the Palestinians as a national group. Thus Palestinians have been in a "strategic defensive" position (W. Khalidi 1991:7), defending their land and homes and defending the idea of their very existence as a people. If the Zionist claim to nationhood, followed by recognition of the State of Israel by the United Nations, frames the conflict between Israelis and Palestinians, then Palestinian claims might be criticized as being purely reactive, mere shallow responses to Zionist claims for nationhood and statehood rather than natural expressions of national essence or a natural right.

In September 2000, in the midst of another round of failed Israeli-Palestinian peace talks, the U.S. House of Representatives voted in opposition to renewed international calls for American recognition of a Palestinian state:

September 27, 2000 WASHINGTON (Reuters). The U.S. House of Representatives approved on Wednesday a bill that would cut off virtually all aid to the Palestinian Authority if President Yasser Arafat unilaterally declares a Palestinian state.

The bill was passed by a vote of 385 to 27, showing wide bipartisan support for the measure, which would sever all aid except humanitarian assistance to the Palestinians and deny U.S. recognition to a unilaterally declared state. "Today's vote reaffirms that the United States will not support any Palestinian entity that is not created through peaceful negotiations with Israel," said Democratic Representative Jerrold Nadler of New York, one of the bill's co-sponsors. A similar measure has been introduced to the Senate but has not yet come up for a vote.

The House action came after Israeli and Palestinian negotiators met separately in Washington on Tuesday night with American envoy Dennis Ross, the main U.S. mediator, to try and bridge gaps between the two sides on some of the most difficult issues left in the Arab-Israeli peace talks. . . .

The Palestinians earlier this month agreed to delay a declaration of statehood for at least two months to allow more time for difficult negotiations toward a lasting Middle East peace accord.

But the Palestinian Central Council has set November 15 as the date it will decide when to make the declaration that Arafat had originally vowed to make as early as September 13.

"The Palestinian threat to declare an independent state unilaterally constitutes a fundamental violation of the underlying principles of the Oslo Accords and the Middle East peace process," said New York Republican Representative Benjamin Gilman, chairman of the House International Relations Committee. "That threat continues unabated," he added. . . .

In addition to withholding aid, the House measure would urge other countries to join the United States in withholding recognition of a Palestinian state and would downgrade the status of the Palestinian office in Washington.[9]

As I write these words the Palestinian quest for a politically meaningful recognition goes on. President Mahmoud Abbas recently brought a resolution to the United Nations asking that Palestine be recognized as a state. In November 2012, the United Nations voted to recognize Palestine as a "non-member observer state," up-grading its status from "entity" to "state" (Charbonneau and Nicholas 2012).

RECOGNITION MATTERS

Recognition can have a number of meanings, from recognizing an individual's personal actions or achievements to political recognition of a collective as a nation. There is the recognition bestowed by people in positions of power and the demands of individuals and groups for recognition of their stories, their accounts of the past, of their suffering or their rights. These demands also sometimes seek admission of guilt from others or request that another party recognize their responsibility for a particular outcome in the past and for the future. Despite the varied levels and definitions of recognition, one thing is certain: recognition matters. Official political recognition can have very real outcomes in people's lives. It can mean the difference between receiving or being denied international aid. It can lead to partnerships in the international community and economic or military alliances. It can mean being granted a passport and the right to vote. Or it can mean violent hostility being defined as war rather than as terrorism, police action, or insurgency. In any case, it is not surprising that the idea of the right to be recognized, to one's collective self, to one's own story, and to having that story recognized, carries an almost unequivocally positive value in contemporary politics and peacemaking.

Stories of collective selves are often stories about the past. Yet recognizing particular versions of the past can also be one of the ways enemies are produced. These versions of the past can construct enemies as national categories (e.g., "the Israelis," or "the Palestinians," understood as "the parties to the conflict") by defining specific intersections between a people, a contiguous territory in which they live, and sovereignty, their right to control that territory. This, in turn, is often justified by narratives about origin, conquest, negotiation, sacrifice, divine bequest, or victimhood. But the enemies that are produced as external to each other can also be joined by internal Others, by people who share beliefs or interests across national categories, and by people who think or act in ways that don't seem especially concerned about national borders at all, or who care more about residing in a territory than about sovereignty over it, or who question the idea of well-defined peoples or nations. Recognizing some ways of telling the past and leaving out others squeezes some people into national containers while pushing others out. This process produces both enemies and spoilers to peace processes.

Spoilers are those groups who are produced as the "outside" of peace. They include, in this case study, people who are seen as religious extremists and blamed for undermining rational negotiations between the national groups taken to be parties to a conflict over territory and sovereignty. Rather than conceptualizing such spoilers as the *cause* of stalled peacemaking, though, they should be considered a *symptom* of the contradictions inherent in the concept of the nation-state itself and the secular constructs that support it. One of these constructs is a particular kind of social order in which territory is imagined as space, people are imagined as demographic units within that space, and sovereignty is imagined as a rational necessity for making decisions about the rights of particular people within this space and for entering into negotiations between similarly defined national groups.[10]

STORYTELLING, DIALOGUE, AND PEACEMAKING

There was a drought in the jungle and all the animals had gathered to drink at the trickle that remained of the river. Shere Khan, the tiger, arrived, boasting that he had killed a Man. The others shunned his behavior, but he spoke of this "right." Mowgli, who was new among them, was confused and asked the elephant, Hathi, to explain.

"It is an old tale," said Hathi, "a tale older than the Jungle.
Keep silence along the bank, and I will tell that tale . . ."

—Rudyard Kipling (1995/1897:72)

If you live here, you have two choices: either you go for the religious
version that God promised the land to the people, or—if you're not
religious—you go for the version where the U.N. recognized Israel.
Or, if you move away to England, like my brother, it doesn't matter,
and you don't need a story anymore.

—Israeli High School Student (2000)

We all tell stories of our past and present to ourselves and to our
children to explain the way things are, how they got this way, who
we are, and what we believe in (Dalsheim 2003). The narrative form,
the way in which we tell stories, imbues events with meanings and
morality (White 1980:17). The story of the Israeli-Palestinian conflict narrates two[11] parties to the conflict, with heroes and villains
locked in a struggle that may end in triumph for one and destruction or defeat for the other; but within the framework of contemporary peacemaking, it culminates in these two *national* groups—after
long processes of gaining recognition as national groups—arriving
at some compromise to end the conflict.[12]

There seems to be a broad consensus among peacemakers that
mutual recognition is an important step in resolving conflict.[13] But
the question, of course, is what or who precisely is being recognized,
and by whom. Franz Fanon (1967), for example, recalls an instance
of recognition in which "the other, the white man had woven me out
of a thousand details." He tells of a moment when a child sees him
on a bus and calls out "Look, Negro!" Seeing him, recognizing him,
not ignoring his existence. Then the child adds, "Mamma, see the
Negro! I'm frightened!" Fanon is recognized but also demonized at
the very same instant.

Recognition in the case of the Israeli-Palestinian conflict—like
other nationalist conflicts—means *two* social groups recognizing each other, constructing themselves as separate and distinct
from each other in the ways that are thought to matter most, while

subsuming internal differences deemed of lesser importance. In the words of Herbert Kelman, director of the Program on International Conflict Analysis and Resolution at Harvard, it means that each group must accept "the other's nationhood and humanity" (Kelman 2004:112), a perspective from which nationhood seems to be directly related to humanity itself.[14]

Dennis Ross, a senior diplomat in a number of recent U.S. administrations and a key player in Israeli-Palestinian negotiations, also explains the central importance of understanding that each party to the conflict has its own story to tell, a story of the past that is integral to collective identity. He devotes an entire chapter of his recent book to these narratives (Ross 2004). As Ross presents them, they are not history, but narrative interpretations of the past that represent each of two national groups as victims of past injustices who deserve recompense through national sovereignty.

It is interesting to note which interpretations of events become the ones a senior diplomat like Ross includes and excludes. These exclusions derive in part from the limited contours of a particular secular telling of history, and as a result, the narratives have a disciplinary force, participating in the production of enemies, enemies of peace, and spoilers of peace processes.

Ross's book opens with a series of maps. His mapping of the conflict begins with the 1947 United Nations partition plan and the 1949 Armistice line, which seems to mark this as a specifically modern conflict. Were it otherwise, he might have begun with a biblical map of the People of Israel in the Land of Israel. Yet, the Israeli narrative that he tells explains that for

the Israelis, their national movement, Zionism, is a natural response to the tragedies of Jewish history. Ever since the destruction of the Second Temple in Jerusalem in 70 A.D., Jews had been dispersed and without a homeland. Dispersal had made Jews weak and vulnerable, and led to repeated expulsions and devastations . . . Zionism meant creating a homeland for the Jews that could be a safe haven. (Ross 2004:15–16)

Ross recognizes that "the Israelis" (produced here as direct descendants of the Ancient Israelites) begin their telling of the story in A.D. 70. He tells a narrative of "the Israelis" in which Israelis are synonymous with Jews, even though this experienced diplomat is surely aware that not all citizens of the modern state of Israel (Israelis) are Jews, and that indeed some of them identify as Palestinians.

These are two small examples of how the narrative form and its implementation can be made useful for nationalism, for conflict, and seemingly for its resolution. Narrative requires choosing a beginning that frames the contours of conflict and its resolution. So, for example, if the Israeli story begins in ancient times and recognizes today's Jews as the inheritors of the Land of Israel, that is quite different from a story that begins with European Jews arriving at the end of the nineteenth century and settling in a land that was inhabited by other people. Each framing also necessarily attributes causality in different ways and leads to different conclusions. I will say much more about the role of narratives and the narrative form in Chapter 3.

"The Israeli narrative" Ross presents goes on to discuss the leadership of the Zionist movement in Europe and Jewish immigration to Palestine in the 1880s. But there is no single unitary Israeli narrative that encompasses the stories of all the citizens of Israel, nor is there a single narrative that encompasses the stories of all the Jewish citizens of Israel: the stories of Jewish citizens who came to Israel as refugees from Nazi Europe, or from North Africa or Latin America, or from Russia or Ethiopia during the 1990s, or those whose genealogy can be traced to Jerusalem centuries back in time. Sociologist Uri Ram (1995) wrote about how Ben Zion Dinur, the historian and Israeli Minister of Education in the early years of the state, constructed a unified story for the Jewish people that would be suitable for the new nation-state and could be used to educate its children, creating a shared memory (Dalsheim 2003). The Zionist narrative was molded into a story of unity and continuity despite the very different experiences of Jewish groups in distinct periods and distant locations. It is a narrative that has since undergone revision, but school history textbooks are still criticized for how Arabs, Palestinians, and Jews of Middle Eastern and North African descent are represented or omitted from the story (Dalsheim 2003; Podeh 2000; Raz-Krakotzkin 2001).

Whether one agrees or disagrees with Ram's analysis of Dinur, it should be clear that the very idea of the existence of *"the* Israeli narrative" is a fiction because, like *all* historical narratives, it is necessarily partial and inherently limited. Ross's version of the past is very much like what one might find on an Israeli government website or in the curriculum for teaching history in public schools, at least in secular public schools.[15] Among that which is missing from Ross's story of conflict and from his Israeli narrative are important differences and complications involving ethnicity, gender, and class. Missing also is the understanding that God gave the Land of Israel to the people of Israel (e.g., Genesis 12:1) and that this is their reason for being there (for the geographical boundaries of this gift, see Genesis 15:18; Exodus 23:31; Deuteronomy 11:24).[16]

Ross tells a similarly secular and homogenizing Palestinian narrative, although it begins by explaining that the "Arab and Palestinian narrative is actually two narratives which have similar roots and converge in certain respects." But, Ross goes on to say, "the Palestinian narrative is ultimately distinct, and informed by a different set of experiences" (Ross 2004:29). Here the diplomat is careful to represent the Palestinians as a people, lest their claim to sovereignty be undermined. But in so constructing the Palestinian people we miss the ways in which, for example, some of the people so named live in northern parts of what is now Israel while their relatives live in what is now Syria, to say nothing of differences in religion, class, gender, or ethnicity.[17]

Nathan Brown (2007) writes of the competing and conflicting voices expressed in the process of developing a Palestinian curriculum when the Palestinian National Authority assumed control over education in the West Bank and Gaza in 1994. The process he describes is in many ways strikingly similar to the process of homogenizing and nationalizing identity through school curricula that Ram describes for the Israeli case. According to Brown, "Palestinians confront vexatious issues involving their history, territory, identity, and neighbors; there is simply no consensus among adults about how to understand any of these matters" (Brown 2007:344). But because there was a need to represent these issues to children, adults decided to simplify and present a more unified picture. However, Brown also shows that the Palestinians who were involved in developing this curriculum were aware of the problematic homogenization of a multiplicity of experiences and identities in the name of national unity. Indeed, some saw this as an opportunity to "create a new and more critical kind of citizenship" in which they might make room for individuality and democratic values (Brown 2007:345). The Ministry of Education, however, modified some of the work of the body they commissioned to write the curriculum, and a more homogenizing version of history ultimately ended up in the Palestinian curriculum. While the committee recommended a rather secular approach to religious identity (as in Taylor's [2007] definition of a secular age), the Ministry ultimately reworked the proposal to emphasize religion (Islam) in particular. And, while the committee recommended a version of Palestinian identity that emphasized its connections and continuities with other nationalities and peoples rather than stressing difference, the Ministry decided on a version that emphasized the distinctiveness of Palestinian identity (Brown 2007:346).

Despite all the complexities of identity and historical experience, the connections to other nations, and the desire of at least some Palestinian intellectuals to create a more critical or plural version of what being Palestinian means, Dennis Ross chooses a unifying and secularized version of Palestinian identity. What makes Palestinians distinctive, according to Ross, is their particular historical experience, not language, religion, or ways of being and believing. What makes Palestinians is not something intrinsic; their distinctiveness derives from the ways in which they were treated by others.[18] This is one way of narrating Palestinian-ness, and it seems particularly useful for conflict resolution, as it calls upon historical wrongs that might be set right through a process of negotiation and compromise. (Indeed, a history of mistreatment, suffering, and exile is also one way to narrate Jewish collective identity and establish the grounds for the need and right to Israeli nationhood.) However, it also clearly reinforces the framework of conflict itself, reinscribing the fiction of two distinct national groups, two enemies produced through the conflict and through the processes of recognition that presumably lays the groundwork for peace.

Ross is concerned with what a third party needs to know to successfully mediate a peace deal. He explains that Zionism is a modern political movement founded to provide a safe home for a persecuted people. He does *not* say that the Jews are living in Israel because it is the Land that God gave them, and it is therefore their right and their duty to live on this Land, or that by returning to the Land they will hasten the coming of the Messiah, which will ultimately bring peace to the world. This too is a narrative of peace and peacemaking, very different from the one Ross tells. It is one told by religiously motivated Jewish settlers living in post-1967 Israeli-occupied Palestinian territories. Ross's Israeli narrative forgets that God promised the Land to the Jews and in so doing removes at least two perspectives held by some people involved in the conflict.[19] First, it does not account for those ultra-Orthodox Jews who reject modern, political Zionism and therefore sometimes form alliances with Palestinians, disturbing the appearance of two enemies, two parties to *the* conflict.[20] Second, it does not account for those religious Zionists now considered among the spoilers of peace, those religiously motivated settlers who believe that peace will come when God's will has been done, and God's will includes the People of Israel (Jews) living on the biblical Land of Israel according the Torah of Israel (Dalsheim 2011; Feige 2009; Lustick 1988; Zertal and Eldar 2007). For Ross, what is important to know about religiously motivated settlers is that they have gotten in the way of the "land for peace" formula, which is based on United Nations resolutions calling for the withdrawal of Israeli armed forces from territories occupied following the 1967 war (Ross 2004:26).

Ross's Arab and Palestinian narrative is also a particularly modernist, secular narrative of nationalism that cannot possibly include all the perspectives and stories of those it claims to represent. In particular, we hear no religious voices, certainly no Islamist narrative (see Lybarger 2007).[21] Rashid Khalidi writes that "from a radical Islamist perspective, Palestinian-centered nationalism is tantamount to heresy, splitting as it does the Islamic *umma*—a word which can mean community, or people, or nation in different contexts—into warring nations" (1997:148). Such voices, like some of those missing in the Israeli narrative, are marginalized as spoilers to potential peace. They are spoilers of a very *particular* peace—one based on nineteenth-century ideas of nation-states—in that they undermine the international political order of bounded territory, security, and defense. The secularity of Ross's perspective then delegitimizes the claims of some people involved in this conflict and denies their narratives of peace at the same time that it reinscribes two enemies: the Arab and the Jew,[22] the Palestinian and the Israeli, each with internal differences and inconsistencies removed, erased, and absorbed into a single unified trajectory.

DECONSTRUCTING, RECONSTRUCTING

It might not seem surprising that high-level diplomats or politicians participate in hegemonic constructions of a national order (that the world is organized into discrete nations represented by states). Indeed, some political analysts claim that this is the moral path of international relations and foreign policy, in which sovereignty is one of the "implicit international norms" that should guide the ethics of foreign policy (Telhami 2004:84). But the reinscription of nation-states and nationalism also takes place at the level of grassroots peacemaking. It seems that our taken-for-granted understanding of the nature of social groups—even among those of us who have learned to deconstruct race, ethnicity, gender, nation, and so forth—has a direct influence on peacemaking. It is as though all the lessons of the socially, historically, contingently constructed nature of collective identity are forgotten, set aside, or applied partially and selectively when it comes to processes of conflict resolution.

Much of the critical scholarship on Israel/Palestine has been aimed at deconstructing the nation as a natural social formation and laying bare the processes through which Jewish nationalism (in the form of modern political Zionism), in particular, has been produced in the selective pasts of historical narratives, archeological productions of facts, schooling, architecture, mapping, and other semiotic and material devices.[23] Such deconstruction removes the veneer of naturalness and allows us to view the seams and scars from cutting and pasting, from pulling apart and recombining, that build enemies through the production of national collectivities.

This kind of theorizing, of course, sets the stage for the possibility of deconstructing Palestinian nationalism as well. Yet many scholars and activists who promote deconstructing the nation-ness of Israel find this prospect extremely problematic, and it has led some to conclude that whether or not the deconstructive theorizing is accurate in general, it must be abandoned in the case of Palestine in the name of social justice.[24] I would suggest that such a position is not only inconsistent, but can also be read as another form of colonizing. At the very least, it is a cunning form of disempowerment based in the sensibilities of a secular age that value the moral importance of recognition.

THEORY FOR PRAXIS

A commitment to liberal humanism in the secular age[25] and secular nationalism interferes with the possibility of practicing liberal humanistic beliefs in cases like this. It is best understood as what Elizabeth Povinelli (2002) calls the "cunning of recognition." I borrow this term to indicate a situation in which the moral sensibilities that provide impetus to recognize a people and rectify past injustices may unintentionally undermine the goals of achieving increased freedom and social justice.

Zvi Bekerman (2007), Professor of Education at the Hebrew University of Jerusalem and longtime peace educator and researcher, discusses a case that occurred in a joint peacebuilding encounter group session that included Palestinian and Jewish Israeli university students. In that session, two of the Jewish Israeli students espoused the deconstruction of national identity, but this move was rejected by the Palestinian students. While some Jews[26] might aspire to deconstruct national identities, Bekerman explains, "none of the Palestinians harbored such aspirations" (Bekerman 2007:31). He points out that this is enormously problematic because "the Jewish quest to de-essentialize national identities had the effect of silencing the voices of Palestinian participants in the dialogue process" (ibid.). "The nation-states scheme has become so powerful," Bekerman writes,

> that, like language in the Sapir–Whorf hypothesis, nationalism seems to shape and direct our most basic paradigmatic conceptions, both of society and individual identity. When these elements are not accounted for in peace educational efforts, they risk consolidating that same reality they intended to overcome. (Bekerman 2007:27)

And yet, after deconstructing individual identity and collective national identity using the tools of poststructuralist critique, Bekerman then sidesteps his own deconstruction to adopt a "postpositivist realism" in order to "rescue praxis from theory" (Bekerman 2007:34). It is worth considering Bekerman's argument closely, as he works out the details and reveals the thought processes involved in arriving at the notion that theory is good for theorists but not for *real* life, an idea often expressed or enacted among peace practitioners, politicians, activists, and scholars.[27]

Bekerman explains the constructed nature of identity in general and national identity in particular, a way of thinking about the nation that has become almost taken for granted in some scholarly circles in the post–Benedict Anderson era of imagined communities.[28] Drawing on the work of Homi Bhabha and Stuart Hall, Bekerman explains clearly and succinctly that "identity as a unitary and autonomous construct has come under attack as being a product of exclusionary power relations" (2007:26). Identity, following Bakhtin, George Herbert Mead, and others, Bekerman writes, is a "monologic posture which tries to overcome through domination that which is 'by nature' dialogic: the self and identity" (ibid.). Social identity and its constitution are products of power relations, which establish dichotomous hierarchies, Bekerman writes. The powerful "attain the status of essentiality while the weak are reduced to the rank of an unfortunate but necessary accident" (Bekerman 2007:26), and the nation-state and nationalism have developed precisely on these conceptions of identity.

Bekerman recalls the work of numerous scholars who have uncovered the "powerful machinery" developed by the nation-state, often in the form of mass educational efforts that market universal literacy and have succeeded in making the national appear natural.[29] Of course, in addition to this work and the power it wields, Bekerman also reminds us that theoreticians have pointed to the structure of nation-states as "one of the cruelest systems on the historical scene" (2007:26).[30]

For the community to be imagined in its national oneness, borders had to be widened and groups lumped together through homogenizing efforts; culture has to be reified and the individual—and his relation to the sovereign—strengthened so as to undermine the power of smaller communal identifications. Concealed behind the promise of universal equality was the sovereign's demand to have none other than individuals, stripped of any group affiliation, under his rod (Bekerman 2007:26–27).

Yet despite this "cultural tyranny" of the nation-state that Bekerman masterfully exposes, he ultimately concludes that this kind of theorizing gets in the way of peace education. On the one hand it must be taken into account, but on the other it interferes with praxis. This conclusion seems contrary to his argument. Because of his deep awareness of the hegemonic constructs underlying education and attempts at peace education, the language he uses raises important questions about the power of an epistemology that we cannot seem to escape.

This is one of the reasons he is skeptical of the usefulness of such encounter groups more generally. The underlying problems of liberal and even radical[31] humanist sensibilities are revealed as Bekerman *recognizes* Palestinians and their reluctance to deconstruct their essentialized identity, but in that very moment of recognition the (previously deconstructed) nation in its fantastic purity is once again reinscribed—naming once again "the Jewish" and "the Palestinian" participants—setting the stage for the very same arguments (who was here first, who belongs to this place, to whom does this place belong, who did what to whom, and who should pay) and the very same fears that one nation will reign over another.

Rescuing praxis from theory is not uncommon among social and political activists more broadly, who are often frustrated when the theories that inspire their thoughts and activism are met with disdain among the population groups the theories aim to empower or liberate; when theories aspire to improve lives, but those whose lives might be directly affected are suspicious, unconvinced, or denounce the theories as worse than meaningless, indeed counterproductive to their goals and desires.[32]

The first result of abandoning theory that deconstructs the naturalness of national belonging, of course, is the risk of reproducing the social imaginary of national collective identity as a unitary group, the kind of group that can be recruited by nationalist ideologies to fight and to die for the cause (Anderson 1983:7).[33] This reduction of multiple forms of being and belonging often fails to take into account the uneven ways in which members of a national group are positioned to suffer and sacrifice for the cause, depending on their socioeconomic as well as cultural place in relation to the powerful against whom they struggle for national independence. Weaker populations tend to be more dependent upon those they struggle against and also often suffer greater losses in anticolonial or nationalist conflicts. Of course, who is weaker, and how much has been suffered, depends very much upon the framing of the conflict. So, for example, while Palestinians may see themselves as the weaker group, victimized by a powerful militarized Israeli state funded by the United States, Israelis may see themselves as victims of Arab aggression and terrorism, a tiny vulnerable state surrounded by larger and more numerous enemies.

Beyond the reproduction of national identities lies a problematic framework in which the idea of abandoning theory is couched in a voice of evolutionary progress, resonating with rhetorical forms through which colonial and other systems of domination have been justified—hence my suggestion that this recognition might itself be a form of colonial knowledge. As such, this evolutionary trope raises red flags about recognition's liberatory potential. Bekerman's argument unwittingly employs an evolutionary discourse of civilizational progress that contributes to the production of Palestinians not only as distinctly different from Jewish Israelis, but as not quite as mature as the former. This underlying notion of progress may in fact prevent even a critical thinker like Bekerman from moving away from nationalism as a necessary stage of development.[34] He writes that

> Palestinians . . . might see in [the deconstruction of essentialized national identity] an impediment to their own national aspirations and thus . . . find it unacceptable *until such time* as they might renounce nationalism *after* having achieved their own nation-state (i.e. only after they have their own nation-state could they consider a perspective that seeks to overcome it) (Bekerman 2007:31, emphasis added).

Bekerman suggests that Palestinians may have to proceed through nationalism and national sovereignty prior to seeking a perspective that might overcome it. Some of the Jews in the encounter group he described seemed to already be on the other side of that transition, but there are Palestinians elsewhere who also seek alternatives to the nation-state.[35] When national groups are anthro-pomorphized, imagined as growing bodies moving through infancy to adulthood, domination of one nation by another is rhetorically rationalized since the group in infancy is not yet ready for self-de-termination. But in this case, maturity is linked implicitly to the ability to *deconstruct* national identity. The context of the discourse remains limited—it must be played out within the chessboard of nations and nationalism—which inevitably, to paraphrase Walter Benjamin, plays favorites for the already powerful.

Benjamin offered a critical analysis of social democratic theory that was "formed by a conception of progress . . . in keeping with the infinite perfectibility of mankind" (Benjamin 1968/1940:260). His writing stands as a warning that a system like fascism could succeed because its opponents treated it as a historical norm, a necessary stage through which we must progress. Benjamin's warning is so pre-cisely applicable to this case because he was concerned that a taken-for-granted belief in an idea of progress that entails always moving toward something better may ultimately undermine even the radical political activists of his time. Such may currently be the case for na-tionalism despite the plethora of scholarship analyzing its dangers.

HUMANIZING ENEMIES

"Storytelling" can be a powerful way of introducing a human el-ement into the dialogue. It can transform enemies into human beings.

—Harold H. Saunders (1999)[36]

Forgetting, I would even go so far as to say historical error, is a crucial factor in the creation of a nation.

—Ernest Renan (1990/1882)

Dialogue groups are one strategy employed by grassroots peace-makers to "humanize" enemy groups in each other's eyes, encour-age mutual understanding, and move from enmity to peaceful coexistence. But telling stories in encounter groups is not always transformative in the ways peacemakers desire (Helman 2002).[37] Dialogue groups might complicate monolithic narratives when they are structured around a different axis, like parenthood or the loss of relatives to the conflict. However, alliances built in these ways also sometimes collapse in the face of all sorts of challenges. Participants often face social pressures from within their own communities or at their places of employment. And when violence emerges, people who have begun to form friendships through these groups may retreat from them, overtaken by uncertainty or fear.[38]

The highly moral moment of recognizing the subaltern as they name themselves is the same moment that reconstitutes two categories of humanity, two enemies, two nations. It is the moment in which even a critical or radical democratic sensibility might embark on a troubling path of supporting dual nationalisms that could ultimately result in efforts to transfer population groups out of a particular territory—whether this be the removal of Palestinians through house demolitions, legal struggles over property, or the expulsion of Israeli settlers from post-1967 territories—or separate the two by a border or wall that sometimes cuts people off from their relatives or from their places of employment.

It might seem like an overreaction to suggest that something so simple and morally compelling as recognizing the subaltern as they name themselves might lead to such extreme outcomes. However, it is precisely these kinds of outcomes both here and in other times and places that have lent urgency to the theoretical analyses of identity and nationalism that Bekerman sidesteps.

Let's step back for a moment and consider how this happens. It begins with the seemingly highly moral moment of recognizing collectives, in this case two national groups. Then a whole set of practical questions ensue. Who will receive passports, and what factors will determine the issuing of passports? What language will be taught in schools? Should each national group have its own state? If each nation has a state, what happens to the people of the "other" nation? And what happens to "other" people? These questions are hardly new. Hannah Arendt (2003/1948) raised such questions, of course, as have scholars of postcolonial nationalism, pointing out that what at first seems liberatory can ultimately have devastating effects.[39] Indeed, for the case of Israel and Palestine the specter of partition (as in India or Cyprus), population transfer, displacement, and refugees is all too real already. Consider, for example, a recent statement by Israeli Foreign Minister Avigdor Lieberman, who was quoted in a Philadelphia Jewish newspaper as saying, "Minorities are the biggest problem in the world." When asked if Arab Israeli citizens (Palestinians) should be removed, he reportedly said:

> I think separation between two nations is the best solution. Cyprus is the best model. Before 1974, the Greeks and Turks lived together and there were frictions and bloodshed and terror. After 1974, they constituted [sic] all Turks on one part of the island, all Greeks on the other part of the island, and there is stability and security.

When reminded that these people were removed forcibly from their homes, he replied, "Yes, but the final result was better." Later, Lieberman explained, "Israeli Arabs don't have to go . . . But if they stay they have to take an oath of allegiance to Israel as a Jewish Zionist state."[40]

This, of course, is also the logic behind removing Israeli settlers from their homes in post-1967 Israeli-occupied territories. While removing settlers may seem morally justified to right the wrongs of the past and the injustices of the present for Palestinians, it is also part of the process of partition. Having recognized nations in the name of justice, we may also set the stage for purifying national territory in which liberation turns to ethnic cleansing, returning us to the question posed by Gil Anidjar that opened this chapter: "Is the enemy the cause of conflict or its effect, or product?" And is the enemy not also the product of conflict resolution?

The humanist sensibility of recognizing differences ultimately undermines Bekerman and seemingly leaves him with no way out of this predicament except to abandon dialogue groups in favor of dealing with practical or "real" issues, what some might argue are the "doable" problems that might be dealt with first (see Povinelli 2002:13, on Michael Walzer) or that might lead to the kinds of outcomes that dialogue encounters cannot. In particular, Bekerman is concerned with actual structural changes that would improve the lives of Palestinians, which he says "cheap recognition by politically correct multiculturalists" will not (2007:29). He is not alone in this. A similar stance has recently been taken by political activists around the world who want to end the Israeli occupation of territory conquered in 1967 and have called for divestment and boycotting of goods, products, services, cultural performances, and the Israeli academy. There have been long and intense discussions and debates about the productiveness and usefulness of such political actions. However, when all is said and done, the most potent argument in favor of divestment and boycotting has often been that this is what "the Palestinians" want. In other words, it amounts to "our" recognition of Palestinians as a people with a goal, who *should* have the right to decide for themselves, and the idea that "we," the highly moral humanists, *should* recognize them and follow their lead.[41] They are the underdogs, the subaltern who have been oppressed and we—so that we can look ourselves in the mirror—will do the right thing by following their lead. (The Jewish people suffered great injustices and in 1948, following the horror of the Nazi Holocaust, asked the United Nations to recognize them as a nation entitled to sovereignty in their own territory. And "we," the highly moral members of the international community of nations, knew that we *ought* to recognize them and their legitimate right to sovereignty in their own territory.)

This is another form of the cunning of recognition that Elizabeth Povinelli (2002) describes in her work on Aboriginals in Australia. For Povinelli, the cunning occurs when indigenous land claims are recognized on the basis of what the courts consider an authentic Aborigine. Australian multiculturalism, Povinelli writes, based on the recognition of differences, is the new content of an Australian nationalism that removes settler guilt for past injustices suffered by the indigenous and inscribes a highly moral nation.[42] Yet, it does so by calling on the indigenous to embody what amounts to an impossible Aboriginality that may actually prevent many from making claims to native land title. The courts have defined what constitutes an Aboriginal identity for the purposes of making legal claims to land, a definition that requires a traditional way of being that cannot possibly be attained in the Australian present and certainly not given the nature of the colonial past.[43] Aborigines making claims to ancestral lands find themselves in an uncanny position of having to be some fictional indigenous character from the past in order to win their rights to land. The result, Povinelli explains, is that "national failures to provide even basic economic and social justice" are translated into "local failures of culture and identity" (Povinelli 2002:56).

The case presented in this chapter, while different, is no less cunning. It allows us to maintain our moral constitution through recognizing cultural differences (presumably beyond the empty recognition of political correctness) at the same time as it works to maintain the system that produces those binary distinctions that form the parameters of conflict within the limited imaginings of territorial nationalism.

In the Israeli case, recognizing Palestinian nation-ness means acknowledging the ground on which Palestinian nationalists have carried out their struggle. Yet recognizing Palestinians as having to go through this process produces them as an anachronism, out of time, people of the past who have, at the very least, not yet gone through the same process and stages that "we" have as a (constructed, imagined) people. And because they have not yet arrived at this stage of modernity, they feel vulnerable and threatened.[44] One can hardly ask a people to deconstruct their national identity and imagine a post-national identity if they have *not yet fully* achieved nationality, which means sovereignty in their homeland and the redistribution of territory—especially if the idea of sovereignty has come to be considered an internationally recognized norm, an expectation that is presumed to be both a right and a good.

Bekerman ultimately suggests the "creation of regional people forums in which to discuss and locally negotiate land redistribution," at once opening up the possibilities for imagining a peaceful future through local processes and at the same time closing down some possible alternatives by appearing to remain within the underlying episteme of secular territorial nationalism (Bekerman 2007:34). Those of us involved in the work of building peace, both bottom up and top down, may be unable to practice peacebuilding beyond the limits of ethnic, territorial nationalism even once we have theoretically deconstructed its naturalness. Our moral constraints require recognition of others as they define themselves, self-determination in the broadest sense. This moral self lives by a code of tolerance, respect, and acceptance of differences that is based in an Enlightenment idea that society should be organized through rational understanding.[45] It encompasses a hope or desire that some consensus might be reached through rational discussion and debate but tends to run into roadblocks when differences are incommensurable, unbridgeable, and irreducible, and conflict remains. The case of recognition here is not so much a matter of unbridgeable differences. It is a case of humanist morality, recognition, and peacemaking undermining themselves when they work for increased human freedom and the flourishing of all humankind without having freed themselves from the insidious cultural tyranny of nationalism.

Chapter 3

History, Histories, Alternative Histories, Alternatives *to* History

> The historical narrative does not, as narrative, dispel false beliefs about the past . . . [it] figurates the body of events that serves as its primary referent and transforms these events into intimations of patterns of meaning that any literal representation of them as facts could never produce.
>
> —Hayden White (1987:45)

History is a complicated endeavor. It is not simply a matter of discovering and recording events of the past. Historians worry and argue about how to present the past and, of course, the discipline of history with its rules and constraints is only one way of remembering. According to Hayden White, the narrative form of presentation that historians employ to tell the past is problematic because while historians seek objectivity, the narrative is inevitably moralizing. This chapter examines historical narratives, alternative histories, and alternatives to history. As we saw in the previous chapter, peacemakers from top-level diplomats to grassroots-level peace educators and facilitators of dialogue groups are aware of the importance of mutual recognition of the parties to conflict and of the stories they tell. However, not all versions of the past can be included, and every narration depends on exclusion to achieve a sense of coherence. This chapter considers stories that are often left out or marginalized in conventional peacebuilding narratives in Israel/Palestine, which tend to remain within the confines of secular nationalism.

The narrative form of historical writing has come to be intuitive and perhaps even inevitable (White 1987:1; 1980:5). Yet this form of representation raises a number of problems for recounting the past. To narrativize is to moralize, to bring coherence, reality, truth, and objectivity to events of the past (White 1980).[1] One way this happens is by bringing together disparate tales and producing unity, as we saw in the cases of Israeli and Palestinian school curricula in the previous chapter. Another way this happens is by making stories appear to tell themselves. Historical narratives such as those in school textbooks can make their stories appear as real, or as the single, objective truth, by removing the subjectivity of an ego from the text (White 1987:3). The events seem to tell themselves *as truth* when the narrator is removed. This is not a problem when the story is presumed to be myth or fiction. Narrative only becomes a problem, according to White, when it is employed to give sequences of real events the form of a story (1987:4).

One way of avoiding such a problem might be to reinsert the voice of the narrator. Another might be to tell more than one version of a particular past, to allow for alternative or even conflicting narratives to reveal the subjective nature of any telling. This, as we saw in the previous chapter, was Dennis Ross's strategy, telling two different stories of the Israeli-Palestinian conflict to show how the parties of this conflict "see the world the way they do" (Ross 2004:15).

This approach seems fair and impartial, but Ross's telling does something else as well. It says: Look, I know that people have different ways of interpreting events, and I'm not going to fight with them over those interpretations. Instead, I'm simply going to show you that I understand that they have a point of view, and I will recognize their point of view and ask that they recognize each other's point of view. This is a polite, relativist move, which in the case of minority histories Dipesh Chakrabarty calls "anthropologizing," because it does not necessarily, and in some cases cannot, tell history from *within* the beliefs of the people who are represented (2000). And Chakrabarty is concerned that such anthropologizing might count as "good" history but will not have the effect of subverting powerful versions of the past and will therefore fall short of the goals of liberation or social justice for the subaltern.

Although some might criticize Ross's strategy for being open to a kind of hopelessly endless relativism,[2] such a telling cannot be criticized for assuming an authoritative voice on the single or true meaning or significance of events.[3] Indeed, it seems more just, more fair, more objective. But what is hiding in this innocence is a kind of repetitive Althusserian interpellation of subjects—in this case, collective subjects. It is a move that reproduces the parties to conflict, once again reinscribing enemies in the process of trying to make peace.

Althusser is known (and his theorizing is often discarded) for his seemingly dated structuralist analysis of repressive and ideological state apparatuses. But in that same long essay (Althusser 1971), he also provides an important and nuanced understanding of how ideology works. If Marxist notions of ideology might be interpreted as removing agency from the subject and *acting on* subjects who have "false consciousness," Althusser demonstrates how the subject is *produced* by, in, or through ideology. Bridging Marx's ideas about ideology and the psychological insights of Freud and Lacan, he explains how ideology gets into our heads, how it powerfully inhabits us, and how ideology can be understood as a structure/system that we inhabit in turn. Ideology, in this sense, is so powerful because it speaks us, names us, but at the same time gives us the illusion that we freely choose to believe what we believe, to be who we are, and to name ourselves. Ideology speaks *to* us as agentive subjects as it also *subjects* us to itself.

Althusser famously illustrated this process by talking about the idea of hailing, or interpellation. He tells a story in which a person is walking down the street and a policeman calls out, "Hey, you there!" Even without calling the person by name, the person turns around, responds, recognizes himself as being hailed. And this moment is both one of subjective self-recognition (it is I being called) and the moment in which one is subjected to the state through ideological apparatuses. This example is meant to illustrate the means by which ideology works, but its oversimplification is misleading because, according to Althusser, an individual is always already an ideological subject. Derrida (2008) gives some insight into this double process of naming and answering the call:

> one must know . . . that if everything begins for us with the response, if everything begins with "yes" implied in all responses ("yes, I respond," "yes, here I am," even if the response is "no") then any response, even the most modest, the most mundane, of responses, remains an acquiescence given to some self-presentation. Even if during the response, in the determined content of a reply, I were to say "no"; even if I were to declare "no, no, and no. I am not here, I will not come, I am leaving, I withdraw, I desert, I am going to the desert, I am not one of your own nor am I facing you," or "no, I deny, abjure, refuse, disavow, and so on," well then this "no" will have said "yes," "yes, I am here to speak to you, I am addressing you in order to answer 'no,' here I am to deny, disavow, or refuse." (Derrida 2008:313)

Ross is aware of the subjective nature of historical narratives, so instead of speaking in an all-knowing voice he *names* the parties, the ones who interpret the past. And the moment the someone is named—the collective someone in this case—that someone is also constituted as a particular someone, an autonomous and choosing someone, one who interprets the past and is part of the collective defined by that past, and one who might be held responsible for that past, while the educative processes through which that collective someone is produced are disguised, hidden, forgotten. Sometimes, these processes are made clear when a "mistake" is made.

THE PEACEMAKER

Once upon a time there was a peacemaker in the Israeli-Palestinian conflict—or at least, there was a young woman who wanted to be a peacemaker. Fittingly, perhaps, if we wanted to use the conventions of Arabic folktales, we might begin, There was and there wasn't—*kaan wa makaan*—a peacemaker. This young woman came to Israel in the midst of the first Palestinian uprising (*Intifada*) against Israeli occupation and began working for an NGO bringing together groups of Israelis and Palestinians, young and old, parents and children, teachers and students, to encourage them to meet and talk and get to know each other, and then to discuss issues of conflict. These meetings were generally prefaced with preparation sessions where people spoke about their own collective identities and about their beliefs about the other group. This NGO aimed to create an environment in which these parties to conflict—who under everyday circumstances might be afraid of or hateful toward each other without ever meeting—could hear each other's stories, really listen and understand. And, as a peace worker, the woman herself was subject to a process of working through her own collective identity or identities—that is, to name the groups to which she belonged or with which she identified. Just as a psychoanalyst undergoes analysis, so a peacemaker undergoes the processes she is learning to employ.

On one occasion, the peacemaker was asked to identify herself. Indeed, she was instructed to reveal her sense of collective belonging. To engage in peacemaking, she was told, one must first be aware of one's own positionality in the conflict. When her supervisor asked her to name herself and explain her belonging, she said, quite simply, "I am my mother's daughter." At that point, the supervisor, a social worker and a very patient person by profession, began to lose her patience with the young peacemaker-in-training. That was the wrong answer! Actually, the supervisor said, it might have been acceptable as a beginning, but the peacemaker was stubborn and refused to go beyond her sense of belonging to her immediate family. She refused, the social worker thought, to identify herself as

Jewish, and as an American. Clearly, she was an American Jew and as such, she really would have to reveal what her relationship as a Jewish American was to Israel. Without this kind of acknowledgment, how could she become aware of her own biases, her subjective position on this conflict?[4] And, to proceed as a peacemaker, such self-knowledge was critical.

But the unfortunate peacemaker had a biography that didn't quite fit the social worker's framework. The peacemaker had had no formal Jewish education, her family never belonged to a synagogue or Jewish community center, nor had she ever learned Hebrew, as so many American Jews did in preparation for their Bar or Bat Mitzvah. Never having been trained in these ways, the peacemaker did not know she was *supposed* to have had a relationship to Israel, a particular take on the conflict, or a sense of belonging to the place. How on earth could someone be a peacemaker in the Israeli-Palestinian conflict without understanding, accepting, recognizing (answering the call, in Derrida's terms) one's own role in it?

From the point of view of the social worker, most people either do or *should* know "who they are." That is, with respect to particular local narratives, in particular contexts, most people should have been successfully schooled in their collective identities. According to the social worker, their parents, their communities, their churches and schools would have taught them. So that when they are named (interpellated), when their collective name (American, Israeli, Palestinian, Jewish, Arab, Muslim, Christian) is called out, they recognize themselves, admit agentive subjectivity, and recognize as their own the label applied to them.[5]

Yet, even then, there are some who struggle against the powerful meanings attached to their collective name. They express a desire to be recognized as members of a particular collective and at the same time to narrate their own past and thereby their own collective identity differently. And some historians have taken up the project of telling those stories that have been left out or marginalized, as part of a move to democratize history and thereby help to achieve social justice. Such narratives, however, despite all good intentions, do not necessarily pave the way toward peaceful resolutions. Sometimes, in fact, they become part of the conflict in the form of competing truth claims, including struggles over who has the right to tell the stories of the collective past.

ALTERNATIVE HISTORIES, SUBALTERN PASTS

Recognizing histories of minority, oppressed, or colonized groups has often taken the form of adding voices and stories to tales of the past within a historicist framework, adding voices that were previously removed, silenced, marginalized, or forgotten.[6] Such additions sometimes present accounts that are at odds with or undermine more powerful narrations. Indeed, they may be recalled precisely in order to privilege a way of telling the past that might serve a different set of interests. Revisionist histories are an important part of recognition not only of peoples but of truth. Quests for truth are also part of who "we" are as post-Enlightenment subjects, concerned with the rational and the role of the rational in achieving a greater common good. We believe that if we can only find out the real and full truth of what transpired in the past, we will surely find salvation or liberation. But when we uncover additional stories about the past, these stories also become part of current struggles. They fuel battles between socially constructed groups, as the past is always revealed through the lens of the present.[7]

HEBRON STORIES

> We read the past differently, see the present differently, dream about the future differently.
> —Haim Hanegbi (quoted in Campos 2007)

I could tell you that Hebron is located in the hills of Judea, south of Jerusalem, and that a small group of about 500 religious Jews live there because of their commitment to the biblical significance of the city. I could also tell you that Hebron is the largest Palestinian city in the occupied West Bank, with a population of more than 150,000, and that there is a struggle over real estate there between radical Jewish settlers and the city's Palestinian inhabitants. I could tell you that settlers have been occupying houses and removing Palestinians, and that the Palestinian shops in Shuhada Street have been closed by the Israeli military to protect those aggressive settlers, in a move that amounts to ethnic cleansing. Or, I might say that observant Jews, returning to the city of their ancestors after having been removed following the 1929 massacre, have been protected from current acts of violence and terror by closing those shops and moving the Palestinian market to another place in the city.

I could tell you a number of stories about Hebron, but I could probably not get away with claiming that the settlers in Hebron should be thought of merely as innocent victims, let alone as subaltern themselves. From the perspective of postcolonial scholarship, to apply the term "subaltern" to religiously motivated settlers in Israeli-occupied Palestine would be considered a misuse of the word. These settlers are part of the colonial invasion and domination of Palestine and party to the ongoing displacement of Palestinians. Indeed, they are at the forefront of expanding Israeli territory by incrementally removing Palestinians from their homes, sometimes through the use of violence and harassment. However, if we can suspend our sense of offense, even for just a moment, there might be something to be learned about theories of representation, the idea of subalterity, and about the case at hand, by imagining these settlers as subaltern themselves.[8]

Each of the following texts aims to set the record straight, and each is speaking to other versions of the past. In some sense, these stories both claim to speak for a subaltern group, to tell the truth from the point of view of those who have been misunderstood, maligned, marginalized, or silenced. And both, unlike Ross's versions, move beyond the confines of the secular nationalism that currently provides the framework through which the Israeli-Palestinian conflict is generally understood and which sets the parameters for its resolution. What follow are not Israeli-versus-Palestinian conflicting versions of the past, but different Jewish narratives of the Jewish community in Hebron.

There is a link to Wellesley College historian Jerold Auerbach's (2009) book, *Hebron Jews: Memory and Conflict in the Land of Israel*, on the website of Hebron's Jewish community.[9] Auerbach explains that the history of the Jewish community of Hebron is deeply rooted in the biblical narrative. The community lives in a cluster around the cave of the patriarchs where Abraham and Sarah, Isaac and Rebekah, and Jacob and Leah are entombed. This tomb, Auerbach writes, is the oldest Jewish holy site in the world. The connection to the biblical narrative is clear, as Chapter 1 opens with the voice of God speaking to Abraham: "'Go,' the voice commanded. 'Leave your land, and your father's house, for the land that I will show you.'" This is the beginning of the story of the Jews of Hebron. Auerbach recounts the story of Abraham and his purchase of the site for Sarah's burial. If claiming rights to a place depends on having been there first, then a story like this would surely prove longevity. Or if claiming territory depends on legally acquiring the land in question, then this story proves that too, for Abraham purchased the land where Sarah was to be buried and the transaction is documented in the biblical text. Of course, all this depends on whether or not one accepts the idea that "the Jews," or the specific community of Jews in Hebron today, are the descendants of Abraham and Sarah, and on whether or not one accepts the Bible as historical record. Auerbach is acutely aware of the controversy over Hebron and the anger the current Jewish community there draws. The opening line of his book is this: "No Jews are as relentlessly reviled as the Jews of Hebron." If they are so hated, Auerbach suggests, it is because they act on their belief in their right and responsibility to live in this contentious city.

Auerbach's mission for his text is to "set the record straight," to explain the Jews of Hebron, to state their case. If narrative has the power to persuade, this is clearly his goal. However, there are counter-narratives as well. Michelle Campos, a historian at the University of Florida, writes about Haim Hanegbi (quoted at the beginning of this section) and other descendants of Hebron Jews[10] who claim that the "settlers [currently] living in the heart of Hebron" do not have the right to speak in the name of the "old Jewish community" of the city (the old Yishuv). Hanegbi and other members of The Association of Hebron Descendants claim they are the true descendants of the Old Jewish community of Hebron. "These settlers," they say, "are alien to the way of life of the [indigenous] Hebron Jews, who created over the years a culture of peace and understanding between peoples and faiths in the city" (quoted in Campos 2007:41). This declaration, Campos tells us, challenges the "widely accepted Zionist metanarrative that saw Hebron as a central symbol of Jewish persecution at the hands of bloodthirsty Arabs. In 1929, sixty-seven Jews were massacred in Hebron," she writes. They were killed in one of a series of countrywide clashes, "making Hebron a political/national sacred site" (ibid.). In effect the entire Jewish community was destroyed in 1929, because those who were not killed were exiled from the city. Thus, Campos writes, the story of Hebron and the 1929 massacre became another chapter of exile and return, a trope so central to a broader Jewish and Zionist narrative. But Auerbach (2009) claims that most Israeli Jews, and Jews more generally, have forgotten the significance of Hebron:

> Jewish history and memory are inextricably entwined, and no community of Jews is more tenaciously committed to the preservation of historical memory than the Jews of Hebron. But their determination to remember in the very place where Jewish memory may be said to have originated, places them at the epicenter of a polarizing conflict within contemporary Israel . . . It involves nothing less than the identity and boundaries of the Jewish state and the definition of legitimacy within it. Hebron Jews are widely condemned by legions of critics for misguided political and religious fanaticism that could propel

Israel into a disastrous holy war with Arabs or a tragic civil war between Jews. Yet they remain fiercely determined to remember what most Jews have long since forgotten. (p. 4)

"Remember and do not forget" (Deuteronomy 9:7). Hayden White writes that memory as such is not enough to constitute meaning. "Events," he says, "must be not only registered within the chronological framework of their original occurrence but narrated as well, that is to say, revealed as possessing a structure, an order of meaning which they do *not* possess as mere sequence" (White 1980:9). The creation of that structure by the narrator and its presentation *as a revelation* of structure to the reader demonstrate that "every historical narrative has as its . . . purpose the desire to moralize the events that it treats" (White 1980:17–18).

The way in which we tell stories of the past matters. White describes the narrative as having a central subject, a well-defined beginning, middle, and end, as well as a turning point in the story that signals its central point or lesson—its moral punch line. The narrator's choice about where the story begins sets the stage for its moral lesson. Auerbach begins with Abraham and Hebron, which is quite different from beginning with Jewish immigration to Palestine in the late 1800s. If claims are to be made about the right to the land, to live there, to possess the land and have sovereignty over it, and if such rights are understood to be determined by who was there first, then when and where the story begins is enormously important.

Now, justice has taken the form of peace negotiations in Israel/Palestine, and the place (in history, in geography) where memory starts and narratives begin have implications in determining what is "right." Who has the right to the land? Who was there first? Who can claim legal title? But why are these the bases upon which such decisions are made? For now, I will simply say that in the same way that Durkheim (1997/1933) argued that what counts as crime is determined by what is punished—that is, we cannot determine what crime is through *a priori* assumptions, but only by looking at what people actually do—so rights to possession are similarly arbitrary. The arbitrariness of such determinations means that the arguments about having been there first and proving possession go on and on potentially without end. This may be good for the discipline of history, but is this "good" for resolving conflict?

Auerbach tells us that "Jewish memory may be said to have originated" in Hebron, implying that Hebron is the foundation of Jewishness itself (Auerbach 2009:4). This is a story of the very place where Jewish memory originated, or the story of the very first characters in Jewish collective memory. But if the story of the Jews starts with Abraham, so do many other stories. Abraham is claimed as a spiritual ancestor by Christians and Muslims as well; and in that case, why not start with Adam and Eve? Abraham is the father of Ishmael as well as Isaac, so remembering this patriarch is also significant to the memory of Arabs more generally, whether Muslim or Christian (or, one might add, Jewish).[11]

There are other places in time and different biblical characters that might be considered the beginning of Jewish history and memory. If Abraham is the father of three monotheistic faiths, then specifically Jewish memory might be thought to have started with Moses. And, of course, the memory of Jewish Israelis might be thought to have begun with the first Aliya, when Jews began immigrating/returning to Palestine in the late 1800s. But to begin with the Jewish Aliya in modernity would be to begin where Palestinians often tell this tale, and it would be to deny continuity between today's Jews in Hebron (and the rest of Israel) and the biblical ancestors. Yet the battle, for Auerbach, centers around intra-Jewish politics in modernity. It is about reminding the Jewish community, Jews everywhere, about what they have forgotten, and reminding them about their historical connection to the sacred sites in Hebron, to the tomb of the patriarchs. Indeed, we might conclude, based on this beginning, that the significance of this Hebron story has nothing to do with struggles between Israelis and Palestinians. It is not about contemporary conflicts over real estate there, or justice for Palestinians, or about the potential for a peace agreement. It is about reminding Jews of the specifically Jewish significance of this place. And place, as some of the settlers I interviewed made clear, is central to their being.

Indeed place (*makom* in Hebrew) is another word for God (*ha makom*, the place). For the settlers of Hebron, like those in the Gaza settlements of Gush Katif who have since been removed, it is important to understand one's relationship to place because this relationship is integral to who you are, to what it means to be Jewish, and to fulfilling God's commandments by living on the Land He promised to the Jewish people. It is there that they must live and live according to His commandments in order to hasten the coming of the Messiah. On a recent visit to the Jewish community of Hebron, I encountered a woman who told me a story about the importance of living there.

This woman came to Israel with her parents from the United States because of their devotion to the Holy Land. They settled in Hebron, but she moved to another place after marriage. She and her husband were considering moving back to Hebron, but she feared for the safety of her children and consulted with the wife of a prominent Hebron rabbi, a man considered to be the founder of the contemporary Jewish community there. The *rebbetzin* (title used for a rabbi's wife) convinced her that it was worth the danger to live there because of the importance of living near the biblical ancestors. The *rebbetzin* told her a story about a man who had come to Hebron but decided to leave and go back to the United States. "He got on a plane and flew to New York and no sooner did he get off the plane than some 'Kushi' (black person)[12] robbed him and killed him! That's it. He died! There is danger everywhere you go and in the end it is all in God's hand. Now, when you think about it," she said, "if you have to die, isn't it better to die for the ancestors (*ha-avot*) here in Hebron than to just die for something as meaningless and humiliating as being robbed by some Kushi?"

The same story that Auerbach tells and that underlies the story the *rebbetzin* told this young woman, with its biblical beginnings and its biblical framing of contemporary human groups, also speaks to issues of rights and justice in the present and future. If the question of Israel/Palestine is one of possession, dispossession, of place and displacement, then determining possession and placement is crucial. And if the Jews were here for centuries, then the land should be returned to them and Palestinian dispossession either becomes trivial in comparison or is itself a result of an earlier injustice and therefore is not dispossession at all. Auerbach's telling seems to reflect the ways in which the Jews in Hebron today narrate themselves on their website and in their museum (see Feige 2009). Of course, the extent to which this narrative will persuade the reader of the righteousness of the settlers' project in Hebron will depend at least partially on the audience itself.

Michelle Campos writes that such remembering is very partial and selective.[13] She contends that the Zionist appropriation of the story of Hebron remembers the violence of 1929 and that that story is used for ultra-nationalist purposes. However, it should be noted that Auerbach and contemporary Hebron Jews are narrating a religious story about remaining on the Land and living near biblical ancestors. This tale can and does provide content for those arguing for Jewish sovereignty, but living near ancestors on the Holy Land does not necessarily imply *political* sovereignty, as we shall see when we return to the story of the Rabbi that opened this book.

Campos (2007) offers a historical narrative based on one prominent man's memoirs. It tells an alternative story about the relationship between Jews and Arabs prior to the establishment of the state of Israel. The memoirs of Yosef Eliyahu Chelouche, an influential businessman and prominent figure in the local North African Jewish community, is an account of how the Jews lived together with their neighbors in Palestine prior to the first Aliya, when European Jews began migrating (or returning) to Palestine. The story Campos tells begins with Chelouche's memoirs of life in Jaffa in the late Ottoman period. These memoirs, she writes, "offer us insights into the ways in which indigenous Palestinian Arabs and Jews inhabited a shared landscape." They were written in the hope that they might "awaken those who would deal with the question of relations with the neighbors in a different manner and with different maneuvers, in the manner and maneuver of the locals, who have great experience in neighborly relations, to repair to the extent possible that which is distorted" (Chelouche, quoted in Campos 2007:42). This account is careful to distinguish between indigenous Jews—those who lived in Palestine before the first Aliya—and those of European descent who came later. It sets up a story in which native Jews lived in relative harmony with their Arab neighbors because they shared a set of cultural norms and knew how to live together. It was only when the Ashkenazi Jews began to arrive—foreigners who came from Europe to the Middle East, to a culture very different from their own—that trouble began between Jews and Arabs. The Ashkenazi Jews did not know how to interact with their neighbors. They behaved in ways that might be insulting, and they looked down upon the local Arabs and wanted to change them and make them more like Europeans.

While a small number of Ashkenazi Jews were longtime residents of the town, many of the victims of the 1929 massacre came from abroad, Campos writes. They were "neither native to the place nor known to the local residents" (p. 55). Many, according to Campos, were there as students in the yeshiva and they "commonly had misunderstandings with the locals and engaged in violations of the local cultural code" (ibid.). These Ashkenazi Jews were part of the Zionist movement to establish a sovereign Jewish state in Palestine. This, according to Campos, is why the violence broke out, and this is the reason for the 1929 massacre of Jews in Hebron. It was, she explains, misrepresented as neighbors killing neighbors (p. 57). Instead it was a case of locals killing outsiders, and was aimed against the Zionist movement.

The story of Chelouche is filled with ambiguity. He worked for the Zionist movement to convince local Jews to join, and he tried to persuade his Arab neighbors that the movement would be good for everyone and that they had nothing to fear from it. However, Campos explains, Chelouche was also critical of some of the Zionist movement's racist beliefs and practices.

If Auerbach's narrative aimed to remind all Jews of their biblical past, especially to remind secular Zionists[14] of their ancient connection to the Holy Land, and presumably to unite them, the story Campos tells makes clear distinctions between Jews of different backgrounds. It calls into question the continuity between the current Jewish community in Hebron and earlier ones. In this sense it also reveals the constructedness of the national collective. It makes these distinctions in order to claim the authority on which to speak about the past, to focus on a very different interpretation of events, one that does not frame Palestinian Arabs as murderers of Jews, but rather places the blame on Zionist settlement and on Ashkenazi Jews. This interpretation provides a framework in which Jews and Arabs once lived harmoniously and therefore could presumably live together peacefully again. "[M]ost of Hebron's Jews," Campos emphasizes, "were in fact saved and spared by their neighbors" (p. 57).

This story is also about rights, but not necessarily about the right to possess land. Focusing on a different time period and providing a different interpretation of events, this story is about the *right to tell* the past. Emphasizing a period of stability and good neighborly relations, this narrative frames the events of 1929 as an understandable anomaly, a reaction to Zionism and the attempt to gain political sovereignty. The massacre in Hebron should not be read as indicative of the eternal character of Palestinian Arabs. That violent outburst was an aberration, a temporary interruption of stability and good neighborly relations.

WHO CAN BE SUBALTERN?

To be subaltern means to lack or be denied access to power. More specifically in the case of postcolonial scholarship and cultural studies, it has come to mean the inability to speak in a hegemonic discourse, and therefore to be excluded from self-representations connoting agency. Subaltern studies seeks a solution to the problem of colonial domination that is exercised through forms of knowledge and cultural practices, through forms of representation and telling history. If colonization and political domination more generally are accomplished through more than direct physical force, then decolonization means more than winning wars of independence or the removal of foreign troops. It can include trying to undo the ways in which the powerful have written history and generated knowledge about the people and places they have colonized (Fanon 1967; Said 1978). Decolonizing includes a range of processes like regaining control of history textbooks in which local or subaltern representations of the past are included in order to recognize "a people" making claims for political independence and sovereignty, or to seek retribution for past injustices, or more generally to gain the independence to define one's self (Spivak 1988).

If being subaltern means exclusion from dominant discourse, then surely this definition applies to the members of the contemporary Jewish community in Hebron. It is not that they cannot speak *in* a dominant discourse, but that the dominant discourse is not their own. They can perhaps adapt to it or translate themselves into it, but the secular nationalism that is the ground of contemporary peacemaking is not their voice, not their worldview. So, to what extent is the term "subaltern" useful in such a case when considering stories about the past?

On the one hand, these settlers cannot express themselves to the hegemonic secular[15] in their own voice, and they therefore fit one definition of subalterity. Making themselves intelligible requires translating themselves into the terms of more powerful others; when settlers speak to outsiders they often represent their concerns in terms of issues of security, national or communal heritage, or national continuity between earlier and later Jews in Palestine in ways that coincide with a broader secular nationalist imaginary.[16] On the other hand, they are part of the colonial project in Palestine. Indeed, they are currently either blamed or credited for driving the conflict by being "spoilers" of peace—and therefore subaltern in yet a different way in their exclusion from secular political processes seeking peace through territorial exchange. If they have close ties to highly positioned political power and are driving the conflict and state decisions, then perhaps they are part of the hegemony. But if they are constantly throwing sticks into the spokes of state-sponsored peace negotiations, pushing things off track and causing endless problems, then they are the subaltern who desire a different sort of hegemony (in the Gramscian sense). If their ways of being and believing, their sense of the importance of living with biblical ancestors, cannot speak persuasively on the secular international political stage, then in terms of postcolonial and subaltern studies, they are clearly subaltern. They claim they have been misunderstood, their voice(s) marginalized, maligned, demonized, or even silenced.

But if these settlers, these persistent, effective, and sometimes violent colonizers and expropriators of territory, can therefore be categorized as subaltern, what does subaltern mean? What does naming a particular group of people "subaltern" do? And under what circumstances should we enter into an endeavor to restore the voice or agency of such subaltern peoples? If subalterity means having been denied the right to speak for one's self, to define one's self, then justice requires restoring that right, as we saw in the case of the Palestinians in Bekerman's study who are (represented as) not yet ready to deconstruct their national identity because they are still in the process of building it. If this right is to be respected, if restoring justice means that subaltern Palestinians should *not* have to deconstruct themselves, then does this also mean that religiously motivated settlers should also be granted this right? If the lack of access to hegemonic discourse is the defining factor of subalterity, and if both groups of Hebron Jews represented in this chapter claim that their perspectives, interpretations, and understandings of the past have not been recognized, does it not follow, from the point of view of subaltern studies and its quest for social justice, that both of these narratives should be recognized?

THEY ARE NOT TEMPLE BREAKERS!

Campos's telling of the past is very much like a story told by Ashis Nandy about another conflict situation in which people who are sometimes considered eternal enemies instead regard each other as morally upstanding, and as people to live with rather than fight against or to separate from. Nandy (1995) has written extensively against the limits and dangers of secular nationalism. He argues against the limits and potential danger of historicism as well, offering ways of looking at the past that do not necessarily participate in the interpretations of cause and precedence that fuel nationalist struggles. Nandy suggests that traditional or religious communities can emphasize the moral constitution of themselves and those who are construed as their enemies through non-historicist interpretations of the past (Nandy 1995). His argument moves beyond the idea of *adding* voices or stories to the historical mode of constructing the past and instead points to the importance of alternatives *to* history.

One case he discusses involves the dispute over the destruction of the Ayodhya temple and the Babri mosque in northeast India. The dispute has to do with what happened at the place where violence triggered by the Ramjanmabhumi movement in India reached its climax on December 6, 1992. On that day a controversial mosque at the sacred city of Ayodhya, which many claimed was built by destroying a Hindu temple that stood at the birthplace of Lord Rama, was demolished to avenge a historical wrong. The controversy surrounds questions of whether or not there was a temple that was destroyed by the builders of the Babri mosque, and whether or not this Ayodhya is really the Ayodhya of Rama. Nandy explains that these questions are important for secularized Indians but not for the devout millions who have made pilgrimages to this sacred city for centuries.

In this case, rather than arguing endlessly over what actually happened, whether there is proof of the temple's existence, or whether some people are "true" Hindus or true Muslims, he shows how the *puranic* textual genre of the Hindu tradition (a traditional form of telling the past) is not concerned with the objective historical truth of the past, but is a narrative of morality.

Contemporary Indian Muslims, for example, deny that they are temple breakers ("It was not us!"). They have not claimed, as they conceivably might, that their forbears destroyed Hindu temples *and* that they are proud of that past as a measure of their piety. Nor have Muslims affirmed their *right* to break temples, or even to retain mosques built on demolished temples. They have not sought protection for the Babri mosque without insisting that the mosque had *not* been built on a razed temple, or without insisting that what Muslim marauders did in India is what marauders always do and such vandalism had nothing to do with Islam (Nandy 1995:63).

Nandy tells us that most of the Hindu residents of Ayodhya have customarily considered these kinds of denial by Muslims about anti-Hindu violence in the past to be an important moral statement. To these Hindus, such denial is a reaffirmation of a specific kind of moral universe by Muslims, which may be more acceptable than the interpretations offered by Hindu nationalists. In this mode of storytelling, the past is truly the past, and present social relations must be based on construals of shared morality, rather than of history.

One might argue that this is what Campos's telling of Chelouche's story does. It is about Jews who don't think the 1929 massacre in Hebron is indicative of Palestinian (or Arab or Muslim) morality—or their "essential nature"—more generally. That violent event is read as an exception, an aberration due to specific circumstances, and should not be used to justify separation or removal of Palestinians. But if Chelouche tells a tale of morality quite similar to the one Nandy tells of Hindus and Muslims in India, his story, like Auerbach's, also does something else: it moves outside the parameters of secular, territorial nationalism. Auerbach, in the name of contemporary Hebron Jews, recalls the ancient past and explains why it is so important for Jews to live near the biblical ancestors. We could say that Hebron Jews' self-conceptualization as descendants of Abraham continuing God's commandments to the patriarch is very like Ranajit Guha's (1994/1983) peasants who speak of supernatural agency in their lives. As with the Indian peasants, this motivation has to be translated into secular nationalist talk in order to be heard at all, but it also works against them. This might be the "authentic" voice of the settlers that would speak if the subaltern voice could be heard, and this is part of the reason why they cannot say some of the things that the "crazy" Rabbi does, if they want to be influential in secular politics. Although Auerbach expresses concern that giving up sovereignty of this territory could prevent Jews from praying at their holy sites, his story of Hebron Jews is not primarily about national sovereignty. Indeed, it is critical of secular Zionism for forgetting the importance of the Holy Land to the Jewish people. The so-called crazy Rabbi who was introduced at the opening of this book also emphasizes the Jewish connection to the Holy Land in a way that moves beyond the limited parameters of territorial nationalism.

PASSION FOR THE LAND

The "crazy" Rabbi's passion for the Land and the Lord places his ideas beyond the current social and political order, and beyond well-known categories of conflict in Israel/Palestine, making his actions and words fall within the category of the crazy. Among different sorts of Israeli nationalists/Zionists, the Rabbi is marginalized in different ways. Those on the left wing of politics, who are often secular or antireligious, find him eccentric—sometimes amusing, but often annoying. While they might applaud his ideas about living with Palestinians, they find his actions contradictory because he feels so strongly about Jewish presence in all of the biblical Land of Israel. Some of that Land, they say, must be relinquished to the Palestinians for their state. Thus, non-Zionist and anti-Zionist members of the left wing of Israeli politics also find this rabbi and his ideas problematic, because from their perspective he cannot claim to support Palestinians and at the same time support Jewish settlement in post-1967 territories. Those on the right wing of politics, who are often supportive of territorial expansion, and therefore of the settlements in post-1967 occupied territories, see this rabbi as a traitor. The right wing usually includes religiously motivated settlers such as the Rabbi himself. However, many religious settlers are adamant about Israeli sovereignty, and many see Palestinians as dangerous enemies.

"Zionism must undergo a process of feminization," the Rabbi sometimes said. "The land is feminine and sovereignty is masculine. We must become closer to the land and let go of our tight grip on the reigns of sovereignty. We must not be afraid to let go." He often spoke about his many meetings over the years with those in the Palestinian community who were considered Muslim extremists. "They are not like you and me," he said. "Do not misunderstand. I do believe we must talk to them, but I do not think they are angels . . . They practice violence and brutality and do not sanctify human life as we do." Nevertheless, the Muslim clerics with whom he had met shared his deep belief in God as the only true Sovereign. And this, he said, can be the basis for living together in the Holy Land, albeit each according to his own practices. He hoped that Jewish settlers could take the role of what he called an "outstretched hand" toward the Palestinians by bringing Jewish and Palestinian communities physically closer to one another, like interlacing fingers. This may seem like a very strange idea, since we so often hear of violent behavior reported between settlers and Palestinians. Still, the Rabbi maintained his determination and is convinced that this is the right and righteous path.

It is interesting to note that at least some of the Jews in Hebron today—including recent settlers of American and European descent who, according to the people Campos describes, have no right to speak about the Jewish past in Hebron—also speak about good neighborly relations. On a recent visit to Hebron I was introduced to a man who lives in a dilapidated trailer in one of the tiny Jewish neighborhoods in Hebron. He is a political activist and known to be an agitator.

He sometimes organizes antagonistic marches and demonstrations through Palestinian neighborhoods and towns in Israel that result in injury and destruction. But when I asked him about some of the recent reports of violence in Hebron, he told me this was most definitely *not* carried out by the local Jewish community. The Jews of Hebron are not violent, he said, and if tires were burned in a struggle to hold on to a particular building that Jews had moved into, those fires were set by people who came from outside the city.[17] In addition to this depiction of the current moral character of the Jews of Hebron as desiring good neighborly relations, other stories appeared in the Israeli press. Hebron Jews were quoted speaking about good relations with their Palestinian neighbors, about going to Palestinian dentists, for example, or shopping together in the same supermarket.[18]

Palestinians in Hebron have also reportedly denied being violent toward their Jewish neighbors.[19] When asked about the 1929 massacre, Hebron Palestinians said that violence was carried out by people from outside the city. Both Palestinians and Jews in Hebron make these claims about their own moral constitutions, denying participation in violence against each other. It was not us, they say.

ALTERNATIVE FUTURES?

Should particular pasts, marginalized or not, blot each other out? When you see the Jewish community in Hebron today, you may want to tell them they are drawing on the *wrong* past, because that past has them imprisoned, literally, inside walls and guarded by soldiers, surrounded by emptied dwellings where their Palestinian neighbors once lived. For some of them, their present might encourage them to move beyond nationalism/anti-nationalism because of the sacredness of the place and the importance of being there. Should diplomats like Dennis Ross, or grassroots activists recognize only particular pasts or privilege previously marginalized tales? Or, might there be room for all the multiple ways in which people understand their pasts to be recognized in the present and taken into account for processes of making peace?

Being attentive to minority or subaltern pasts poses a challenge to maintaining the heterogeneity of many pasts without reducing them to any overarching principle that speaks for an already given whole (Chakrabarty 2000:107), an already given whole like "the nation": the Palestinians, the Israelis, or the Arabs and the Jews.

Nandy recommends moving beyond historicism and suggests focusing on moral discourses that move beyond secular nationalism. But Chakrabarty insists we should make room for *all* the various ways of telling the past, even though historians do not have a form that can accomplish such inclusiveness. Nor do we have a social order that proceeds from such inclusive heterogeneity.

All three narratives recounted above—the "crazy" Rabbi's embrace of territory at the expense of sovereignty; the Old Yishuv story of neighborly relations between Hebron's Jews and Arabs; and Auerbach's story of the centrality of the tombs of the patriarchs to Jewish experience and even the survival of the Jewish state— interfere with hegemonic social and moral orders of nations and states, the rights of peoples to sovereignty in their own territory. They interfere with the premises of the two-state solution in different ways, spoiling the ability of the people currently in power to get what they want without trouble. Each tale points to a different specific solution: remaining on the Land without political control; a one-state solution for all residents; or permanent Israeli sovereignty over the West Bank, and then some.

Chapter 4

Anachronisms and Moralities

> Global social movements, like the unprecedented global movement
> against the Iraq war in 2002–3 or the ongoing World Social Forum
> gatherings, already herald a world that is beyond the logic of na-
> tional liberation—even as the settler colonial hold over Palestine
> remains as a relic of an antiquated era, and therefore appears espe-
> cially intolerable.
>
> —Mohammed Bamyeh (2010:62)

If being stuck within nationalist consciousness appears to be an
impediment to human liberation and peaceful coexistence, then
perhaps thinking beyond nationalist or state-ist solutions could
offer an alternative. Peacemakers like Zvi Bekerman are sometimes
involved in community efforts in educating for peace. They might
organize encounter groups to reduce tensions between enemy factions on the ground and to address what have come to be thought
of as symbolic, cultural, or identity issues. Some peacemakers,
like Dennis Ross, advise politicians in applying diplomatic pres-
sure or economic sanctions or negotiating treaties. But sometimes
peacemakers have a broader vision for change beyond the end of

local fighting. Peace can mean freedom from war or the cessation of armed physical violence. It can mean the end of conflict and a renewed sense of security or stability. For many, peace also means social justice, structural changes, or making amends for the past. But whatever peace means for those who seek it, it always connotes better lives.

One way of thinking about better lives is to think about life free of subjugation altogether. Writing about anarchy as a liberating form of social order, sociologist Mohammed Bamyeh falls off the usual grid of left wing and right wing, or progressive and conservative, politics.[1] Rather than focusing on resolving specific conflicts, Bamyeh has been concerned with the bigger question of how to conceive of social order without domination. His quest for liberation through anarchy might marginalize him in many different kinds of communities just like the so-called crazy Rabbi at the opening of this book, even though his belief in human sovereignty also makes him very different from that rabbi. And in much of his work, Bamyeh advocates something that is also different from ordinary peacemaking. He is neither a politician nor a local activist, yet he is deeply concerned about Palestine and about liberation for the Palestinian people. Why does Bamyeh express special concern for the Palestinians? What makes liberation for them any different than for the rest of us? According to Bamyeh, the Palestinians should be of special concern because their oppression is a "relic of an antiquated era," and this makes their need for liberation all the more urgent.

In Chapter 2 we saw how "cunning recognition" of Palestinians produces them as an anachronism: as people who *still* need national liberation despite the inherent cruelties of nationalism.[2] This chapter deals with ideas about time and about being out of time, ideas that also constrain the ways we think about peace, morality, and belonging. It is about the relationship between the idea of anachronism and the production of moral orders, about how temporality can draw moral and social boundary lines.[3] Ideas about time are everywhere and nowhere. They enter into our thoughts so profoundly that they disappear, becoming little more than a backdrop for other perceptions, like water for fish. We value certain kinds of changes as forms of progress, as moving forward toward something better than what we've known in the past. Our temporal conditioning is so deeply ingrained that many of us live with a sense that progress toward something better occurs naturally through the passage of time. We admire "forward thinking" and admonish ideas and practices that are "backward." To arrive at such conclusions means thinking in terms of a linear progressive temporality, which can produce a largely unconscious and often unspoken animosity toward different ways of being in time. Despite decades of scholarly analysis and critique,[4] this temporal conditioning remains so pervasive, like the taken-for-grantedness of nation that we encountered in the previous chapters, that it too can affect our thinking about social justice, peace, and human liberation. It, too, can shape the production of enemies and spoilers to peace processes.

RELIC OF AN ANTIQUATED ERA

In the quote that opens this chapter, Mohammed Bamyeh characterizes the logic of national liberation as something that will soon pass as global social movements herald a new stage in history. And at the same time, he writes about the settler-colonial hold over Palestine as a thing of the past. Such temporal thinking can provoke anger at some people because their ways of living are considered a thing of the past. It can also evoke pity for those who have been unjustly left behind as history sweeps by them.

Some "people out of time" arouse anger, revulsion, and condemnation. We despise them, and that revulsion prevents us from engaging with them, mimicking the very colonial impulses that progressive and radical theorists and activists struggle against. The "despised" I am referring to here are religiously motivated settlers in post-1967 Israeli-occupied territories,[5] who are seen as anachronistic for at least three reasons: their actions belong to a pre-state past, their beliefs are not modern,[6] and their temporal ideology is abhorrent. I begin with these settlers because in the current political milieu they are often considered by liberals and progressives to be the locus of evil, the people who must be moved so that peacemaking can go forward.[7] They are an obstacle for peacemakers like Dennis Ross. But they are also a bone in the throat for post-nationalist radical thinkers like Mohammed Bamyeh:

> "This is the twenty-first century, how could this be happening now?" The words belong to a resident of the town of Jenin in the West Bank, reached by a radio station on his cellular phone in the spring of 2002 amid the slaughter wrought by the Israeli military Operation Defensive Shield . . . In an age of globalization and reduced sovereignty, the time of nations and their states seems to be passing. Yet over Palestine today hovers a logic fully out of joint with its times. The old-fashioned colonialism that had devoured Palestine shows no signs of relenting. If anything, the opposite is happening. Today we witness a far more fanatic religious attachment to a greater "Eretz Yisrael" than had been the case half a century ago.
>
> The tragedy of modern Palestine, beyond all the horrors and suffering associated with it, is doubly tragic in that it appears to have been caused not by any necessary logic of history but rather by countertimely events. (Bamyeh 2003:825–826)

The entire tragic situation belongs to the past, and this temporal placement makes the situation especially intolerable. But Walter Benjamin teaches us that "The current amazement that the things we are experiencing are 'still' possible . . . is not philosophical. This amazement is not the beginning of knowledge—unless it is the knowledge that the view of history which gives rise to it is untenable" (1968/1940:257). In other words, Benjamin warns against precisely the kind of temporal ideology that lies behind Bamyeh's words.[8] On the one hand the religious zeal for *Eretz Yisrael*, which of course refers to the influence of religiously motivated settlers, is an abhorrent thing of the past. And on the other hand, Palestinians have been left behind by the sweeping tides of history that have granted to most other nations the reality of territorial sovereignty. "Thus it would seem natural to argue that Palestine must be allowed to resume its rightful but long-postponed march along the path of decolonization and independence. Yet, in Palestine we confront the possibility that even this seemingly modest proposal may now be out of date" (Bamyeh 2003:826).

Bamyeh suggests that the language of nationalism is *not* the answer for Israel/Palestine. Instead he recommends reimagining the collective through agreement on a common narrative that might form the basis of a possible resolution.[9] He recalls the work of Ammiel Alcalay (1993), who writes about an alternative past preceding the constitution of distinct categories of Jews and Arabs as *enemy* others. In many ways, this is precisely the kind of move that Benjamin's theorizing calls for, recalling a different past, an alternative that can provide a basis on which to rebuild the present. However, remaining entrenched in categories of national belonging, Bamyeh calls for justice to right the wrongs of the past and for a new collective narrative that would bring these *two* separated nations together. The common narrative Bamyeh recommends understands Zionism itself as part of the process of removal of Jews from Europe, a cruelty that continued the work of the Nazi Holocaust while also creating a new tragedy for the Palestinians. Writing of Zionism, Bamyeh asks,

> was there a more anti-Semitic act than removing the Jews from Europe into Palestine after the Holocaust—in effect completing the work of the Holocaust, and in the process creating another entangled regional crisis elsewhere in the world when the reparation for Jewish suffering ought to have taken place in Europe? (2003:827)

Many scholars view Zionism as a reaction to nineteenth-century anti-Semitism in Europe. Others contend that the modern political discourses of nation-states and anti-Semitism in nineteenth-century Europe are related to Zionism in more profound ways (Halevi 1987:155–157). That is, rather than thinking of Zionism only as a reaction to anti-Semitism, it has been argued that these ideologies share a common set of conditions that allowed them to emerge. The racist theories of the nineteenth century that classified the Jews as a race (genealogically tied together as a people rather than as a group who could choose affiliation with a religious institution), and the conditions that created the need and the right of citizens to rule themselves, underlie the combination of nationalism and democracy in which self-rule is a right granted to a people. These are the same conditions in which two peoples—the Jews as a nation and the Palestinians as a nation—are constructed against each other, vying for sovereignty over the same territory.

But this alternative narrative potentially produces another enemy. In this scenario, people of Palestine/Israel might imagine themselves in opposition to "Europe." This brings us back to Anidjar's question about whether enemies precede conflict, are produced through conflict, or as I ask, whether they are also produced through conflict resolution. What is most problematic for peacemaking in Bamyeh's theorizing is that to arrive at this new collective historical narrative, and to concentrate on concrete grievances arising from past injustices, we must "dismantl[e] the blinding religious mythology with which this concreteness of things is covered up" (2003:828). In other words, we must relegate particular kinds of religion to the dust heap of history.

Such dismantling, of course, discards the cultural meanings of some of the people involved while it honors the cultural meanings of others. This move has the potential to continue cycles of violence, because to make amends for having silenced and oppressed Palestinians, it requires silencing or marginalizing other groups.

The common narrative Bamyeh suggests might provide a new collective narrative for *some* of the variously situated people directly involved in this conflict. It might work for some secular and left-wing Israelis and Palestinians in particular locations.

But there are others, including some religiously motivated settlers and religiously motivated Palestinians as well, who would
be removed from this narrative, left behind, as it were. Bamyeh,
much like many left-wing and secular Israelis, considers the religious idea of the right and responsibility of the Jewish people
to the Land of Israel to be a strange perversion. He speaks about
religious extremism among Palestinian Muslims and Israeli
Jews as resulting from the mistakes of politics and diplomacy
(Bamyeh 2003:829)—like Gramsci's idea of the "morbid symp-
toms" that appear in the interregnum between changing hegemonies (Gramsci 1971:276). This provides the alibi for ignoring,
marginalizing, or neutralizing particular groups, a position that
may undermine his own goals of *human* liberation, by dehuman-
izing the morally repugnant others (Harding 1991) whose beliefs
and practices seem to belong to the past.

SPACE, TIME, MORALITY: THE NATION
AND ANACHRONISTIC SETTLERS

Who are these repugnant Others who are perceived as belonging to
the past? Before returning to Bamyeh's ideas about human liberation, perhaps we should revisit the Jewish community of Hebron—
an important focal point of the religious zeal for *Eretz Yisrael* that
Bamyeh criticizes—to consider in some detail the ways in which
religiously motivated Jewish settlers are construed as anachronistic. Hebron is sometimes thought of as a concentrated microcosm
of the conflict in Israel/Palestine. Sometimes it is imagined as a microcosm of Israeli occupation in post-1967 territories, sometimes as
a microcosm of the settler-colonial project in Palestine, and sometimes as a microcosm of a Jewish state surrounded by Arab enemies.
As we saw in the previous chapter, there is even conflict over the
historical narrative of Hebron Jews.[10] One of the most ancient cities
and one of the most contentious places in Israel/Palestine, Hebron
seems like a good place to begin to think about how anachronism is
deployed in the production of moral communities.

Sarah's lifetime—the span of Sarah's life—came to one hundred and twenty-seven years. Sarah died in Kiryath-arba—now Hebron—in the land of Canaan; and Abraham proceeded to mourn for Sarah . . . Then Abraham rose from beside his dead, and spoke to the Hittites, saying, "I am a resident alien among you; sell me a burial site . . . that I may remove my dead for burial." And the Hittites replied to Abraham, saying to him, "Hear us, my lord: you are the elect of God among us. Bury your dead in the choicest of our burial places; none of us will withhold his burial place from you for burying your dead." Thereupon Abraham bowed low to the people of the land, the Hittites, and he said to them, "If it is your wish that I remove my dead for burial, you must agree to intercede for me with Ephron son of Zohar. Let him sell me the cave of Machpelah . . . Let him sell it to me, at the full price, for a burial site in your midst."

. . .

Ephron the Hittite answered Abraham . . . saying, "No, my lord, hear me: I give you the field and I give you the cave that is in it . . ." Then Abraham bowed low before the people of the land, and spoke to Ephron in the hearing of the people of the land, saying, "If only you would hear me out! Let me pay the price of the land; accept it from me, that I may bury my dead there." (Genesis 23:1–13)

Ultimately Abraham pays for the land, and the biblical text is explicit about this exchange all taking place before witnesses:

So Ephron's land in Machpelah, near Mamre—the field with its cave and all the trees anywhere within the confines of that field—passed to Abraham as his possession, in the presence of the Hittites, of all who entered the gate of his town. And then Abraham buried his wife Sarah in the cave of the field of Machpelah, facing Mamre—now Hebron—in the land of Canaan. Thus the field with its cave passed from the Hittites to Abraham, as a burial site. (Genesis 23:17–20)

The Avraham Avinu neighborhood in the Old City of Hebron is astonishingly beautiful. Avraham Avinu means "Abraham Our Father"; the neighborhood takes its name from its proximity to the tomb of the patriarchs where Abraham bought the plot of land to build the tomb for Sarah. The high stone facades have been cleaned and refurbished, old places brought back to life. What's astonishing about the beauty of these old buildings is that Hebron is often written about in the news these days. It is a violent place, where Jewish settlers clash with Palestinians, burning tires in the streets and setting houses aflame.

But here, in Avraham Avinu, everything is quiet. A few small children are out with their mothers. One rides a little scooter; another has just leaned his bike against a wall. A toddler tumbles and begins to cry as his mother calmly makes her way toward him, calling out soothing and comforting words: "You're alright. It's alright. You can get up. Come on, now." Walking through narrow passageways leads you to the neighborhood where apartments are tightly squeezed into very limited space. Everyone here knows everyone else—in such tight quarters, how could it be otherwise?

On this hot summer afternoon, a visitor has arrived and the women, in their long skirts and covered heads, chatting about what to make for dinner this weekday afternoon, figure she must be looking for the synagogue. But she walked right past it! Tourists who visit Hebron always want to see the Avraham Avinu Synagogue. This is the city of Abraham, and Abraham and Sarah are known for inviting strangers and guests into their tent (Genesis 18). Recall the story of the three strangers for whom Abraham prepared a great feast. Recall that those strangers turned out to be angels, messengers from God. Abraham is known for his hospitality (*hahknassat orchim*), and the current Jewish residents of Hebron speak about carrying out this tradition in honor of the patriarch. Visitors, they say, must always be greeted and treated well. One never knows when a visitor might be an angel or a prophet—like Elijah, for whom an extra place is set at the Passover table, or the celestial visitors who arrive at the Sukkah each evening.

Visiting the Avraham Avinu neighborhood on that warm summer day, I had not given much thought to the synagogue. Although I had seen the bustling Palestinian side of the city, I had never been to this part of Hebron. Now I wanted to know about the people inside the walls and fences, the ones who were said to throw their trash down onto their Palestinians neighbors, the ones whom even some other religious settlers in the West Bank describe as crazy extremists. I wanted to see how the members of the Jewish community in Hebron lived and what they thought about their situation. But now that the women mentioned it, I wanted to see the synagogue too. Except for the plaque marking the entrance, one might not know a synagogue is there. You have to duck down to get through the tiny door, but the inside is breathtaking. The synagogue was built in 1540 after the Ottoman conquest of Palestine, and its interior has been completely restored, with domed ceilings and arches much like they may have been then. It has a simple splendor and an atmosphere that inspires awe.

Outside, the children are still playing down at the other end of the street. Well, it's not really a street, but more like an alley. No modern vehicle could drive through these passageways. The alley opens up to a little playground looking very new, its bright colors out of place among the ancient stones of the old city. This playground and others like it throughout the Jewish community of Hebron were built from donations given by external supporters of the community, perhaps American or European Jews or Christians who believe in the importance of a Jewish presence in the Holy Land, and here near the tomb of the patriarchs in particular. There is soft rubber flooring so children won't get hurt if they fall from the monkey bars or from the brightly painted slide. There is seating around the edges of the tiny playground so mothers or older siblings can look after the little ones. I took a seat there and watched the children play. The sun was beginning to set on this very warm June day. It is a relief to sit in the shade provided by the surrounding buildings that form an enclosure around this playground at the end of the alleyway, an enclosure that seems almost like an inner courtyard, or maybe more like a fortress. The stone buildings conjure up images of earlier days, days of living inside walled cities like the Old City in Jerusalem, reminding us of a very distant past.

But looking up to the rooftops, one can see the camouflage netting around a small wooden shack perched on top of one of the old buildings. There's an Israeli soldier up there, his automatic weapon slung over his shoulder, guarding the women and their children, and now guarding me too. The soldier looks down and smiles for a moment. If you look up almost anywhere in the Jewish community of Hebron, you will see fencing or walls, barbed wire, and cameras keeping watch, soldiers on guard. But on the other side of those walls, the idea that those inside need protection seems absurd. To many of the Palestinians of Hebron these settlers are aggressive and violent. It is they, the Palestinians, who need protection from the settlers for their personal safety and property. And many Israelis would agree.

Some Israelis find it very difficult to understand why these Jews would want to live in Hebron. It's scary. The road to Hebron from Jerusalem winds through Palestinian refugee camps. For many Israelis this is enemy territory, or in the very least, a place where they do not feel welcome. But it's also a place where people drive as though there were no traffic rules, passing on the left and the right, driving much too fast for the poor roads. Beyond the refugee camps, after passing through the large Jewish settlement of Kiryat Arba, a modern town named after the ancient town of Hebron, you drive through nearly deserted streets heavily guarded by Israeli soldiers, streets where Palestinians have been removed from their homes and shops to ensure unimpeded travel for the Israelis who live in Hebron and for tourists and visitors to the Tomb of the Patriarchs, the Machpelah. Tourists are always reassured that their busses will be specially equipped to protect them from gunfire. Some Israelis can't imagine wanting to live in a place like this, surrounded by enemies and soldiers, walls and fences, in cramped living quarters, segregated from their Palestinian neighbors, without a sense of freedom. Why would the Jews in Hebron want to live like that? "Like what?"

you might wonder. "Like they're still living in the *shtetls* of Europe!" a secular Israeli once explained to me in exasperation. Not only out of place, then, but also out of time.

The Jewish community of Hebron has been described by some Israelis as reminiscent of the Jewish ghettos of Europe, anachronistic because being confined to restricted, walled-off enclaves amidst non-Jews is a way of life that belongs to a pre-state past. This is the first of the three ways in which religiously motivated settlers are conceptualized as anachronistic. The Hebron Jews are a tiny community of about 50 families and students, their numbers estimated between 500 and 800 people, who are considered to be among the most radical, violent, and aggressive in the effect their community has had on the Palestinians who lived and owned shops in and near the Jewish settlement.

Secular and left-wing Israelis often ask, both rhetorically and disparagingly, why these Jews would want to live as though they had gone back in time to the days before modern nationalism brought liberation to the Jews, creating a state where they could live freely and flourish economically and culturally. Part of the secularist ethos of Jewish nationalism, modern political Zionism, is precisely about individual freedoms in contrast to the world of European *shtetls*. In Israel people can run their own lives, free to be Jewish without assimilating to a hegemonic gentile culture or to the confining elements of Orthodox religious beliefs. One older kibbutz woman, among the founding members of her community, was adamant about the importance of being freely Jewish. She spoke to me about the importance of being free to express one's Jewishness in any number of ways, and of still being Jewish even when one does not pray, attend synagogue, or keep kosher. Israelis can wear bikinis on the beach and spend Saturdays in coffee shops and restaurants rather than in synagogue (precisely the activities that religious settlers sometimes point to as indicative of a lack of values among the secular). They can celebrate Jewish holidays freely and according to their own interpretations. And they don't have to live in those crowded conditions, walled off in ghettos from surrounding communities.

Another way in which religiously motivated settlers are seen as anachronistic reaches even further back in time, beyond Jewish history in Europe. Many of the Israelis who support a two-state solution see religious settlers as threatening to the possibility of peace with the Palestinians because their beliefs about the sanctity of the Holy Land threaten the possibility of territorial compromise. Religious settlers, on the other hand, often see themselves as bravely redeeming God's ancient promise to the Jewish people. Other Israelis see these actions as the theft of Palestinian land, the construction of homes in politically contested territory, the exercise of face-to-face violence against Palestinians, and the destruction of their property. Religiously motivated settlers are acting on the knowledge that God gave them the Land, and that it is their right and their responsibility to live on the Land according to the requirements of the Torah in order to fulfill their duty as Jews and hasten the coming of the Messiah. However, many left-wing and secular Israelis as well as other religious Jews question the authenticity of these beliefs *as* Judaism, dismissing the idea that religious settlers could actually believe these things. They doubt the sincerity of this belief and argue that the ideas themselves are not really Jewish, claiming instead that the settlers use religion instrumentally for political purposes.[11] This ideology, secular liberals argue, is employed to justify extreme territorial nationalism. Thus, for example, Larry Abramson recalls "participating in anti-occupation and anti-settlement demonstrations as far back as the early 1970s in which our slogans equated the concept of sacred land with idolatry, a political theology we condemned as diametrically opposed to true Jewish—and even Zionist—values" (2009:284).[12]

Religiously motivated settlers are also despised as anachronistic for their temporal ideology. In other words, their *beliefs about time* make them a particularly repugnant and inauthentic thing of the past.[13] Even worse perhaps than recreating the ghettos of Europe, religiously motivated settlers live according to a temporal ideology and a social imaginary[14] in which biblical ancestors have a vital role in contemporary life. Religious settlers think of themselves as living biblical stories in the present. In this sacred temporality, time is not exclusively linear, and among the faithful Jews in Hebron and elsewhere, time is experienced as cyclical or as a spiral relationship between past and present. Each year and each season the past is repeated, yet changed, as the faithful move closer and closer in their relationship to God, watching the divine plan unfold and bringing redemption nearer.

During my fieldwork (Dalsheim 2011) in the former settlements of Gush Katif in the Gaza Strip, the rabbi of a girls' high school (*ulpana*) in Neve Dekelim, the largest community in the settlements, speaking at a Purim event prior to the disengagement, reminded his audience that "what happened then is in fact now." The story of Esther, retold on the holiday of Purim, tells a tale in which all reason and logic in the world is turned on its head and one can no longer distinguish good from evil. "This," the rabbi said, was "precisely what is happening now." The disengagement plan was devoid of all logic; the world had turned upside down and nothing made sense when a Jewish government would consider removing Jews from the Land of Israel. "There is no difference," the rabbi explained; "then is now. And anyone who does not understand this is sorely mistaken." Secular narratives that are constrained by the contours of a linear progressive temporality cannot contain the ideas expressed by this rabbi, and the behavior of those settlers who did not make practical arrangements for their removal from the land could then only be interpreted as irrational or purposely defiant.[15] Although parallels can be found, for example, in social scientific thought that seeks stable patterns or universal rules to explain human history and uncover a greater truth in "human nature," or predict the ways in which these forces will eventually be worked out,[16] the rabbi's predictions of repeated patterns—"then is now"—seemed absurd from a specifically linear, progressive temporal perspective.

I interviewed a number of left-wing secular Israelis who explained their disdain for religiously motivated settlers by recalling their interactions with settlers while guarding them as soldiers in the reserves. These recollections illustrate conflicting temporal ideologies. Some of the most disturbing stories came from Hebron, where soldiers told of settler children throwing stones at an elderly Palestinian woman laden with packages. Why don't these children, who are being raised in a deeply religious manner, offer to help the old woman with her packages? One soldier who grew up on a kibbutz but now lives with his wife and children outside Tel Aviv said he asked the children what they were doing: Why were they throwing stones? What had the woman done to deserve this? The children explained that they were throwing stones in retribution for the Arab massacre of Jews in Hebron. That was in 1929; now it was 2005. The soldier was confused and outraged. A stone memorial placed in a wall of the Muslim quarter in the Old City of Jerusalem marks the site where a Jewish man was killed in the 1990s, presumably by local Palestinians. The placard reads: "On this spot Elhanan Aharon Atteli was murdered by the evil ones . . . By the spilling of his blood, we shall live on." This is followed by: "Remember what Amalek did to you on your way" (Deuteronomy 25:17). The Amalekites are depicted in the Bible as a tribe of nomadic people who attacked the Israelites during the exodus from Egypt (Exodus 17:8–17). They appear in other places in the text, and the interpretations of what is required by the injunction to "remember Amalek" are varied. In this case, the term has come to stand for any and all those who are considered "enemies" of the Jewish people.

In Hebron there is a museum commemorating the 1929 massacre discussed in Chapter 3. As we saw, there are arguments over this history and its meanings, arguments over who has the right to represent this past and who should determine the implications of this past. The museum in Hebron enters this fray of representations because of the particular way it commemorates 1929 and because of how that representation speaks to other representations. Bakhtin (1981) taught us about the interconnectedness of texts, about dialogism and intertextuality. In examining the novel as a form of representation, he allowed us to understand how all representations speak to other representations, increasing their significance and their meaning. A text is never meaningful only in and of itself. It is meaningful in context, and this context consists of other representations, previous ones and different ones. A text—which can be any form of representation, whether a history book or a museum exhibit or a movie or the stories people tell each other—can also influence and change the meanings of other texts, other representations, other interpretations of events.[17] And, if they alter the narrative, as Hayden White has shown, they also influence the weight of the moral imperatives emerging from those narratives. This is one reason that representation matters so much.

The women in the Avraham Avinu neighborhood asked me if I had already seen the museum. They directed me toward the Beit Hadassah neighborhood and told me the museum might still be open even though it was getting late. When I got there I found that Beit Hadassah is more like an apartment building than a neighborhood, and I wasn't quite sure what to do. But as I walked up the steps to the entrance of what had once been a hospital or clinic, but was now called a neighborhood, an elderly man emerged from the stairwell. He began telling me how he lives here now with his daughter and her family. The people here are all very good people, he said, and he is glad he could join them and live here. He was sure his daughter would unlock the Hebron Heritage Museum downstairs.

I felt like I was imposing, but the man's daughter smiled, got the key, and led the way to the museum. Having to tend to her own children, she apologized for having to leave me for a little while. I did not spend much time in the museum. Maybe that was because I felt I was inconveniencing others, but more likely it was because of my visceral response to its imagery.

I entered a dark place underneath the building that had been converted from a hospital into apartments, then moved through an archway into a dimly lit cavern where the faces of the victims of the 1929 massacre are illuminated from behind as if lit by flames. A pile of stones inside another small arch, signifying destruction and loss, was lit from below with red light. The dark brick arches like openings glowing from within, the fiery light making visible the portraits of murdered men and women. The sense of being inside an oven at

Auschwitz was overwhelming. I could not stand it. I could not stay. The imagery was horrific and the claustrophobic conditions made it unbearable. I quickly made my way back outside and thanked the young woman for unlocking the museum, although I wasn't feeling very grateful at all. Their commemoration of a tragic event in Hebron's history seemed to be framed clearly in terms of another far more comprehensive one in Europe. Whether that framing emerged from the settlers' understanding of temporality, or from a more cynical and self-conscious attempt to play on the disciplined sensorium of the broader universe of Jews in Israel and abroad who had been touched by the Holocaust, didn't matter much to me as I stepped out of the building into the fading sunshine.

The memorial to 1929 in the museum in Hebron is very much like the representation of Amalek recalled above. It too tells a story that creates continuity with Jewish pasts of persecution and brings those pasts into the present as forever and ongoing, producing a story of persistent and eternal anti-Semitism. Time, in this case, is not linear, progressive time; this time is cyclical and spiraling, and place is spiraling too.[18] The past *is* the present, the forced abandonment of the Gaza settlements is the time of Esther, 1929 is the Holocaust, and Amalek is the Palestinian woman in Hebron.

From within a linear progressive temporality, representations in which the past *is* the present are anachronistic. Such ideas and the people who espouse them seem irrational. But if you suggested to the Jews of Hebron that 1929 is *not* now, they might point to attacks by Palestinians on Jews in the West Bank, or attacks on Jews in Argentina or anywhere in the world and tell you that you are mistaken. Your ideas are irrational and *you* do not understand.

Cyclical temporality emphasizes the enduring features of the world. In this case, one of those enduring features is anti-Semitism. One need not be a member of the religious settler community or a religious Jew or religious at all to realize that beliefs in such enduring features or patterns or rules of human society are widespread. Indeed, even those of us who interpret certain settler behaviors as anachronistic sometimes understand the world or ourselves or human behavior in cyclical terms. We surely understand seasons and calendars this way. But more importantly, we often invoke our sense of collective identity in these terms. We've been attacked by terrorists, we say after the devastation of the World Trade Center in New York, and we recall Pearl Harbor 60 years before. But we rebuild and remain strong, and we tell ourselves we will always come back, we will not be beaten because we are a good people who help each other in times of trouble. We stand together against evil in the world. Sometimes when natural disasters like storms or earthquakes strike, we speak of the strength and endurance of the community in ways that also reflect our understanding of the continuity and stability or dependable characteristics of our social group.

Even more striking, perhaps, are the ways in which members of national groups—including secular and left-wing Israelis—represent themselves to themselves and their children, collapsing the past into the present through museum exhibits, field trips to battlegrounds, or high-school history lessons. Sometimes this is accomplished rhetorically through a simple slippage between the word "they" and the word "we." I have written elsewhere about high-school history trips among secular and left-wing Israelis from kibbutz schools to the cemetery at Kibbutz Kinneret and to the Palmach Museum (see Dalsheim 2004, 2005). In these cases heterogeneous groups of high-school students became "descendants" of the socialist Zionist founders of the State of Israel. Teachers or tour guides telling historical tales about members of the first kibbutz communities at Kinneret and about a pre-state militia at the museum sometimes slipped seamlessly from the pronoun "they" to "we," collapsing distances in time and place. And with the same rhetorical move they erased the specific, personal, and family histories of students who included new immigrants from the former Soviet Union and Latin America and other places, as well as the grandchildren of Middle Eastern and North African Jews whose past is not that of the socialist Zionist founders of the state (Dalsheim 2004, 2005). There were also times in high-school history classes when teachers used the pronoun "we" to include themselves and their students, who were asked to take responsibility for past actions carried out in the early years of the state, constructing a continuous national collective (Dalsheim 2007).

In like manner, social scientists and political and social activists seek patterns. To learn from history and from the experiences of others, peacemakers look for regularities, social processes that are repeatable in other places at other times. In some cases, social psychology is applied in peacemaking based on a generalizable framework of a broad understanding of human behavior, as when the importance of recognition is stressed as crucial in peacemaking processes. Or when reparations partially make amends for past injustices and an enduring "we" is produced, a unity through time of a moral people who take responsibility for the past. Or when rules of human behavior are used to predict political outcomes, trying to understand why people rebel or how uprisings can be ended. So, too, the Jews of Hebron seek patterns, and they have come to see that some people have hated Jews since the time of Amalek. Thus, Amalek, 1929, and the Nazi Holocaust, the death of Shalhevet Paz in Hebron in 2009, the murder of a Chabad rabbi and his wife in Mumbai in 2011, the killing of a husband, wife, an 11-year-old, a 3-year-old, and a baby girl in the settlement of Itamar also in 2011, the 2012 shootings that killed four people at a Jewish school in Toulouse, France, are all part of a much longer list that reveals the enduring nature of anti-Semitism and its ever-present danger.

From within this settler point of view, the reasonableness of attributing violent acts to enduring anti-Semitism is self-evident. It is the assumption that such hatred is part of the past, or that such current violence is a temporary aberration that might be made part of the past, that is anachronistic thinking.

OUT OF TIME

Of all the ways in which settlers are considered anachronistic, perhaps the most significant has to do with perceptions of 1948 and

1967. Some Israelis and members of the international community view settlers and settlement itself (not only in Hebron) as a set of practices that might have been necessary in the days before the State of Israel was established in 1948, but as unnecessary now (post-1967). Practices such as setting up outposts under cover of darkness to avoid detection by authorities (then the British, now the Israelis) to expand Jewish territory through settlement are out of time. They do not belong in the now. Their time has run out. Left-wing and secular Israelis express animosity toward contemporary settlers in post-1967 territories and to the settlement project there. They are angered by the violence, the force, and the danger they perceive arising from this ongoing territorial conflict with Palestinians for which post-1967 settlers are often blamed. However, it seems that they are also angered by the particular way in which some religiously motivated settlers perceive and represent themselves and their project as a continuation of or even the same as pre-state settlement.

The former Jewish communities in the Gaza Strip portrayed themselves to the outside world in a number of ways through newspaper articles, public protests and private discussions, museum displays, and films. One particularly interesting example was a film produced by the people living in the Jewish communities of Gaza before they were forcibly removed by the Israeli government in the summer of 2005. It is a good example of what some critics see as conflating 1948 and post-1967. The film, *Between the Sand Dunes,* produced by Gaza settlers just prior to the disengagement, was primarily employed as part of the campaign to garner support among Israelis for their cause; however, it did not inspire a sense of solidarity among left-wing, secular Israelis. Indeed, it provoked quite the opposite reaction. When I showed this film to left-wing kibbutz members who lived near the Gaza Strip and to left-wing political activists in other parts of the country, it infuriated people for a number of reasons, including the idea that these settlers and their project belong to the past.

Between the Sand Dunes is a carefully constructed and edited representation of the religious settler community. It was one of the productions shown to visitors, including schoolchildren, who came to a museum and visitors' center in the Gaza settlements prior to the disengagement, which is where I first saw it. The film depicts scenes that evoke a positive self-image, one that creates a sense of comfort, solidarity, or "home" among like-minded viewers, including members of the nationalist religious camp in Israel and some more right-wing secular Israelis as well.

The film depicts life in the settlements of Gush Katif, focusing on the beautiful seaside landscape, the crimson sunsets, and rows of palm trees. It emphasizes the industrious settlers who worked hard developing agriculture in the arid and non-arable sand dunes, showing vast expanses of greenhouses. It tells of the special techniques of planting and raising vegetables and flowers in the sands of the Gaza area. It zooms in with close-ups of the innocent faces of young children, with their large, deep brown eyes and endearing smiles. All the while a melodious song in the background lends an atmosphere coinciding with the innocence in those eyes. A voice sings, "Here is a strip of land that kisses the waves. Here, where people live with love, and in their hearts there is hope . . . here people preserve the sanctity of the land . . . Here in the Land of Israel!"

There is one short scene of horror and burning, an incident in which Palestinians from the surrounding area had attacked the settlers. Otherwise, there were no Palestinians in sight, no large brown or blue eyes of Palestinian children or men and women at work. Their presence, the enormous population, so much greater than the Jewish population of Gaza, was hidden from view, very much like the Palestinian population from within the Jewish community of Hebron.

The images in *Between the Sand Dunes* provoke outrage among those opposed to the settlement project in the Gaza Strip and the West Bank. For example, I was once invited to speak about the impending disengagement, then an issue of current events, to a group of fifth-graders at a school in Jerusalem. When I showed this film to the class their history and civics teacher, who is also a left-wing political activist, told me of his outrage, but methodically analyzed the film with his students and pointed out the problems of how the film represents the issue. Not only did the film make it appear as though there were no Palestinians except for violent terrorists, but the Israeli flag was also repeatedly shown flying above it all as though this was *the* story of the entire nation, of all Israelis. The teacher was offended by this representation that certainly did not reflect his position, nor that of all the children in the class, which included Palestinian citizens of Israel.

The gap in emotional responses to the sights portrayed in this film is an indication of the cultural training of the senses. Reading the landscape, like reading a text, involves interpretations that are based in previous training, learning, and reading experiences (Starrett 2003). Interpretations are intertextual, drawing on previous knowledge and codes and falling back on learned narratives. Variously situated groups read their own moral superiority into these representations as they create and re-create their identities in the process. Religious settlers and their supporters identified positively, seeing the settlers as hardworking, pious people carrying out the work of God against all odds. Secular, liberal, and left-wing viewers expressed outrage and identified themselves as diametrically opposed.

People who were infuriated by the images in the film rejected them first of all because the force and military might that made those settlements possible is missing from the depiction. Kibbutz members I interviewed who lived in the surrounding communities, some of whom protested against the Gaza settlements, explained that such force *was* necessary in pre-state years to ensure the survival of the Jewish people but was excessive and unnecessary *now*.[19] They were infuriated by the particular way this story is told because it so closely resembles the way the pioneering socialists portrayed themselves in pre-state years.[20] The film depicts a hard-working, honest people who till the soil and make the desert bloom. The people in the film have built a beautiful, simple, idyllic community, for which they have made many sacrifices, including physical injury and loss of life, as they stand firm against a violent enemy. There is something uncanny about this film that the uninitiated might miss. If it were in black and white, some of the clothing were different, and the religious elements were removed, this film could be a newsreel portrayal of kibbutz life in pre-state and early state years. From the point of view of kibbutz members, descendants of the Socialist Zionists who established the state, these settlers have stolen and perverted their pure and honorable story (Dalsheim 2005). These settlers are living practices that belong in the past, practices that *had* to take place in the years before there was a state and an army, at a time when there was no other choice. In the early days, settlement was essential, and while there was force and violence involved, that was necessary *then* to establish a state and preserve the Jewish people. *Now*, anti-settlement activists told me, there is a state and an army and these practices are excessive.

Religiously motivated settlers in post-1967 Israeli-occupied territories are an anachronism and must be brought into the present of the national collective by being removed from their homes and moved across the geographical divide into morally acceptable territory. Some of those who protested against the settlements carried signs that read "and the sons (children) shall return to our borders," a play on the biblical quote (Jeremiah 31:17) *"vay shavu banim l'gvulam"* (literally "and the sons return to their borders," also translated as "and your children will return to their territory"), implying that these settlements are beyond the legitimate borders and constituted a moral transgression. This idea also ironically seems to imagine these settlers as somehow in exile. It is almost as though the political redemption of the nation hinges upon returning these sons of Israel to the pre-1967 borders.[21] Of course, the residents of Gush Katif in the Gaza Strip would quickly point out that the establishment of *their* communities did not require the removal of Palestinians. Unlike some of their brethren in the kibbutz communities inside the borders of the pre-1967 Green Line, they did not build their homes on the ruins of Palestinian communities. And settlers in Hebron would claim that, just like Abraham, they purchased and hold the deeds to the places where they live.

All of these depictions—the commemoration of 1929 in Hebron, the reference to Amalek, and this film that equates post-1967 settlement with pre-1948—are important because they have the potential to reinterpret the past and lead to moral imperatives that are different and even contradictory to other stories about Israel/Palestine. Peacemakers, even faith-based peacemakers, are hard pressed to include these multiple depictions in peacebuilding processes. They may stress the importance of recognizing that different factions have different interpretations, but building a peaceful community around incommensurable interpretations with varying moral imperatives is far more difficult. Faith-based peacemakers often stress that religion need not be violent and demonstrate how it can also be a transformative force in peacemaking (Abu-Nimer 2003; Appleby 2001/1996; Coward and Smith 2004; Gopin 2004; Little and Appleby 2004). For example, Marc Gopin (2002), an American Orthodox rabbi, writes that religion can bring peace to the Middle East. But such peace, in the case of Israel/Palestine, means condemning settler acts of violence against Palestinians even if those acts are supported by settler interpretations of the past (see Gopin 2004).[22]

This difficulty with multiplicity is something I will return to later in the book, but thinking about these depictions and about religiously motivated settlers as anachronistic, morally repugnant, and threatening to the possibility of peace and security has a disciplining force for international scholars, activists, and liberal or left-wing Israelis. It prevents engagement with the settlers, even making research difficult because the researcher's own moral integrity can be called into question as somehow supporting Occupation or as sympathizing with settlers and not with Palestinians. It is often considered morally acceptable to cross the border into Occupied Territory to meet with Palestinians, but wrong to have anything at all to do with religious settlers. It is wrong to make any purchases in these settlements because doing so supports the settlement project.[23]

Thinking about settlers as anachronistic also participates in producing the "outside" of peace as it reinscribes a moral community that is separate from these settlers. Such thinking works in concert with two kinds of narratives about Israel/Palestine and the moral imperatives they imply. It supports what might be considered the mainstream secular Zionist narrative about the need for a state for the Jewish people and the importance of maintaining a Jewish state for Jewish survival. That narrative can support the idea of a two-state solution as it recognizes national sovereignty as the means for liberation. But because it places less importance on the religious attachment to the Greater Land of Israel, it can also allow for territorial compromise. Thinking about settlers as anachronistic also supports an anti- or non-Zionist narrative, one that might be considered mainstream among Palestinians. That is the narrative of settler-colonial invasion, which suggests that justice requires postcolonial liberation.[24] The settler-colonial narrative can support a two-state solution as well as a one-state solution. Its moral imperative is ending colonial rule, which can mean the end of the State of Israel as a Jewish state (one-state solution) or Palestinian independence and sovereignty next to an Israeli state (two-state solution). Both these narratives depend on the linear progressive temporality that marginalizes other experiences of time and place as continuous enactments of loyalty to the Torah and the universal Sovereign. Viewing such ways of being and believing primarily from within a progressivist temporality can mean focusing on the comforting campfire, whose flames make all else appear as nothing but shadows.

RECOGNIZING HUMANITY IN ALL ITS COMPLEXITY

Mohammed Bamyeh, introduced at the opening of this chapter, offers another narrative. Bamyeh, like Ilan Pappe (2000) and others, suggests a third way, a bridging narrative between a Zionist narrative and a settler-colonial narrative. Bamyeh is well versed in the contesting narratives that frame the conflict in Israel/Palestine and understands deeply the relationship between these narratives, identities, and conflict. Because of this understanding, he suggests that another narrative is needed, one that can unite the people currently in opposition. The idea of finding a joint narrative, a new story that can retell the past in such a way as to unify those engaged in conflict, is not unheard of among peacemakers. The idea is to renarrate divisive versions of the past and recast former enemies as united toward a new goal once they understand they are victims of the same conflict situation, or even of the same oppressor. So, for example, prisoners in Irish jails from both Republican and Loyalist militias could come to see that they had been manipulated and fought against each other only to their own detriment. Now they would be the leaders of nonviolence and work together to build a peaceful Northern Ireland.[25]

Bamyeh is convinced that Palestinian suffering is caused by a particular oppressive system that should have long since passed from the world. This is the "settler-colonial hold over Palestine" that "remains as a relic of an antiquated era." And yet, he suggests that the settlers—meaning all Israeli Jews, not just settlers in the Occupied Territories—should also be considered tragic victims. They are the victims of European racism and anti-Semitism.

What moral imperative does this narrative suggest? How does it compare to the alternative historical narrative Michelle Campos tells of the Jews of Hebron that we considered in Chapter 3? The narrative Campos tells sets up Ashkenazi Jews (part of Europe) in opposition to Mizrahi Jews and Arabs in Palestine, thereby undermining the way in which Jews and Arabs are produced as enemies. But it also inscribes a new set of oppositions: local Jews and Arabs against Jews from Europe. Does Bamyeh's narrative lead somewhere else? If the people involved accepted his narrative, it might set up "Europe" itself as a common enemy to the people of Israel/Palestine, or at least European racism and anti-Semitism. Gil Anidjar (2008) writes of the category "Semites" as one that seems to have dropped from our vocabulary. Such a category could include Arabs and Jews in Palestine/Israel, those excluded from a European imaginary.

This idea works with Bamyeh's alternative narrative. But, as I've already suggested, like any historical narrative Bamyeh's too would be necessarily partial, and it necessarily excludes religiously motivated Jewish settlers who would once again be produced as spoilers. The question we are left with is whether Bamyeh's thinking about Israel/Palestine fulfills his own ideas of achieving human liberation. Bamyeh asks that we reconsider what Franz Fanon's thinking about human liberation from colonial domination might have to teach us about the struggles for liberation faced today. Fanon was writing in the 1960s and was concerned with colonial subjugation. Today's struggles are both inescapably global, Bamyeh explains, and intensely local. In one way the main struggles of our time are waged against unimaginably abstract forces rather than "old, clearly discernible agents of colonial power," but in another way they are "deeply earthly and even personal" (Bamyeh 2010:53). Yet, despite these differences, he suggests that Fanon's concern with liberation involving "all sectors of the personality" (Fanon 1963:310 in Bamyeh 2010:53) provides a useful framework in which to think about current struggles for liberation. The challenge, according to Bamyeh's interpretation of Fanon, is to focus on the disorders that impede our ability to "recognize the humanity, in all its complexity, of our own selves and others" (Bamyeh 2010:53). Liberation, he writes, is a matter of "introducing a perspective into the world that makes such ways of seeing possible."

While reiterating the intolerability of the anachronism of the Palestinian situation, Bamyeh also calls for a different strategy to achieve human liberation. He writes about the global social movement and the idea of local actions and solutions rather than a universalist appeal (such as uniting the workers of the world, or anticolonial nationalism). His thinking is compelling, and if the repugnance for certain anachronistic others could be set aside, one might consider applying his insights to local situations in the space of Israel/Palestine in ways that would *not* necessitate a reversion to the anachronistic strategy of national liberation. Indeed, we might take a cue from the flexible ideas about citizenship found among some religiously motivated settlers, like the "crazy" Rabbi whose story opened the book, which are strikingly similar to an idea recently espoused by a "crazy" Palestinian that I will discuss in greater detail in Chapter 5.[26]

Recognizing humanity in all its complexity must surely include recognizing the humanity even of the despicable anachronistic others who live in the past, surrounded by walls among biblical ancestors. The idea of focusing on the local that social theorists and activists promote for liberation in the globalized present holds the potential to make room for all kinds of differences that would not have to be submerged in a single unifying temporal narrative, nor in a single universalist resolution to the local conflict in Palestine/Israel.

Bamyeh and other social theorists turn to local struggles that are united not by a particular version of a new world order but by local people struggling to take back control of their everyday lives (e.g., local food, micro-investment, environmentalism, native peoples' claims). But somehow, in Bamyeh's Palestine, "local" seems to mean reconfiguring the social order in a singular, unified way for all the various population groups that would be directly affected by such a solution. A new collective identity—victims of European persecution and domination—would emerge from a new historical narrative. But if local is the new global, why remain within the parameters of a predefined location and a unified narrative? A resolution and way forward for the residents of Gaza and Sderot might not be the same as what the residents of Jaffa and Tel Aviv require. The people who identify as Bedouin in the Negev and the Galilee might have different ideas about the past and present and what recognizing their humanity might mean. And, of course, those who identify as Jewish and Palestinian residents of Hebron surely have their own ideas of how they might go forth together or separately.

The idea of multiple local solutions might be unappealing to those who are concerned about the relative power relations of those involved (see Boyarin 1996:202–203).[27] But there are many different kinds of asymmetries. That those asymmetries are not taken into account when we talk in bare terms about "power" does not mean they are not vitally important. If we take only some kinds of "power" into account, the goals we have for social justice will always continue to be blocked. Some will argue that to achieve justice, "the powerful" or those who have benefitted from the settler-colonial formation must give something up, return something, or make amends to those who have primarily been the victims of settler colonialism. Yet this might be one of the false historical lessons against which Benjamin warned us. His critique of the thought that is "nourished by the image of enslaved ancestors rather than that of liberated grandchildren" (1968/1940:260) suggests we should take care not to simply act in ways that we think might ensure that that our ancestors will not have suffered, struggled, fought, or died for no reason.

What look like binary divisions between categories of settlers and natives, colonizers and colonized, or even powerful and powerless are never quite that simple or straightforward (Cooper and Stoler 1997). Settlers in the Occupied Territories are in a position of relative power vis-à-vis Palestinians, because they are supported by the Israeli state and its army and by Israeli governments from both the Right and Left, which have for decades built infrastructure, permitted the construction of homes and communities, and protected those communities (Zertal and Eldar 2007). But the population of Israelis who make their home in the Occupied Territories includes people of greater and lesser means, those who could not afford housing elsewhere, and those who are un- or underemployed (Dalsheim 2008). Oren Yiftachel (2006) calls such communities "development towns" rather than "settlements," even though some of them are located in the Occupied Territories. Development towns are communities primarily composed of members of weaker population groups (Khazzoom 2005), including *Mizrahim*, Jews of Middle Eastern and North African descent and heritage, and more recently immigrants to Israel from Ethiopia and the former Soviet Union, many of whom struggle with ethnic and economic discrimination in Israeli society. Thinking in terms of Fanon

(1963/1961, 1967), it is important to bear in mind that even if we could easily distinguish between the powerful and the oppressed, the people who fit into each of those categories should be thought of as negatively affected by colonization in different ways. Like Memmi (1967) and later Nandy (1983), Fanon understood the effects of colonization on the colonizers as well as on the colonized. As Bamyeh points out, Fanon argued that decolonization includes healing the disorders that prevent *all* of us from recognizing our own and each other's humanity. Postcolonial scholars have argued that the "decolonization" of the colonizer (like the colonized) would require a radical psychological shift and deconstruction of a narcissism based on illusory identity. Decolonization involves a change of mind, not only the end of the colonizer's control. Colonizers have to recognize the humanity of the colonized, which in this case might mean recognizing that the injustices suffered by Palestinians involve their colonizers having to give up their homes, their sovereignty, their privilege. The idea is that colonialism, because of its brutality and inherent injustice, creates "monsters" out of men.[28] It results in the colonized who hate themselves because they internalize the way the colonizers see them. They hate their "primitive, uncivilized" selves and want to become like the colonizers, but since they never can, they continue to hate themselves. It creates colonizers who accept the colonial system and believe it is right, but also colonizers who refuse—who feel bad about the situation and think it's wrong but participate in the system anyway, sometimes justifying this as a lack of choice.[29] Rather than think about domination as a vertical hierarchy of power, Bamyeh's invocation of Fanon to recognize the fullness of humanity and heal the disorders that prevent such recognition requires recognizing the scattered nature of hegemony (Grewal and Kaplan 1994), allowing us to consider gender, ethnicity, class, or other differences that complicate simply binary divisions of power.

An important part of postcolonial theorizing has been to show that domination has worked through colonial knowledge that produced the colonized as a homogenized, undifferentiated horde of uncivilized primitives, while the colonizers could be individuals with differences among them. Thus, Memmi wrote that "the colonized is never characterized in an individual manner, he is entitled only to drown in an anonymous collectivity" (1967:88). To recognize "humanity" then meant to see beyond that binary distinction and see the colonized as having their own culture that is not necessarily less, but different, and also to see them as people with individual differences. So to turn the tables and paint the colonizers as a powerful and brutish but undifferentiated horde is precisely to *mimic that very colonial impulse* that Fanon, and later Bhabha (1994), wrote against.

The call to recognize our own and other's humanity has primarily been about the "colonized," or about whichever group the critical theorist thinks is being dominated. But to take this idea seriously really requires more. As I have suggested, the difficulty of taking this call seriously is partly conditioned by the ways in which morality is intertwined with ideas about time.

Relegating our despised Others—Jewish settlers, in this case—to the past is possible only if we subscribe to a linear historicism in which human destiny flows inevitably toward liberation through territorial ethno-nationalism. By accusing settlers of temporal derangement—their actions, their beliefs, even the kinds of communities in which they live have been superseded by more acceptable forms of being and belonging—the secular Left hopes to pull the Jews of Israel back within their proper boundaries and thus redeem history by setting into place those two last, small pieces of the world map of nation-states: Palestine and Israel. (It makes little difference whether these last pieces are two ethno-national states, one bi-national state, or one state for all its citizens; the point is that such states are both inevitable and desirable as culminations of a necessary logic of history that has been freed of the untimely blockages of settlement and allowed to flow freely once again.) Only the cessation of settlement will accomplish the goal of pulling both Jews and Palestinians into the right places on both the landscape and the timeline.

But those who want to commit themselves to thinking beyond models of rights and belonging organized around state formations must recognize the puzzle and the opportunity that thinking about religious settlers provides. Expelling them from the moral community by condemning them as anachronisms that have halted the flow of history means that we lose the critical ability to question the very nature of the historical narrative of ethno-nationalism, the destructive nature of which we condemn in the idealized Other of the settler just as surely as we hold it out as a bright promise of civilization and progress to the disenfranchised.

Chapter 5

Local Solutions: Collaboration, Cooperation, Coexistence

Tell me a story, great-aunt,
so that I can sleep.
Tell me a story, Scheherazade,
so that you can live . . .
    It was a dark and stormy night
    [and we] sat around the campfire . . .
    and this is the story she told:

—Ursula Le Guin (1980)

Once upon a time there was a Palestinian Arab sheikh. He was the leader of a large community whose members held him in high esteem, yet Palestinian elected officials claimed he had no authority to speak for Palestinians. The Sheikh lived near Hebron, the city where Israeli settlers terrorize Palestinians, squat in their homes, and cause their places of business to be shut down. By most accounts, he should consider those settlers his arch-enemies, yet this sheikh erected a special tent on the outskirts of his town, furnished with soft cushions and handwoven carpets, where he welcomed these settlers and their supporters, some of whom were politicians who came from distant lands. He offered strong black coffee to his guests and, when they were seated and comfortable, he spoke about being neighbors and about living together in peace. He said the word "peace" over and over again, as if to make certain there would be no misunderstanding of his intentions, but he never quite said what he meant. This sheikh had no interest in dividing up the land between Israelis and Palestinians. Indeed, he was convinced that good Muslims such as himself could *never* part with Muslim territory; it was forbidden by Islamic law.

Someone who takes such a stance might be considered an uncompromising hard-liner, a fundamentalist, and a spoiler of peace. And yet, some of the Jewish settlers who came from communities where fear and hatred of Arabs is said to be rampant said this sheikh was a good man, a friend, and a man of peace.[1]

A character like this sheikh, who crosses established ideological and political lines and talks about peace with the worst enemies of his people, seems entirely fictional. But this sheikh is a very real character who lives at the edge of contradictory moral orders, an edge that marks the boundaries of the acceptable.

The Sheikh has been discounted because, it is said, he does not represent the Palestinian people and has no authority to speak for them. A spokesman for the Palestinian Authority responded to the Sheikh's work by saying "any efforts not approved by Mr. Abbas [president of the Palestinian Authority] could not have any outcome when it comes to final negotiations." I asked a long-time Israeli peace activist about the Sheikh after a story about him appeared in the *New York Times*. The activist, who has worked for decades promoting cooperation between Israelis and Palestinians, said he had never heard of the man. It seemed strange that this veteran peace activist, who seemed to know everyone who was anyone on the peacemaking scene, would not know about the Sheikh. But then, when I asked him to speculate, he suggested the Sheikh was likely one of a number of Palestinian Arabs in the hills south of Hebron whom the Israeli authorities set up as the Village Leagues in the 1970s. "There were these village leagues created by Israel, of people who got benefits and privileges because they collaborated with the Israeli authorities, and the Occupation, and security people. And they got licenses and permits and . . . there are the same kind of people there [now] who are not Palestinian nationalists, they don't represent the Palestinian cause . . . It is unfortunate," he said, "that the *New York Times* gave them coverage." This sheikh is not a nationalist, and his activities are not worth mentioning, let alone celebrating, because he is nothing more than a collaborator.

THE LOCAL

In the last chapter, we saw Mohammed Bamyeh thinking about local solutions in reference to the global social movement. Many other social activists also point to the ways people are organizing, defying national categories to solve some of the dilemmas they face. People are creative. They make use of the resources and knowledge available to them, and the Sheikh, in the story above, is a local leader who is looking for local solutions to local problems. Yet while some sorts of local solutions seem very appealing, others are deemed criminal and still others are discounted as worse than criminal. They are traitorous, immoral, and counterproductive to the needs of the people and to the larger goals of peace and justice.

Despite all kinds of restrictions, cooperation between Israelis and Palestinians and movement across the Green Line is constant. For example, there have been very successful cooperative efforts across the border to supply automobile parts inexpensively to those who need them in the Palestinian territories. When someone needs a part, an order is placed across the border in the internationally recognized territory of the State of Israel. There, in Israel, there are plenty of parts to be found, often attached to currently owned vehicles. The supplier will locate the parts, remove them from a vehicle, and transport them across the border to be sold at a good price in an automobile repair shop in the Occupied Territories or the Palestinian Authority. In fact, some Israelis will travel across that boundary

to get their cars repaired at a lower price than they could in an Israeli garage. If some people are benefitting from this trade more
than others, this is not so different from the way normal market
mechanisms work.[2]

The Sheikh who hosts settlers in his peace tent is not accused
of theft nor of engaging in criminal activity like those who cooperate across borders to supply automobile parts. According to reports
in the *New York Times*, the *Jerusalem Post*, and the online edition
of *Speigel*, the peace tent is the continuation of earlier efforts by
this local leader, who says that he comes from "a generation that
lived with the Jews peacefully in a brotherly relationship" (Lazaroff
2012). This sheikh is reportedly an outspoken critic of the Palestinian Authority and is respected on the streets of Hebron because he
is the descendant of a dynasty that stretches back nearly a millennium (Rudoren 2012). He said he began hosting Jewish settlers in
his home in 2008. A spokesperson from the Jewish settlement in
Hebron said that he had been meeting privately with the Sheikh for
a number of years. In 2011, another group of Jewish residents from
the settlement in Hebron and some of their supporters were hosted
in the Sheikh's peace tent (Hawley 2012).

The Sheikh is discounted not only because he does not represent
the national interests of the Palestinian people, but also because of
the particular people he invited into his peace tent. From the point
of view of left-wing and mainstream peace seekers, the people who
came to the tent are suspect, either not truly interested in peace
or interested only if peace means their own continued dominance.
They promote the coexistence of a rider and his horse. The Sheikh
invited settlers from Hebron and a settler leader from another
part of the Occupied Territories. He invited right-wing politicians
from the European Union and reportedly has ties in the United
States with right-wing Christian televangelist John Hagee. Taken
together, this group of visitors might be described as religious extremists and supporters of the right of Israel to expand and for
Jews to settle in that expanded territory. This sheikh is therefore
not only collaborating with Israeli authorities (something Fatah has

also been accused of) but is also courting the very worst enemies of the Palestinian people, those who are directly involved in removing Palestinians from their land, a process that has been equated with their destruction.[3]

However, this sheikh reportedly feels betrayed by those who claim authority to speak for him and is deeply frustrated by what he describes as a corrupt Palestinian Authority that has done little to help his native Hebron (Hawley 2012). He is not alone in that sentiment.[4] Let's say, just for the sake of argument, that he is a collaborator with the Israeli security forces. What might that mean? According to the settlers from Hebron who were invited to his peace tent, on one occasion the Sheikh was able to intervene and prevent the destruction of a Jewish holy site (Wilder 2011). In return we might imagine that he was granted certain privileges for the people he represents.[5] He might have gained permits for himself or for members of his extended family to travel or to build. Maybe he received monetary benefits. He might, through this collaboration, be protecting the homes of members of his community, attempting to ensure that their land will not be taken away for Israeli military exercises or to build additional Jewish settlements (Falah 2003; Hanafi 2012; PeaceNow 2012). He demonstrates loyalty to and acts on behalf of the extended families he represents and in so doing appears to undermine the integrity of the national group to which he is supposed to belong.

In so doing, he enacts a space in which hegemonic structures— including those of the dominant Israelis as well as those of the official Palestinian political order—are represented, contested, and inverted. Michel Foucault called such spaces *heterotopia*, literally "other spaces." This chapter focuses on the remarkable heterogeneity of ways in which people in Palestine/Israel are establishing "other spaces" where sets of relations and oppositions that we have come to take for granted are at once mirrored, challenged, and reversed (Foucault 2008/1967). This conceptualization allows us to think beyond the stale and unsuccessful models and processes that have made Israel/Palestine into a seemingly intractable conflict.

BEYOND THE CAMPFIRE

Some people come up with grandiose plans to change the world, spur a revolution, or create new political arrangements between Israelis and Palestinians, while others work within given systems, whether through official, formal channels like the court system or through back channels and in the shadows. This kind of working-within can be thought of either as collaborating with the enemy, or as "weapons of the weak" (Scott 1985), everyday forms of resistance.[6] But the idea of everyday resistance implies a single overarching hegemony that can be contested in numerous ways. In the case of Palestine, this has meant struggling against Jewish settlement and Jewish sovereignty of the land of historic Palestine. It has been conceptualized through one of two major narratives struggling to define the conflict: either the Palestinian people resisting the colonization of Palestine or two national groups vying for sovereignty over the same territory.

The story of the Sheikh does not quite fit into a model of resistance in either of these two narratives. However, if we imagine at once a more complicated set of power relations and the conditions of possibility in which those two narratives have come to struggle for hegemony, we can see what is at stake in the actions of the Sheikh. He and others whose stories form this chapter contest and invert different elements not only of the single hegemony of Jewish sovereignty in Palestine, but also of scattered and overlapping hegemonies that emerge from more fundamental conditions. Thinking Israel/Palestine through the notion of heterotopia opens a window through which to explore a set of actions already taking place in Israel/Palestine that might otherwise be discarded as criminal and traitorous, or simply as marginal and unimportant.

Heterotopias, according to Foucault (2008/1967), are spaces of contestation, where sets of relations and oppositions within a given social system that we have come to take for granted are reflected and challenged at the same time. The term resonates with but is quite different from utopia. If utopias "present society itself in a perfected form," they are also "fundamentally unreal." Utopias are imagined perfect societies. Foucault conjectured that heterotopias, on the other hand, actually exist and can likely be found in every culture. They are real places that are "something like counter-sites" in which the "real sites . . . that can be found within the culture" are reimagined, or reconfigured. (Foucault 2008/1967:17). Unlike utopias, heterotopias do not necessarily demonstrate models superior to the existing social order they contest. Although many theorists have used the term to analyze contemporary social space, especially cities, what distinguishes heterotopia need not be physical space (Low 2008). Heterotopia can also be marked by a conceptual border around rules and practices that are distinct from powerful norms. It may encompass a location for otherwise unacceptable practices, but it also, and more importantly, enacts subversions of powerful relations, norms, and practices. Heterotopia, then, is a way of conceptualizing what might be found beyond the blinding light of Le Guin's (1980) metaphorical campfire of hegemonic norms and practices. But rather than being the simple binary opposite to a single all-encompassing hegemonic system, heterotopia is a way of thinking about the other sides of scattered hegemonies (Grewal and Kaplan 1994), the complex and uneven ways in which power relations are organized.[7]

The idea of scattered hegemonies arises from an analysis that complicates universalized or essentialized notions of identity and difference. Feminists, in particular, realized that the issues of inequality and subordination that women faced could be very different in different locations and contexts. While forms of oppression may be layered, such that a Palestinian woman might be struggling against male domination in her family and village, she might also be struggling against Israeli domination of Palestinians (Hasan 1993).

So, while patriarchal society is based on the domination of women, not all women will be denied access to power in identical or equivalent ways, nor will all women always be subordinated to all men in every circumstance. Thus, Caren Kaplan wrote that to be effective, "feminists need detailed, historicized maps of the circuits of power" (1994:148). Social class, race, education, location, and other factors come into play so that, for example, a woman professor at an elite university will be relatively powerful in relation to a male professor at a community college seeking funding for a research project, but she might still face gender discrimination at work. In the same way, the issues Palestinian citizens of Israel face can be very different from those faced by Palestinians in the Occupied Territories, and different still from those living in refugee camps in Lebanon. This scattered nature of hegemony has led many activists to suggest forming coalitions around particular issues rather than around identity groups.

The idea of heterotopia opens up a conceptual space for thinking about the ways in which such scattered forms of hegemony are contested. Each instance might challenge a different kind of hegemony or a different aspect of power relations, such that different heterotopias may even be counter-sites to each other. However, resisting or contesting taken-for-granted relations is not enough to qualify as an example of heterotopia.

The stories of thieves and collaborators recalled in this chapter not only represent and invert power relations in the broader society; more specifically and maybe more importantly, they appear as heterotopias that mimic aspects of the hegemonic systems that determine what count as peacemaking, negotiation, and coexistence, while at the same time undermining the conditions that produce certain kinds of activities as peacemaking in the first place. Those conditions are not eternal. They must be produced, reproduced, and enforced, partially through the disciplining of unacceptable behaviors.

One of the ways in which these conditions are undermined and then disciplined is when family or local allegiances take precedence over loyalty to a national group. Recall the story of the peacemaker in Chapter 3 who, when asked by her supervisor to define her identity, said, quite simply, "I am my mother's daughter." That answer annoyed her supervisor. This young peacemaker had designated her first allegiance to her own family rather than claiming a sense of belonging to the Jewish people or the Israeli nation. In some ways, this sounds very much like what the Sheikh, suspected of collaborating with the enemy, has done. He has designated his allegiance to his extended family, his clan or tribe, the local people to whom he is responsible, and has acted on that allegiance. When family and community take precedence a young peacemaker or local leader may be called a traitor, marginalized as backward, called to order, or simply ignored. The hegemonic norms of peacemaking, it appears, require that one express allegiance to a national community over and above family or local community.

In the case of the young peacemaker, it turned out that her supervisor might have been right. One day, the young peacemaker was out doing her job. She had gone to visit a school in a Jewish town near the Arab village where she was housed. She was going to try to convince the school's principal to participate in the peacemaking program she was organizing. Ada, the principal, first checked her credentials. She wasn't concerned with the young peacemaker's schooling or job experience; she wanted to know if the peacemaker was an Israeli citizen. "You can't just show up from America and think you understand and try to intervene," Ada told the peacemaker. "You have to put yourself in the same position as the rest of us, be a citizen and see how it feels when you and your children have to serve in the army. See how it feels when Arab suicide bombers blow up busses in Jerusalem and then come and tell me if you think we should all just sit down together; if you really think that having meetings between school children will make everything better." The principal was adamant about this and was insulted by the notion that this young woman, who had never been on the front lines, never directly affected by the conflict, would show up and try to tell *her* how to make peace with her neighbors. Behind the indignation

Ada expressed was a disciplining moment. It meant that in order to take part in peacemaking, one ought to enact one's allegiance to the nation. The program was all about bringing people together. It was about providing a space in which members of enemy groups could have a chance to meet face to face, to reduce fear between them and challenge stereotypes. It aimed at allowing people to find their shared interests through discovering their shared humanity. But to do this, one must first declare oneself a member of a particular sort of enemy group.

The Sheikh and his peace tent might be the mirror image of high-level diplomacy between Israelis and Palestinians or of grassroots-level peacebuilding encounters, officially recognized efforts that promote and are legitimized by particular political structures. But those efforts and all the promises made by the political elite have done little to address the local issues of concern to the Sheikh. In mirroring official kinds of peace negotiations in which enemies come together, the Sheikh's efforts are heterotopic because the set of "enemies" who gathered in his tent are believed to be marginal, inappropriate, immovable, or mistaken. From the perspective of the secular nationalist, the Sheikh is speaking to the wrong people, even though from the local point of view, the settlers are far more relevant to what is going on than elites in Jerusalem and Ramallah or handshakes on the White House lawn.

And given the most recent political constellations, one might argue that those settlers are also more relevant to those elite spaces as well. Right-wing and settler groups are represented in the current Israeli government. But at the same time, the two-state solution is being pushed by the international community, and settlers who try to stay on the land threaten the state order of things whether they argue for continued Israeli control over settled areas or whether they try to make arrangements to live within the borders of a proposed Palestinian state. Entrepreneurs who trans-port automobile parts across borders work according to the laws of supply and demand. Their actions reflect the ideals espoused during the Oslo peace process that envisioned a New Middle East, a phrase coined by Shimon Peres that encapsulated the vision of the political elite (Ben-Porat 2006:167–168). The New Middle East was likened to the European Economic Community; it would have open borders and free trade. Peace would pave the way toward economic prosperity. This vision imagined Israel leading the way with new technologies and knowledge that would advance the region as it took a leading place in the global economy. Israel is home to a growing high-tech industry second only to Silicon Valley; this sector is sometimes referred to as Silicon Wadi. But the growing high-tech industry did not come hand in hand with peace, nor did it bring prosperity to the majority of people in Israel/Palestine. The cross-border trade in car parts mirrors the ideals of a New Middle East yet mocks the utopian vision. Car thieves provide a service and resources to the benefit of some and detriment of others, much like the high-tech industry. The car thieves represent the ideals of open borders and free trade associated with officially sanctioned visions of peace, but they also contest and invert the current hegemonic economic formation that has led to mass protests both in Israel and in the West Bank, where Israelis and Palestinians respectively express their anger at elected officials who have brought neither peace nor prosperity.[8]

COLLABORATION, COOPERATION, COEXISTENCE

What should count as a people's national interest is not immediately obvious nor necessarily agreed upon by those who may be immediately affected. Arjun Appadurai, a cultural anthropologist who describes himself as one who grew up "in the elite sections of the postcolonial world" (1993:411), discusses the complexities of nationalism and patriotism based on his own experiences growing up in India. Appadurai explains that his father had joined a group who thought of themselves as Indian nationalists in exile. In 1940, his father had been a journalist working for Reuters in Bangkok, where he met an expatriate Indian nationalist "who split with Gandhi and

Nehru on the issue of violence." The expat, a man named Subhas Chandra Bose, established a government-in-exile in Southeast Asia with the support of the Japanese. Appadurai's father joined with Bose and became the minister of publicity and propaganda. Bose put together an army composed of Indian soldiers whom the Japanese had taken prisoner. They called themselves the Indian National Army and fought a losing battle against the British in 1944. The elder Appadurai must certainly have thought of himself as doing everything he could for the Indian people. Surely he was patriotic, but was he a nationalist?

Arjun Appadurai writes that when his father returned to India in 1945 "he and his comrades were unwelcome heroes, poor cousins in the story of the nationalist struggle for Indian independence. They were patriots," but because of their specifically anti-British sentiment and because of their ties to the Axis powers (specifically Japan), they were considered "an embarrassment both to Gandhi's nonviolence and Nehru's Fabian Anglophilia. To the end of their lives, my father and his comrades remained pariah patriots, rogue nationalists" (Appadurai 1993:413).

The examples in this chapter illustrate some of the processes through which hegemony is formed; they show the struggle for hegemony, contested and competing hegemonies, and layered and scattered hegemonies. To be a collaborator, an accused traitor, or a "pariah patriot," one has to have demonstrated allegiance to a particular group vying for power within a larger collective defining itself as a community (nation). And that oppositional group also has to be one that ultimately lost the struggle for hegemony. And at the same time, to be a collaborator, one has to work with the people who are or will become hegemonic among the *other* group—the colonizer, the competing national group, the enemy. What is especially interesting in the case of Appadurai is that theirs was an elite family. They were not among the poor or economically oppressed. Hegemony is never quite as simple as a single hierarchy. One can be among the elite and still end up on the wrong side of politics.

HEGEMONIES

> [P]reviously germinated ideologies . . . come into confrontation
> and conflict, until only one of them . . . tends to prevail, to gain
> the upper hand, to propagate itself throughout society—bringing
> about not only a unison of economic and political aims, but also
> intellectual and moral unity . . . creating the hegemony of a funda-
> mental group over a series of subordinate groups.
>
> —Antonio Gramsci (1971:181–182)

While imprisoned in fascist Italy in the 1920s, Antonio Gramsci
analyzed the intricate ways in which hegemony can work. He was
concerned with how political domination could be wrested from
the ruling class. In the case of India, Appadurai tells of competing
nationalisms, which he separates by calling one "patriotism"—Bose
and his father—and the other "Nehru-style . . . bourgeois nationalism." He suggests *another* India, with "Japanese connections and
anti-Western ways [that] carried the nameless aroma of treason in
respect to the cozy alliance of the Nehrus and Mountbattens, and
the bourgeois compact between Gandhian nonviolence and Nehru-
vian socialism" (Appadurai 1993:413). Like the Sheikh, in the story
above the elder Appadurai's political involvements were suspect,
considered to be dangerous and opposed to the best interests of
Indian nationalists seeking independence. Bose and the elder Appadurai might be called "spoilers" of the prospects of nationalist
independence. But if their group *had* become dominant, they might
have been considered visionaries.

In Palestine, the Sheikh shares some of the sentiments expressed by Hamas. He seems convinced that Palestinians can never
accept a two-state solution because to arrive at two separate states
requires making territorial concessions. Selling or giving away land
is the worst form of social transgression when a situation is understood as an ethno-territorial nationalist conflict. When two nations both claim the same piece of land, gaining sovereignty, which
has become equated with political if not human liberation, means

gaining or maintaining control of that land. Like Hamas, the Sheikh explains that there are also religious issues involved. Muslims are forbidden from giving up claims to Muslim land (Hawley 2012), just as religiously motivated Jewish settlers explain that giving away land is contradictory to their own religious principles. Yet, unlike the official stance of Hamas, the Sheikh seeks ways of cooperating with his Jewish neighbors.

COLLABORATION

Given his position, and the fact that selling or surrendering land to Jews has been considered the most traitorous form of collaboration, it might seem surprising to hear that ultimately, this sheikh and other Palestinians like him are denounced as collaborators. He is opposed to making territorial compromise and is *not* giving away or selling land. But what, then, does it mean to be a collaborator? What is the difference between collaboration and cooperation, or collaboration and coexistence? Another way to ask these questions is to consider what conditions make the notion of "collaboration" possible. What do we need to assume, and what institutions have to be in place, for the idea of collaboration to make sense, let alone be upsetting or horrifying? What do thieves have to do with collaboration, and what is the difference between a collaborator, a peacemaker, and a spoiler?

In his book about Palestinian collaboration with Zionism between 1917 and 1948, prior to the establishment of the state of Israel, Hillel Cohen (2008) writes of at least four different kinds of activities that have been considered collaboration: selling land, providing information, having business relationships, and protecting Jews against Arab violence. Regev Nathansohn (2010), an anthropologist who studies past relations between Jews and Arabs, writes about household servants who worked for Jewish families in Haifa prior to the establishment of the Israeli state. He tells of Arab childcare workers who offered protection to the children of their

Jewish employers when the Arab riots or revolts broke out in 1929. Nathansohn is not writing about "collaboration"; he is telling stories about how Jews and Arabs helped each other in the past. He documents instances of Jewish/Arab coexistence, what he calls "co-existence from below." Documenting peaceful ways of living together among people who are perceived to be in a state of conflict might provide models of alternative possibilities to what is often considered the "intractable conflict" in Israel/Palestine. But if we think about Nathansohn's stories in terms of the categories of collaboration Cohen set out, simple acts of kindness can take on very different meanings. Actions emerging from interpersonal relationships might be considered the highly moral, humanistic acts of righteous people, but the very same "good deed" can also be read as treason.

Now, for some Palestinian nationalists, "normalization" is what must be condemned. Normalization refers to Palestinian cooperation with Israelis, which some activists denounce as normalizing the Israeli occupation. In the summer of 2013, Palestinians held their "fourth national BDS conference in Bethlehem," as reported on the Electronic Intifada website.[9] BDS stands for boycott, divestment, and sanctions; it is an international campaign calling for the boycott of Israeli goods and corporations that work with Israel, especially those that have ties to Israeli settlements in the West Bank. BDS began as an economic campaign to end the Occupation but then expanded to include a cultural and academic boycott as well. The anti-normalization campaign discussed at the 2013 conference has primarily been directed at the Palestinian Authority, but some activists have charged that certain kinds of peace initiatives are also forms of normalization and should be resisted.

One blogger reported that:

> Several speakers from the platform . . . denounced efforts by Israel and its collaborators to normalize the occupation. Many of those who spoke from the floor demanded the PA make laws to punish normalization. Several said the PA was undermining

boycott efforts through joint initiatives. An-Najah University sity economist Yousef Abdul Haqs said of such efforts: "We have breached our boycott movement."

Samia Botmeh of the Palestinian Campaign for the Academic and Cultural Boycott of Israel talked about efforts in schools to combat normalization initiatives like OneVoice, which target the minds of children, she said. OneVoice is a group founded by Israeli businessman Daniel Lubetzky, which seeks to bring the "two sides" together in dialogue.

Ziad Shuaibi of the BDS National Committee talked about Seeds of Peace, another normalization initiative, which sends Israeli and Palestinian youth on summer camps abroad together. He described how it uses powerful financial initiatives to entice participants, such as potential scholarships in foreign universities and the chance of travel. Normalization is a form of "social engineering" by Israel, he said, concluding: "we will not allow them to occupy our future."[10]

According to this report, what counts as peace or coexistence in some circles is understood as collaboration with the enemy in others. Some of those who attended the conference reported that participants debated the idea of making a blacklist of Palestinians who engage in normalized relations with Israelis. Such a list, it was reported, might include the Palestinian co-director of the film *Five Broken Cameras*, because it was made with an Israeli co-director. This might seem surprising given that the film has been shown to international audiences to gain support for the Palestinian cause, including support for the BDS movement. Nathansohn might designate the collaborative effort to make that film another example of "co-existence from below," but some Palestinians would disagree. It should not be surprising, then, that joint Israeli-Palestinian efforts to end the Occupation are becoming increasingly difficult, or that there are sometimes more Israelis and international activists than Palestinians involved in such efforts (Callan 2013).

If we think in terms of Hayden White's (1980) analysis of the narrative form (see Chapter 3), we can imagine reading Nathansohn's stories about the Arabs who protected Jewish children in a number of ways. White suggested that when history is narrativized it will necessarily embody a moral conclusion. From within a particular Jewish historical perspective, the narrative of these Arabs could be folded into a broader narrative about Jews as perpetual outsiders and victims who are sometimes protected by righteous gentiles who take great personal risks. From within such a narrative, these Arabs could be compared to other brave nonconformists who protected Jews in Nazi Europe, or Arabs who protected Jews from Nazis in Morocco or Algeria, or those who saved Jews from the massacre in Hebron in 1929. One of the important points of these narratives is that such actions are seen as exceptions; they do not suggest that Jews should or can ever rely on such kindness. From this perspective, because they are seen as exceptional, such stories bolster the idea that Jews must rely only on themselves for protection and security. They support the argument for the need to have a state and to be sovereign.

Such actions might be read by some Palestinians, on the other hand, as dangerous acts of protecting an enemy who will ultimately rule over those who helped them, like normalization today. Or perhaps such actions could be read as prudent measures. For those who believed the Jews could not be defeated, it might seem sensible to work with them rather than against them. For others still, perhaps protecting Jewish children in the midst of this conflict could be read as part of a longer tradition of protecting minority populations in Muslim-majority lands—or, on a more intimate level, an honorable personal or professional duty toward those who have been defined as innocents, friends, neighbors, dependents, co-workers, or patrons; or simply as a basic act of human kindness and concern.

Both Muslim and Jewish legal traditions allow for the protection of minority populations as long as they do not seek sovereignty. Offering refuge for Jewish families or children can thus be read as part of a righteous history or as a foolish act by those who did not understand its longer-term implications. Similarly, Jews and Israelis today who offer support and assistance to Palestinians might be considered righteous, highly moral individuals, or they might be denounced as traitors to their nation.

Cohen explains that the period between 1917 and 1948, when "the collapse of the Ottoman Empire and the British conquest of Palestine . . . brought Palestine and the rest of the Middle East into the age of nationalism" (2008:43), was the period when certain previously acceptable behaviors among the Arabs of Palestine became traitorous and unacceptable. Previously, it had neither been unusual nor especially problematic to sell land or to have other economic relations with Jews in Palestine. Perhaps this is what the Sheikh was referring to when he spoke about coming from a generation that lived in cooperation with its Jewish neighbors. But when the political context of the region changed, so did acceptable norms. This was a period of transition from one hegemony to another.

Cohen explains that during this period of transition, selling land, in particular, became illegitimate in the eyes of Palestinian Arab nationalists. It took some time for nationalism to become dominant, but as early as 1911, newspapers began publishing opinion pieces admonishing those who sold their property because land had now taken on an importance beyond the individual or family; now land was of central importance to the nation. It is important to bear in mind that at the same time, early Zionists were making similar strategic decisions about land and labor as they worked to build the foundations of a Jewish state. They aimed to gain more land and to employ Jewish rather than Arab laborers (Shafir 1989). This led to bringing in additional immigrants, including Jews from Arab lands who were imported to replace the local Palestinian Arabs as laborers, as Jewish landowners worked to establish an economy that would not be reliant on local Arabs. So, rather than simply inquiring into the definition of a collaborator, we should ask under what conditions certain actions are considered acceptable and what makes the very same actions count as collaboration or treason in a different context (see Dudai and Cohen 2007). When does economic cooperation, sharing information, buying and selling property, protecting people from acts of violence, or meeting with people to talk about peace become an act of betrayal?

DEMOCRACY AND DEMOLITION

There once was a grassroots peace activist named Jamal, who lived in the Negev Desert near the Bedouin town of Kuseife. Jamal was a teacher in the Kuseife school, but he did not consider himself a Bedouin. He said he was a *fallah*, the descendant of farmers who worked their own land. And in the mid-1980s, when the Israeli government established the town of Kuseife as part of a larger state project to sedentarize the Bedouin, he refused to move there. According to Jamal, the town was beset with all sorts of social problems and, in any case, he was not a Bedouin but lived on the land he owned, as did his father and grandfather before him. I met Jamal while working for an NGO that promoted democracy and peaceful coexistence between Arabs and Jews in Israel. Jamal worked tirelessly for this NGO, organizing all sorts of events. He was committed to its goals. Yet at the same time as he worked with Jewish partners arranging meetings for Arab and Jewish schoolchildren to learn about democracy, parts of his home regularly came under demolition orders from the Israeli Ministry of the Interior.

Jamal was organizing for peaceful coexistence between Arabs and Jews while the Israeli government was destroying his home. They claimed that he was breaking Israeli laws because he had no permit to build outside of Kuseife. He made his home in a village that was not recognized by the Israeli government. So he built it and they knocked it down. Then he would build it again, and they would knock it down again. He kept working with the NGO, which could do nothing about the demolition orders, and kept smiling and struggling to have the place where he lived officially recognized. He told us he was never angry at the men who came to knock down the newly

erected walls that would house one of his recently married sons. Instead, he offered them refreshments and acted as a host while he
continued his battle through the courts. Eventually he succeeded. It
took years and years, but ultimately in the late 1990s the homes of
his extended family were recognized as legal. Eventually a clinic and
a school were built for the people living there and the little village
was connected to electricity and running water.

Was Jamal a collaborator for working with this NGO? Was he a
collaborator for seeking Israeli permits to build? Perhaps he should
be considered an outlaw for building without a permit. He might be
considered a nationalist because he would not give up his land. On
the other hand, he could be an expansionist, or even a settler. Was a
Jamal a peacemaker or a spoiler?

I was recently told a story about Ahmed, a Palestinian man
who lived in the Gaza Strip. Ahmed crossed the border into Israel
to attend a meeting of Israelis and Palestinians in a town not more
than 20 minutes away from where he lives. Upon his return to Gaza,
he was arrested, interrogated, and beaten up. According to those Palestinians currently in positions of power in the Gaza Strip, members
of Hamas, this man is a collaborator. The harassment of such people
might be one way in which Hamas can be considered a spoiler of
peace, but it is also part of their own narrative of men such as Ahmed
as spoilers of legitimate authority. But there's more to this story.

One of the Jewish Israeli peace activists who told this story
about Ahmed from Gaza also told me about efforts to help resettle
him. The Israeli peace activist called on his Palestinian peacemaking contacts in the West Bank, where the Fatah party rather than
Hamas is currently more powerful. The Israeli, who has a great deal
of experience with negotiations, thought the West Bank Palestinians might help this Gaza man to resettle. Perhaps Ahmed and his
family could leave the Gaza Strip and move to the West Bank and
be safe there. But the West Bank Palestinians refused. They said
the Gaza man was not a member of their party, and so there was
no reason they should help him. Now we might say that the Fatah
were acting as spoilers, rejecting a Palestinian who has tried to meet

peacefully and work together with Israelis. Did the West Bank Fatah members refuse to help the man from Gaza because he was not a member of their party, or perhaps because, despite their power struggle with Hamas, they too thought of him as a collaborator?

WHO ARE YOU CALLING A THIEF?

> It is a crime to kill a neighbor, an act of heroism to kill an enemy, but who is an enemy and who is a neighbor is purely a matter of social definition.
>
> —Edmund Leach (1968, quoted in Nader 2001)

I once heard a story about an Israeli man whose pickup truck was gone from the parking lot where he left it one afternoon while doing errands. A few minutes after the man realized his vehicle was missing, his cell phone began to ring. It was the man who had his truck, asking whether or not he'd like to have it back. That would require paying a fee, of course. How much would he be willing to pay? The Israeli was furious, "I don't negotiate with thieves!" he said. "Who are you calling a thief?" came the indignant reply.

The Israeli reported the crime to the local police, who were not at all surprised. They knew about a ring of Bedouin thieves who stole Israeli vehicles, and they did not expect to find the truck. Once he'd recovered from the inconvenience and indignity, the man also began to tell this story to his friends. Everyone laughed when he got to the part where the thief says, "Who are you calling a thief!" But one day, when he told the story to his friend Isaac, his friend had another story to tell.

Isaac was a rancher in the Negev. He had tried raising beef cattle, but then switched to raising goats and selling their milk. One evening, Isaac's wife Perach went into town with her friends to attend a performance of classical music. When the performance ended, she returned to her car only to find it wasn't there. Isaac and Perach never got a phone call, but Isaac decided to look into the matter. He knew there was a ring of Bedouin car thieves and thought maybe he could find his wife's car.

Isaac, his wife, and their five children made their home on a piece of land that ran along the inside of the pre-1967 Israeli border, the Green Line. Isaac had friends who were right-wing Israeli politicians, and when he was looking for a place to set up his ranch, he turned to a politician friend who was instrumental in facilitating the permission Isaac needed to live on this land. The government had agreed to give Isaac the land for his ranch for security purposes. His ranch marked the border, which he could patrol. By the time the incident with his wife's car happened, Isaac had been living in this border zone for quite a long time. His closest neighbors were Palestinians who lived on the hills across the valley and across the Green Line from his ranch. His relationship with them did not always go smoothly.

When Isaac first tried raising beef cattle, he would take them out to pasture and leave them to graze some distance away from his house, which at the time was an abandoned British train car to which he'd attached a generator so he would have electricity for a few hours each day. Sometimes he would find that some of his cattle were missing. Or, he would plant trees and find them uprooted. Isaac did not report these problems to the Israeli border patrol or the police. Instead, he drove across the valley that marked the Green Line to the Palestinian village on the other side and looked for the local sheikh. When he found the village leader, they spoke at length. The sheikh hosted him in his home and they came to some arrangements. I'm not sure what exactly was given in exchange, but soon Isaac employed a few men from the village to work on his ranch and purchased supplies for his household in the village—and he stopped losing cattle or having trees uprooted for a while. When these sorts of things would happen again, he'd make another trip to visit with the Palestinian sheikh and perhaps offer something in return for protection.

So, when Perach came out of the concert and found that her car was not where she had parked it, Isaac had some idea of how to proceed. He asked around and finally figured out who might have the car. Then he went to talk to the people. This time, it was a man in a Bedouin town, not far away. Isaac wanted to see the car and the Bedouin man wanted to make sure he could trust Isaac. Each man asked around; the man who now had the car found out that Isaac was not an undercover policeman, and eventually he and Isaac met. Isaac saw that the car was not too badly damaged and negotiations began. Finally an agreement was reached in which goats were exchanged for the car.

Taking a car from a parking lot and offering to sell it back to its owner might seem outrageous. It is a crime. But what counts as "theft" is determined by those who have the power to decide. And "theft," like "violence," is deeply embedded in systems of power. Those of us who live our lives according to the rules of law and order protect the hegemony that determines what is theft and what is violence, what are acceptable forms of removing property, and when causing suffering, pain, or death is punishable.[11] In this case, those rules and laws are established and enforced by the Israeli state, although the hegemony is a broader one.

Jamal, the peacemaker who refused to move into the Bedouin town established by the Israeli government, struggled against the law he found unjust. He broke the law over and over again while contesting demolition orders in court. The man who refused to "negotiate with thieves" upholds the law and order of the state, which he sees as protecting his interests, even though he might oppose the demolition orders on Jamal's house. Indeed, this man would attend protests on Saturdays against such orders, not only on Jamal's house but on many of the demolition orders against "illegal" structures erected by Bedouins in the Negev. The man took his family to visit the unrecognized villages and his children saw the poverty. The Bedouin children in the unrecognized village had no shoes, there was no running water, and people lived in meager huts made of thin sheets of tin. The houses were set off the road on a dusty path. It was extremely hot in those huts during the summer and the dusty path would turn to mud as soon as it rained. This can be called poverty, or it can be called structural violence.

Despite the poor conditions, the people wanted to remain there, but they were not permitted to build and did not have access to public utilities. The men in this village would leave each morning, walking to the main road to catch a bus and go to work for meager wages. Some worked in the Israeli service sector; others were laborers in the housing industry. While they were away, when only their wives and young children were at home, the authorities would come to carry out a demolition order and knock down a tin hut or simple mosque. It wasn't hard to imagine how men like these might decide to take a car from a parking lot and try to resell it either to its previous owner or for spare parts in garages in the Bedouin villages or across the border, mimicking free-trade zones and mocking a vision of peace based on open borders, where the market forces of global capitalism offer scant relief against the broader structural violence that makes their living conditions so difficult.

Are any and all meetings with members of the enemy nation acts of treason? This question brings us back to the episteme of nations and nationalism, and of the notion that peace is tied to justice and that justice can best be accomplished by gaining sovereignty in one's own nation-state. This idea gives primacy to a particular kind of unified, essentialized identity and is hard-pressed to deal with the complexities of scattered, layered, uneven, and overlapping hegemonies. It means allegiance to the imagined national community should take precedence over and above allegiance to one's family and relations with one's immediate neighbors. It can mean that the nation should also take precedence over religious affiliations that might exceed the nation even as religion and nationalism become intertwined.

NATIONALISM AND A SECULAR AGE

Hillel Cohen (2008:48) documents the first assembly of Muslim religious scholars in Palestine, which convened in 1935. The sale of land was the focal point of discussion at that meeting, which resulted in a religious ruling (*fatwa*) prohibiting the sale of land by Muslims to Jews in Palestine. The text of that ruling not only defines such a sale as a direct offense to God and to the Prophet Muhammad, but it also places friendship and family relations in a secondary position. The ruling states that "one who sells land to Jews in Palestine . . . and those who knowingly facilitate and help them in any way, one may not pray for them [at their deaths] or bury them in Muslim graves and one should abandon them and ban them and despise them and not become friendly with them or get close to them, even if they are parents or children or brothers or spouses" (quoted in Cohen 2008:49).

Were the Arabs of Palestine right to try to prevent the sale of their property to those who would ultimately establish a Jewish state in Palestine? With the ongoing struggle over territory, one might think they were absolutely justified. If so, are Israeli rabbis equally justified in making similar pronouncements today against Jews renting or selling land to Arabs? Some contemporary peacemakers suggest that peace can only be accomplished with the implementation of structural changes that would end all forms of discrimination. Were the Arabs of Palestine discriminating against the Jews? Are the Jews now discriminating against the Palestinian Arabs? Are national self-determination and discrimination the same thing in any case? Is the enemy the cause of the conflict or its outcome?

Particular forms of sovereignty determine the extent to which personal, family, or local interests can be pursued. In other words, we might ask what forms of collective sovereignty allow for particular kinds of individual sovereignty. During Ottoman rule neither Arabs nor Jews were sovereign, so they lived as minority groups among minority groups.[12] It might seem as though in order to have such personal/local subjectivities now, national sovereignty must first be attained.

Some scholars (e.g., Boyarin and Boyarin 2003/1993; Rabinowitz 2000) have suggested that peaceful coexistence between Israelis and Palestinians could be accomplished without abandoning allegiance to their respective national communities. They recommend adopting models of living that might be similar to the ways in which Arabs and Jews lived as minorities among minorities in the Ottoman Empire, suggesting that forms of diasporic identity could be adapted to life inside Israel/Palestine. If neither Arabs nor Jews were the ruling group, then what is currently considered collaboration might be considered good neighborly relations. In diaspora it is not necessarily discriminatory for members of a particular ethnic, racial, or religious group to take care of each other, raise funds to provide social services, help each other find work, or live in close proximity to each other in the same neighborhoods. Some of the very same behaviors, according to Boyarin and Boyarin (1993), become exclusionary and racist if they are attached to state power. If neither Arabs nor Jews were the hegemonic group, neither one the sovereign group, then perhaps all sorts of disciplinary processes that inscribe, produce, and reproduce these enemy nations might fade away. That, of course, is also something that many people fear because they fear the precarious condition of being ruled over by another group who might not protect their interests or rights, the condition that Hannah Arendt described for Jews in Europe.

Perhaps it is precisely this fear that leads to reinforcing national identities even, or maybe especially, when people in conflict situations are seeking ways of living together peacefully. If a school program, for example, is designed to bring together Arabs and Jews in Israel, or Catholics and Protestants in Northern Ireland, or Greek and Turkish Cypriots, individuals who declare their first allegiance to their parents or neighbors, or children who just want to be friends with other children, must be molded to fit into the categorizes of existing enemy groups. What happens to children of mixed marriages? What happens to immigrants or children of migrant workers who attend a school participating in an intergroup peace project? How will these children be educated, disciplined, and chiseled into the requisite identities needed for peacemaking? The young peacemaker's project and so many others like it were based on the idea that interactions between members of enemy groups will reduce animosity and help build a peaceful future from the bottom up.

Zvi Bekerman has been studying programs like this for more than a decade now. Ultimately, he writes, when it comes down to a question of peace versus national identity, identity wins (Bekerman 2009). One of his field sites has been a bilingual school in Jerusalem designed to bring Arab and Jewish Israeli students together. This is very unusual in Israel, where there are separate schools for members of these different groups. The Israeli public school system consists of three different streams of education. *Mamlachti* refers to state schools that serve the general, primarily secular, Jewish population, and in which instruction takes place in Hebrew. *Mamlachti dati* are those state schools designed for religious Jews, where additional courses in religious instruction are provided. Arab schools are those state-administered schools in Arab towns and neighborhoods where instruction is given in Arabic, with Hebrew as a second language.

In the bilingual school Bekerman describes, courses are team-taught in Arabic and Hebrew, aiming to maintain a balance of Arab and Jewish children and to allow children to "strengthen their own identities while better understanding their classmates" (2009:75). Even the simplest administrative actions aimed at balance and diversity reproduce and strengthen divisions between the two communities. For example, because the school wants to maintain an "ethnically balanced" student population, each child has to be counted as either Palestinian Arab or as Jewish. So, for example, when a child with a Jewish mother and a Muslim Palestinian father was admitted to the school, the child was counted as Palestinian. According to Bekerman, the emphasis on individual and collective identities in this school "left little space for border crossing" (2009:76) and in fact reinscribed the Jewish–Palestinian divide. Because they are all citizens of Israel, these identity categories are considered ethnicities and Palestinians are the ethnic minority. But these identities inside the borders of the internationally recognized state of Israel bleed into the contested territories beyond those borders, uneasily and unevenly creating two enemy national groups (see Appadurai 2006). Palestinians in the Occupied Territories and the Palestinian Authority sometimes speak disparagingly about Israeli Palestinians. Their lives are easier, some say, and "they have forgotten that they are Palestinian" (Neslen 2011:152). But Palestinian Israelis identify with those across the Green Line, even if they face a different set of challenges as an ethnic minority and as citizens of the State of Israel.

Children in the bilingual Arabic–Hebrew school attend classes together, but separate ceremonies are arranged on holidays. In particular, probably the most sensitive date is the day before Israeli Independence Day, which is commemorated throughout the country as a memorial day for fallen soldiers. Palestinian citizens of Israel do not celebrate Israeli independence. Instead they commemorate their losses in the Nakbah, or disaster, that befell them. In the bilingual school separate commemoration ceremonies are held for Jewish and Palestinian Israelis. Bekerman recalls a situation in which one child, a Palestinian, asked to attend the Jewish Israeli commemoration. And while there are now in Israel a number of events in which Jewish Israelis choose to attend special Nakbah commemoration ceremonies, in this case the child's father was horrified.

Bekerman explains that there are a number of reasons that parents choose the bilingual school, but generally speaking it is not because they want to lessen their children's ethnic/national identity. Parents are very concerned about passing along their nation's history to their children. They might want the children to feel more comfortable in each other's presence, to understand each other's language, and to reduce stereotypical images of members of the other group. However, most parents do not seek assimilation between the groups.

This school and other peacemaking projects like dialogue and encounter groups reinforce and essentialize national identity, and young children are molded into national containers even when they don't quite fit, or when they wriggle and flex and try to explore. So while it is possible to argue either that identity causes conflict or that conflict produces identity, here we see how peacebuilding efforts, which are meant to be the opposite of conflict processes, indeed the *solution* to conflict, also produce identity, and specifically enemy identities. We are not allowed to take part without declaring one identity or another, even if the central issue being negotiated is the nature and extent of conflict between them. If we compare these formalized peace projects to the others stories recounted in this chapter, then we might wonder why an educational effort that reinforces enemy identities should count as peacemaking any more or any less than negotiations that result in trading goats for car parts.

SECURITY/EXCEPTION AND HETEROTOPIA

The tradition of the oppressed teaches us that the "state of emergency" in which we live is not the exception but the rule.

—Walter Benjamin (1968/1940:257)

In Israel/Palestine so much of what is going on seems to be out of proper order. As we have seen, there seem to be temporal, spatial, and moral disturbances of all sorts. Scholars have tried to find ways to characterize its apparently unusual status, its resistance to solutions that seem obvious (one state, two states), and the forms of political authority and rule employed in the space of Israel/Palestine. One line of thought has been to think of Palestine in terms of Giorgio Agamben's theorizing on the "state of exception" (Hanafi 2012; Lentin 2008). Agamben (2005) begins with a particular reading of Carl Schmitt's well-known work on the relationship between the state of exception and sovereignty.

Ronit Lentin (2008) explains that Agamben expanded on Schmitt's idea that the state of exception is integral to modern sovereignty. Schmitt suggested that the sovereign can declare a state of exception in which the normal laws are suspended as a result of a specific emergency (Schmitt 1985/1922). It is the power to declare an emergency that requires a state of exception that produces sovereignty itself. Because Schmitt's thinking is so closely tied to the case of Nazi Germany, Lentin writes, we might too quickly equate the theorization of the state of exception with the Nazi state. Indeed, soon after Hitler took power, he suspended the articles of the Weimar Constitution concerning personal liberties. Since that decree was never repealed, the Third Reich became "a state of exception which lasted twelve years" (Lentin 2008:4). But it is not only modern totalitarianism that can be established through a state of exception. What is more important, for Agamben, is to analyze how the state of exception operates within what we think of as democratic states. Within democracies this power is so important because it works with the consent of the governed. It is a process by which some of the essential liberties of democratic systems are removed, but the restrictions come to be accepted as in fact protecting freedom by protecting the people from some serious threat to their existence. This might be considered an extreme version of Gramsci's ideas about educating consent, which turns "coercion into freedom" (1971:242).

Lentin explains that

> through the state of exception, the sovereign "creates and guarantees the situation" that the law needs for its validity—and this circularity characterizes not only extreme regimes such as the Nazi state, but also the voluntary creation of a permanent state of emergency that has become one of the essential practices of contemporary states, including so-called democratic states (Agamben 2005:2). This involves, on the one hand, the extension of the military authority's wartime powers into the civil sphere, and on the other, the suspension of constitutional norms that protect individual liberties. (Lentin 2008:4–5)

Democratic freedoms are undone, even within so-called democratic systems, through gaining the consent of the governed by invoking a specific kind of fear that also works to create and maintain the boundaries of the national group.

> Agamben's reading of Schmitt's state of exception theory rests not only on sovereignty declaring a state of emergency in which the sovereign both stays outside the law and enacts it, but also on the notion that it *is the nation (in the sense of volk, rather than citizenry or residency within the state's territorial borders) which needs defending from its others.* (Lentin 2008:5, emphasis added; cf. Appadurai 2006)

According to Lentin, then, in this sort of security state, which Agamben takes not to be exceptional but characteristic of contemporary political order, the suspension of certain rights is rationalized as necessary to protect "the people" from external threats. If the state of exception is a security state, instituting "an unprecedented generalization of the paradigm of security as the normal techniques of government" (Agamben 2005:14), we might think of it in terms of Le Guin's campfire. Despite its extensive use of techniques of surveillance, violence, and population control that not only interfere with individual freedoms but also open up the possibility of eliminating those deemed political adversaries—which may be entire categories of people who are not integrated into the political system—this state becomes the norm and the place of comfort. It becomes the campfire. Many people readily accept and even embrace the security state because they have been educated to consent, in Gramsci's terms (1971:310). That education takes place in homes, through television and other media, and in schools. To accept or embrace the security state requires maintaining that which must be protected: the people. The people, in the form of national categories of humanity, are produced through educative processes including official and grassroots peacemaking that ultimately form the basis of ongoing conflict, and theirs are the stories told around the campfire.

The stories in this chapter reveal a complex picture of people, ideas, and actions that seem to threaten and undermine the *Volk.*

Collaborators, thieves, and settlers who meet with local Palestinian leaders to work on local issues without the approval of elected officials challenge and invert the norms of the security state or state of exception. These actors create heterotopias that represent negotiations, market exchange, coexistence, and peacemaking, without necessarily essentializing national identities or reinforcing the contiguity between such identities with territory and sovereignty. Their actions endanger the fragile distinction between categories of enemy national groups in stable territorial orders that are required for the state and the nation, for the conflict, and for official peacemaking.

Just as the bilingual school can only teach children to be tolerant if those children's sense of belonging and allegiance to one of two national categories is clearly affirmed, so it is at the level of international diplomacy. Recall that Dennis Ross insists on recognizing the narratives of the parties to conflict (Chapter 2). It was not a matter of accepting the content of those narratives, but recognizing that the parties *have* a narrative, which is part of what establishes their collective identity as parties to be eligible for international recognition and intervention.

As noted above, Israel/Palestine has been theorized as exemplary of Agamben's state of exception, but I want to point to heterotopias because turning away from the campfire provides additional insight into how the epistemic basis of the security state/state of exception is disciplined and contested. This kind of analysis, to quote Hannah Arendt, is "a complicated process that never produces unequivocal results. It is an unending activity by which . . . we come to terms with and reconcile ourselves to reality, that is, try to be at home in the world" (Arendt 1989:42–43).[13]

So, for Agamben the state of exception is not exceptional at all but instead marks "the dominant paradigm of government in contemporary politics" (2005:2) where "the camp," as Dehaene and De Cauter (2008) argue, has taken over. The camp is the sprawling planet of slums, the growing, raging poverty, and the resulting precariousness of everyday life. It is the security state exemplified by places like Guantanamo Bay, where the rights of citizens are stripped away, or Israel's post-1967 Occupied Territories, where the rules of the state don't quite apply (Collins 2011; Gordon 2008). The security measures imposed in such places bleed over into the rest of society, and ultimately we all live in a state of exception in which our protection by the law and the line between dictatorship and democracy become precarious.

Deheane and De Cauter posit that heterotopia is the opposite of what Agamben calls the camp. Setha Low, in the same volume, then theorizes gated communities as heterotopias because they are enclosed and guarded against fear of poverty and crime, against threats to personal security. Low writes that heterotopias are "places where the technologies and discipline of social order are broken down . . . and reordered"; they are places with a distinct "regimen of rules and practices" (Low 2008:153). And yet her choice of gated communities as an example of heterotopia seems to set up heterotopias as places that *reinforce* the social order of the camp. What is crucial about the camp is not so much the unpleasantness of crime and poverty, which are indeed threatening, but the particular forms of social control that fear of crime, poverty, and other threats enable and reinforce. Gated communities are among the places and practices that reinforce the camp's forms of social control. This is exactly what makes such places fit squarely *inside* the kinds of security states that arise out of states of emergency. One might imagine such communities as perhaps the guards' barracks rather than those of the prisoners, but nonetheless within the camp. Heterotopia, for Foucault, is the *opposite* of the camp, contesting and inverting the hegemonic order and the foundations that make that order possible.

The two terms "security state" and "state of exception" taken together are another way of describing the hegemonic system in place in Israel/Palestine. And like all such systems its asymmetries, acts of discipline, revoking of rights, and production of categories of humanity who are subject to surveillance and control do not occur evenly across population groups or territory. In other words, within its internationally recognized borders, the State of Israel might be considered a security state (see Ochs 2011), while the Occupied Territories might be the primary locus for states of exception where all sorts of rights are stripped away or never granted in the first place. However, even if such characterizations are accurate, a division of such political conditions mapped onto geography would be an oversimplification, since civil and human rights are also precarious for both Palestinian and Jewish citizens of Israel within its pre-1967 borders.

Rashid Khalidi (1997) writes that Palestinian identity is produced at checkpoints. The security/state of emergency that is Israel/Palestine produces identity when identity cards are required for movement and when closures mean an inability to work or visit relatives, impediments to business growth that are responsible for stagnating the economy. Palestinian identity is part of the camp, an element of camp life. But Israeli identity is also produced at these checkpoints. Israeli identity is equally and profoundly an outcome and aspect of the historical European concentration camp Agamben uses as a metaphor for contemporary life, and of the camp as that contemporary life itself, in which the rule of law and morality are suspended. From this point of view, national identities do not develop as liberating forms of resistance, but as structures of practice and meaning whose own hegemonies are contested from heterotopic spaces outside of them.

THINKING OR ACTING BEYOND THE NATION

We need to think ourselves beyond the nation. This is not to suggest that thought alone will carry us beyond the nation or that the nation is largely a thought or an imagined thing. Rather, it is to suggest that the role of intellectual practices is to identify the current crisis of the nation and, in identifying it, to provide part of the apparatus of recognition for postnational social forms.

—Arjun Appadurai (1993:411)

The actions of the Sheikh might not remove Israeli control over the territory or gain Palestinians their own nation-state. But if we can allow ourselves to step out of our current context and see the episteme that gives rise to it, we might realize that his actions contest the current social and political order that gives rise to both conflict and to injustice.

Thinking beyond the nation has temporal as well as spatial and political aspects. In the Ottoman context, Arabs and Jews could work together in some ways. Now that these Jews are representatives of the Israeli state, the behavior of the Sheikh is out of the national order of things. We might understand this collaboration as a heterotopian enactment of peaceful coexistence. But heterotopias "engage temporalities distinct from those engaged in the places that surround them" (Faubion 2008, referring to Foucault 1984:180–183), and so this behavior seems also to belong to the past, just as does the Jewish settler behavior criticized by Israeli leftists in Chapter 4. To many people it seems bizarre, anachronistic, and ultimately senseless.

Recall Zvi Bekerman's description of the force required in order to produce the nation (Chapter 2). "For the community to be imagined in its national oneness," he wrote, echoing Benedict Anderson, not only was it necessary to widen borders and lump together groups "through homogenizing efforts," but in addition "culture has to be reified and the individual—and his relation to the sovereign—strengthened so as to undermine the power of smaller communal identifications" (Bekerman 2007:26–27). The disciplining power of the national order refuses this undisciplined Sheikh and the smaller communal affiliations he enacts. His peace tent is a place that at once represents other sites—other gatherings, peacemaking encounters, negotiations between leaders—and simultaneously contests or inverts those sites. It represents dialogue encounters that Jamal the peacemaker might have arranged between Israeli Jews and Arabs or the kinds of diplomatic encounters in which Dennis Ross might have participated. But it is a meeting that seems to seek the "wrong" kind of peace, a peace out of place in the world order of nation-states.

Such a peace may not address the unequal distribution of land and other resources. It may not create a situation in which Palestinians would gain self-determination. But, then again, what counts as "self-determination" in the first place, and why it should be so celebrated, is not immediately obvious and should not be taken for granted. Is self-determination the ability to make choices as one pleases and to look out for one's self, one's family and community? Is it another way of thinking about agency? Is self-determination distinguished by the right to vote and elect representatives to a governing body? Or is self-determination a matter of being a member of a majority or ruling group in one's own nation-state? I will investigate questions of sovereignty and self-determination further in the final two chapters.

Chapter 6

Beyond Producing Spoilers

What stories? How to count them and give account of them, or better yet, how to be accountable for them?

—Jacques Derrida (2008:312)

The Israeli-Palestinian conflict is not a Greek tragedy, nor is it fated.

—Jonathan Boyarin (1996:46)

Once upon a time there was a scholar who lived in Jerusalem. He came from a prominent, well-respected Palestinian family and often voiced his opinion on pressing political issues of the day. He was a public intellectual and had even been a politician representing Jerusalem in the Palestinian National Authority. This man was a patriotic Palestinian with moderate positions on controversial issues. Not long ago, he had worked with a prominent Israeli to promote a peace agreement that would result in a two-state solution to the conflict in Israel/Palestine. But now, the same man began suggesting something else, something that broke all the unspoken rules. His new idea led to disbelief and outrage among Palestinians and their supporters. This Palestinian intellectual had begun to question the political aspirations of his people, undermining the foundations of their decades-long struggle. Like the Rabbi whose story opened this book and the Sheikh we met in Chapter 5, his ideas violate conventional political categories. They seem to contradict some of the foundational assumptions of the modern order of nation-states that lie at the core of liberal peacemaking.

In 2011, Sari Nusseibeh published a book called *What Is a Palestinian State Worth?* It was a surprising book because Nusseibeh was known for his earlier efforts to promote a Palestinian state alongside an Israeli state. Now he was asking whether such a state is worth the high price of Palestinian suffering. Was the establishment of an independent Palestinian state really the answer to all their dreams? Was it worth the ongoing violence and destruction, the seemingly hopeless struggle? "How much has our killing of each other for so many years moved us toward peace?" he asks (Nusseibeh 2011:44). He wonders "What would a state be for, anyway?," suggesting that to fulfill their natural potential, what Palestinians need is an end to the restrictions imposed by military rule, which is not necessarily dependent upon the establishment of their own state (Nusseibeh 2011:6–7).

Beyond the question of whether the independent state Palestinians have been collectively struggling to achieve for decades is still worth fighting for, Nusseibeh made an alternative suggestion, a suggestion that makes some people think he's crazy and makes others think he's a traitor like the Sheikh. Still others think he's just being provocative and making this suggestion to shock people into realizing its absurdity. For one reason or another, people are outraged by the proposition. And whether or not outrage is what he was aiming for, it seems worthwhile to consider what is it he could possibly have said that would be so deplorable.[1]

Nusseibeh is pragmatic. A state, he says, should be the means rather than the end. And what Palestinians need most right now is the ability to improve their living conditions. They need the ability to move around freely, to find housing and work. Nusseibeh wants to end the restrictions imposed by checkpoints and walls that trap and suffocate Palestinians, making life intolerable by separating them from their families and places of work. To suggest Palestinians be granted such freedoms should not sound outrageous. Many Israelis say they'd be perfectly happy to live without all that security, but some add that there is no choice. Acts of terror were the cause of all these security measures that now make Palestinians prisoners and Israelis their jailers. Israelis certainly do not enjoy the years of military service required of them, the countless years of being called to reserve duty, sending their children to stand guard at checkpoints and man the pillbox towers. Some tell stories about their children's fears in these situations. Often no more than 18 years old, these young soldiers are armed but often given instructions not to open fire. They feel surrounded by hatred, by enemies who want their destruction. They are children themselves and often just don't know what to do, how to respond to Palestinian anger when they're guarding checkpoints or patrolling the maze of alleyways in Palestinian cities.

But what if the security measures in place are there more to protect the symbolic integrity or purity of the Israeli nation than to guard against acts of physical violence? We might approach this question by not only considering razor-wire fences, barriers, and walls with armed soldiers at checkpoints, but by looking at what seem like banal safety measures in out-of-the-way places. In his book *Palestine and Jewish History*, Jonathan Boyarin tells a story about his visit to the ruins of the Palestinian village Bir'im in the Galilee, which is also an ancient Israelite settlement. It is so old, Boyarin explains, that it is mentioned in the Talmud. This site is called Biram on Israeli maps. It is a place where tourists can visit the archaeological site of an ancient synagogue, which is surrounded by the ruins of the Palestinian village. But this place is now a park, and the Israeli Department for Landscaping Improvement and the Development of Historical Sites works to restore and maintain it. There are signs in the parking lot asking visitors to take care, to watch out for their own safety, and to avoid walking on freshly planted landscaped areas. A simple request like "Please don't step on the grass!" in this case also works to prevent visitors from looking too closely, or from disturbing the newly planted shrubs that cover the ruins of the Palestinian village as they walk along a path that leads directly to the ruins of the synagogue (Boyarin 1996:249–250). These are simple safety measures, commonsense requests: "Please don't damage the antiquities." "Please stay on the path for your own safety." But such simple requests are also a continuation of the work of soldiers perched atop a wall surrounding the Jewish community of Hebron that we visited in Chapter 4. In Bir'im/Biram "security" appears in a very different register, but it might be argued that these safety measures also protect the *Volk* (as discussed in the previous chapter). Such measures point to the fragility of the nation and the need to work continuously to protect its purity both through walls and separation barriers and by raising the ruins of some pasts while planting over others.

If the role of a highly securitized state is to protect the nation or *Volk* in this deeper sense, and if Agamben's (2005) understanding of the state of emergency is correct, then highly securitized states like Israel maintain these systems to provide physical security or everyday safety and in so doing also to maintain the nation and the integrity of the national group. Under what circumstances would the nation, as a people, no longer require such protection/production?

In the past Nusseibeh recommended two states, one Israeli and one Palestinian, side by side. Together with Ami Ayalon, an Israeli politician and former director of the Israeli security agency Shin Bet, he devised a peace proposal that was widely circulated among Israelis and Palestinians. Their goal was to demonstrate that peace could be achieved and that most people would agree to the terms. It was very effective, and indeed many people expressed agreement. The idea of two states for two people has become the most popular solution in international politics and diplomacy; by some accounts it continues to be the solution most Israelis and Palestinians favor. However, many analysts contend that it is too late for the two-state solution because of the growth of Israeli settlements beyond the Green Line. It now seems impossible to divide the land, and with it the population groups, into neatly separated national communities. In any case, there is currently no compromise on the table. And now, Sari Nusseibeh reverts to fundamental philosophical questions about life itself and what gives it meaning: "one of the most morally challenging dilemmas facing all of us, whoever we are, wherever we might be" (2011:49). He asks if the value of human life is intrinsic to it, or if its value is produced by something external to it. Does the value of life depend on "a meaning without which life would be worthless?" (p. 50). And does such meaning derive from larger sets of beliefs and allegiances, like religious beliefs or national affiliation? In other words, to paraphrase Benedict Anderson, Nusseibeh asks what sorts of meanings are worth fighting, suffering, and dying for. Is sovereignty in one's own nation-state such a value? Nusseibeh says that maybe Palestinians ought to forget about having a state of their own, at least for a while, and live in Israel instead.

That idea might not seem so outrageous, but Nusseibeh goes one step further, suggesting that Palestinians live in an Israeli state *without* full citizens' rights. He suggests that all of the territory that now makes up Israel, Israeli-occupied territory, the Palestinian Authority, and Gaza could become Israel. Palestinians would be granted many of the rights and privileges provided by the state. They would be able to live wherever they could find housing without geographical restrictions. Likewise, there would be no restrictions on where they could work. They would benefit from social welfare, health insurance, and state services like education and infrastructure. However, they would not have the right to vote.

Nusseibeh says that voting is what scares Israeli Jews and their leaders: they fear the possibility of being outnumbered demographically and outvoted in their own state. So, Nusseibeh suggests, at least temporarily, Palestinians would forego the right to vote. And in so doing he suggests they give up the coveted right to self-rule.

One possible path that, I believe, deserves serious consideration . . . is for Israel to offer Palestinians in the West Bank and Gaza full civil and human rights so long as a permanent settlement has not yet been reached. The result would be an interim step: a single-state but electorally non-democratic arrangement, that is, a mutually agreed-upon conferral by Israel of a form of "second-class citizenship" on all Palestinians currently under occupation who wish to accept it. For those Palestinians this result would be like . . . belonging to the state without being its co-owners . . . (2011:143–144)

If what Israeli Jews really fear is being voted out of power in their own state, losing sovereignty, we might wonder whether Palestinians giving up the right to vote, to full citizenship, might also be a way of protecting the Israeli nation. Might this be another form of protection for the Jewish nation that could take the place of separations, barriers, walls, fences, and armed soldiers at checkpoints? As we saw in the previous chapter, the security state ostensibly provides protection for the members of the nation, and yet at the same time it actually produces them *as* the nation. By keeping out potentially dangerous others, the securitized state produces the national group as those in need of protection. But what if, through the implementation of an idea like Nusseibeh's, the nation in the form of Israeli Jews was no longer threatened? They could not be removed or voted out of their own state by Palestinians because although Palestinians might live among them, they would not have the right to vote and therefore could not gain sovereignty and rule over the Jewish people. Would such a move lead to the end of the highly securitized state?

Might such a move also protect the Palestinian people from the chokehold of the securitized state that keeps them behind barriers and walls in the occupied West Bank? If Palestinians undertook such an arrangement, might this also be considered another form of collaborating with the enemy? Palestinians would work with Israeli Jews, trading full civil rights for the ability to move more freely that could allow them improved economic opportunities and a better quality of life. But this might make them collaborators like the Palestinians described by Cohen (see Chapter 5) who entered

into business relationships with their Jewish neighbors in the pre-
state years. Palestinians in Nusseibeh's scenario would be gaining
certain freedoms by trading away the Palestinian nation's collective rights to self-rule. They might gain as individuals, like those
who profited from the sale of land. But they might be considered
traitors to the national cause, collaborating with the enemies of
the Palestinian people in return for personal gain. Yet Nusseibeh's
idea would require collective action. If the majority of Palestinians
agreed to this arrangement, would it still be collaboration? Should
such an arrangement be considered coexistence, collaboration, or
defeat? Or maybe subversion, counter-conduct, or heterotopia?

Nusseibeh, a secular Palestinian intellectual who studied at
Harvard University, might almost be speaking in the voice of a religiously motivated Jewish settler. His suggestion of second-class
citizenship reminds me of what so many religiously motivated settlers say: We should treat Palestinians well. They are like foreigners
among us and we should treat them as guests. We should be gra-
cious and generous hosts, "but we should not give them our house,
not even our porch!" (Dalsheim 2011:117–130). It sounds like Nusseibeh may have accepted being a foreigner in his own land.

"The advantage of this scenario," Nusseibeh goes on to say, is that
it might be agreeable to "the two sides . . . at least as a transitional
stage" and "would maintain Jewish ownership of the state while
guaranteeing Palestinians their human rights and all services a state
normally provides for its citizens, including their collective cultural
rights" (2011:144). "Cultural rights" generally refer to a group's ability to preserve their language, teach it to their children, and have
it recognized legally, and it means having the right to pass on the
group's traditions and perhaps most importantly their interpretation of their collective past. For Palestinians in Israel this has often
meant having the opportunity to commemorate the *Nakbah*, the disaster that befell them following the 1948 war that displaced them
from the land and led to the establishment of the State of Israel.
Nusseibeh seems to be placing a higher value on language, religion,
tradition, and so forth than on sovereignty. He is suggesting that

cultural rights are more important than political rights, although he gives no reason to expect that the Israeli State would protect such rights.

In addition, Nusseibeh seems to be relying on a progressive notion of temporality that presumes, predicts, or hopes for improvement over time. There is a sense that within the world of real politics, a very limited set of options is available. The Occupation seems to be something temporary that will give way to something better as history unfolds in stages, but particular political options seem to be all that are available or possible "right now." When Nusseibeh suggests improving conditions for Palestinians in the interim he seems to respond to a more widespread sense of limitation among Palestinians and Israelis, a sense of restriction on what might be possible for now, a temporary-ness that requires stages of progress toward an anticipated better future. Nusseibeh's temporary arrangement seems to presume an eventual shift to full rights for Palestinians, to increasing liberation and an end of violence. Of course, as we saw in Chapter 4, Walter Benjamin warned against presuming that the present is nothing more than a passing stage of history moving ever forward toward a better future. And Nusseibeh's suggestion seems particularly troubling because the path forward from there is unclear. How will the second-class citizens achieve equal rights? Who will protect their freedoms? What would turn the ethno-national state of Israel into a place where minority rights are upheld? When Hannah Arendt (2003/1948) asked these questions of European democracies, she found the seeds of oppression embedded in the foundations of political arrangements that seemed to guarantee equality and freedom.

But what is perhaps most remarkable is that whether he intends to or not, Sari Nusseibeh is promoting an idea that, in many ways, is the mirror image of what the "crazy" Rabbi has suggested for Jews who currently reside in Israeli-occupied Palestinian territories, in Judea and Samaria. They could live in Palestine, the Rabbi said, as resident aliens. Like resident aliens in any country, Jews in Palestine would not have voting rights, nor would they serve in the military. They could live on the Land they covet, the land that makes them at one with God. This, for the Rabbi, is what makes life meaningful. Living on the Land is more important than ruling it. Living on the Holy Land is part of how Jews become one with the ruler of the universe. It is part of a greater unity that Jews seek in fulfilling their covenant with the Lord. Living on the Land according to the commandments (*mitzvoth*) is more important than being sovereign, because the idea that humans actually can have sovereignty is sheer hubris. Humility is called for. However, despite surface appearances there is an important difference between these two ideas. The Rabbi suggests Jews submit themselves to God and thereby fulfill an idea of justice, while Nusseibeh asks Palestinians to submit themselves to an injustice for the sake of increased comfort and peace.

THE VALUE OF POPULAR SOVEREIGNTY

What is it about the idea of having sovereignty in one's homeland that makes it an inviolable value? Philosophers and political scientists at least since Carl Schmitt (1985/1922) have written countless volumes on the various forms of political sovereignty, on what sovereignty means, and how it is to be evaluated.[2] But what is perhaps most important to note is that like the apparent naturalness of the nation, the contemporary belief that liberation is achieved through self-rule in the form of popular sovereignty has also become taken for granted as a truism. And yet, according to Yehouda Shenhav, for all the analysis, "sovereignty," which "may be the most important concept of modern political theory . . . has yet to undergo a process of systematic, theoretical critical deconstruction" (2012:149). To begin such a process of deep interrogation would mean to begin by thinking about the foundational ideas on which popular sovereignty rests.[3]

Sovereignty assumes agency—the possibility to act, to decide, to choose. It presumes the ability of human beings to rule their own lives. But both theology and social science point to the ambiguous nature of such self-rule.

CHOICE?

> See, this day I set before you a blessing and a curse: blessing, if you
> obey the commandments of the Lord your God that I enjoin upon
> you this day; and curse, if you do not obey . . .
>
> —Deuteronomy 11:26–28

> See, I set before you this day life and prosperity, death and adver-
> sity . . . I have put before you life and death, blessing and curse.
> Choose life—if you and your offspring would live . . .
>
> —Deuteronomy 30:15–19

> Men make their own history, but they do not make it as they please;
> they do not make it under self-selected circumstances, but under
> circumstances existing already, given and transmitted from the
> past. The tradition of all dead generations weighs like a nightmare
> on the brains of the living.
>
> —Karl Marx (1978/1852)

The presupposition of choice and agency is central to our secular age.[4] It
presumes the ability of human sovereignty, the ability of human beings
to rule ourselves. But the idea of agency is inherently ambiguous. The
foundational nature of the human ability to make choices and to rule
our own lives always includes opposing ideas, both in its religious and
its secular constellations. In religious sources, free will is given (and
also imposed) by God. Yet, at the very same moment that free will is
granted, it is also limited. One is endowed with the ability to choose and
to act but is both given a limited number of choices and commanded to
do God's will. To what extent are human beings free to act given that
they are subject to the will of God, to God's rewards and punishments?
Free will itself might be thought of as a divine imposition that *requires*
human beings to make choices and mistakes in order to become closer
to God. Without choice, the acts are meaningless, but without rewards
or punishments, the freedom would be meaningless. The intimate tension between freedom and constraint is mirrored in secular conceptu-
alizations in which human agency always exists within the limits and
possibilities of social structures and cultural constraints.

In its secular incarnations, for example, Karl Marx's most famous idea is that there are certain constraints upon our ability to "make history." Adam Smith's invisible hand describes a system of freedom and constraint in which the market is the aggregate result of individual choices being made, as rational actors balance their interests and desires through exchange. Weber's iron cage, Durkheim's social facts, Bourdieu's habitus: all engage in different ways with the social and historical constraints on human freedom, echoing the tension found in religious traditions.

The ambiguity of choice finds a solution in splitting its primary features—free will always coexists with restrictions on the exercise of that will—into two parts. The subjective experience of exercising unrestricted free will is maintained by projecting choice's restriction onto others, who are imagined as the originators of restrictions on free choice at the same time that they are positioned as the objects of restrictions that are being imposed upon them. The experience of ambivalence and the practice of imposing limits seem to uphold our own freedoms while projecting constraint onto those whom we imagine as beyond tolerance, because they are themselves intolerant. Such is the case for religious radicals whose behaviors are seen as irrational. These are the spoilers who must be kept in check so that rational peace processes may go forth. Because tolerance is not an organic part of their tradition, the liberal story goes, they can know it only as a political tactic, a way of infiltrating the cultural space of liberal peacemaking in order to undermine its principles.

Despite all this theorizing, people experience life—or interpret their experiences of life—as consisting of the freedom to choose freely and exercise agency. We attach meaning and intentionality to actions, socialize our children in this way, and hold each other accountable for our actions. Sometimes this notion is mitigated, as in courts of law when people are deemed unable to be responsible for their actions, or in cases of social neglect. But in our everyday lives we rarely imagine our mundane actions as constrained by social circumstances, the weight of history, or the will of God. So we separate out what we have learned about the constraints on our actions from our experience of our actions. And we take that experience one step further, contending that human sovereignty in the form of democratic political systems provides the best conditions in which to act freely.

One of liberalism's central presumptions is that human subjects exist prior to the social system, and that the subject has the capacity to freely make decisions based on rational calculating informed by some sense of self-interest. This is the idea behind Kant's notion of perpetual peace, which presumes that given a choice most people would rarely enter into war (see Chapter 1). But also consider John Rawls's idea of the original position in his theory of justice. Rawls (1971) postulates that if we were designing a social system, but we each were denied knowledge of the details of our identity within that system, we would set up just arrangements that protected the rights of everyone, because without further knowledge we might each potentially be in a weak position and therefore potentially vulnerable. This formulation presumes human actors who can and will act rationally[5] and according to their own best interests. Beyond that, it also supposes a subject preexisting the social system, rather than one produced through it, such that the availability of choice and agency becomes central. The very foundations of liberal jurisprudence depend on human responsibility, which is meaningless without this belief in the ability to act freely.[6] Such conditions are foundational to the possibility of popular sovereignty, self-rule in the nation-state, and to the belief that such a system provides the most fairness to individuals and the most freedom.[7] The idea of human agency, free choice, and free will (intention) are integral to democratic systems and to the belief that such systems contain the seeds of human liberation.

Some analysts, political scientists, and peacemakers say that popular sovereignty is currently the most viable answer to injustice, oppression, or seemingly intractable conflict because the world is organized into nation-states now.[8] It might not always be this way, but in the contemporary context people become free by gaining sovereignty in their homeland. Others, however, have been pointing to the erosion of state sovereignty and of citizenship as the locus of rights and privileges. Modern democracy or the idea of popular rule has, at least since the end of World War II, come to be considered one of the foundational conditions of political legitimacy (Sassen 1996:2). It is held up as an international norm, at least formally, in the documents that established the United Nations, and is written into the Universal Declaration of Human Rights. After all, democracy is the system that promises us the power of choice to influence decisions that affect our lives. Even if such choice is limited and constrained by specific social, historical, and political circumstances, who would volunteer to relinquish the possibility of determining one's own collective path, especially after having lived under the oppressive rule of invaders?

Moving away from rule by a dictator or a king endowed by God with the power to rule, or away from rule by a foreign power or colonizer to self-rule, is often considered the best means currently available to achieve liberation. And the belief in a natural order of nations means that the character and essence of the nation is best guaranteed and also best expressed through participation in the polity. As such, it is a value so fundamental that it seems counterintuitive to contemplate arriving at peace without such sovereignty. An arrangement such as the one Nusseibeh suggests seems to bypass justice, which many people count as being at least as important for, if not a requirement of, ending conflict.

And yet the idea of state sovereignty based on the "will of the people" has recently been challenged from a number of directions as a result of contemporary global forces.

> From an exclusive emphasis on the sovereignty of the people and right to self-determination, a shift to rights of individuals regardless of nationality has occurred. Human rights codes can . . . erode the legitimacy of the state if the state fails to respect such human rights . . . In accumulating social, civic, and even some political rights in countries of residence, immigrants have diluted the meaning of citizenship and the specialness of

the claims citizens can make on the state. When it comes to social services (education, health insurance, welfare, unemployment benefits) citizenship status is of minor importance in the United States and Western Europe. What matters is residence and legal alien status. (Sassen 1996:95)

The sovereignty of the state is challenged by global flows of people and capital. Immigrants and refugees challenge the authority of the nation-state, and international capital is far more powerful than individual citizens.

THE ENDS OF SOVEREIGNTY

The so-called crazy Rabbi introduced at the beginning of the book is willing to give up sovereignty. For him it isn't really about relinquishing authority or control over a particular geographical area, because we (humans) have never had such authority. The Rabbi knows there is only one true Sovereign in the universe and we should have faith in Him and realize that it is He who has the power to influence our lives in this land. It is His Land.

Sari Nusseibeh is willing to give up sovereignty. He is willing to forego, at least temporarily, the right of the Palestinian people to self-rule; the modern right of liberty enacted through one man, one vote; the right of citizens to be sovereign in their own state, a state that itself is understood to have a sovereignty of its own within the broader world of nation-states. Nusseibeh does not argue that such sovereignty of men over their own lives does not exist, as the Rabbi does or the Sheikh might (or as members of Hamas might). He does not write about the inherent limits of human sovereignty and the impossibility of agency. Neither does he say that the land is not his to keep or give away, as does the Sheikh. Sari Nusseibeh's arguments are entirely secular and pragmatic, and yet the similarity in the outcome of his ideas to the "crazy" Rabbi's is quite remarkable.

Popular sovereignty depends on socially and historically constructed ideas about collective identity ("the people" who govern themselves).[9] Collective identity may be based on a sense of shared culture or language, but it sometimes imagines some kind of natural or primordial relationship among people. In the case of nations, that relationship can be produced through devices like historical narratives and processes like industrialization and modernization, as well as through conflict and peacemaking. Popular sovereignty and collective national identity depend upon recognition in the international community. But in the case of Palestinians, such recognition may amount to nothing more than cunning recognition: it comes at a moment when the Palestinian West Bank is so divided by Jewish settlements that it looks more like an archipelago than a contiguous state[10]—and that's to say nothing of the distance between the West Bank and Gaza. In addition, even if Palestinians were granted a state in some part of the territory, it seems clear that Israel would agree only if such a state were demilitarized. If this happened, Palestine would be little more than an autonomous bureaucracy serving as occupied territory under another guise. And of course, ultimately, popular sovereignty, collective identity, and recognition all presuppose the possibility of human agency, itself a very uncertain proposition. Taking all of this into consideration, we might conclude that popular sovereignty is itself a fiction or an impossibility. But, as we have seen, our theoretical knowledge is not necessarily implemented in our everyday lives; in fact, Zvi Bekerman recommended abandoning theory for practical action. Accepting the solidity and naturalness of nations seem practical and satisfying, but problems can arise when we adopt the fiction and in so doing undermine our goals for peace, social justice, or human liberation.

Chapter 7

Room at the Campfire

In the Far West . . . they tell stories about hoop snakes. When a hoop snake wants to get somewhere—whether because the hoop snake is after something, or because something is after the hoop snake—it takes its tail . . . into its mouth, thus forming itself into a hoop, and rolls . . . But for the hoop snake with rattles, there is a drawback. They are venomous snakes and when they bite their own tail they die, in awful agony, of a snakebite . . . . I don't know what the moral is . . .

—Ursula Le Guin (1980)

The last chapter opened with a set of questions about which stories to tell, how to enumerate and account for the stories, and how to be accountable for them. But how should we account for the outrage that meets the telling of these stories?

Jonathan Boyarin (1996) tells a story about telling a story about an Israeli and a Palestinian in Jerusalem. His story produced moral outrage among scholars who heard him tell it. The story he told was about a Palestinian plumber working in a Jewish man's house. The plumber knows the current resident well, and teases the

Jewish homeowner by suggesting that the house once belonged to the Palestinian man's grandfather. He realizes that the Jewish man would be horrified at the idea that he was living in a home that ought to belong to the plumber. The Jewish man gasps, and then the Palestinian laughs, "I got you! I got you that time!" (Boyarin 1996:199). This kind of teasing, Boyarin suggests, is indicative of a level of shared assumptions and even intimacy. But upon hearing this fieldwork story, Boyarin reports, some scholars were outraged. The story seemed to suggest symmetry between the Palestinian and the Jew, which Boyarin writes was certainly not what he intended.[1]

People who are outraged by Sari Nusseibeh's idea of Palestinians settling for second-class citizenship without the right to vote might be the very same people who would tell you in other contexts that voting is meaningless anyway. We vote all the time for politicians who promise us one thing but do something else once they're in office. Who can trust them? Consider the case of Israelis electing Ariel Sharon over Amram Mitzna in 2004 because Mitzna was in favor of a disengagement plan that would remove Israeli settlers from the Gaza Strip and Sharon was opposed. Then Sharon was elected and implemented the disengagement plan himself.

Palestinian citizens of Israel have the right to vote in Israeli elections, and yet many of them have become disheartened. The Arabs of Israel make up about 20% of the population and they suffer disproportionately from poverty, unemployment, and other social ills. The government does not invest in their villages and towns to provide the kind of support they need. Many of them say that the ability to vote has not led to improvements in their lives. There has yet to be an Israeli government that includes Arab parties in its coalition. So, in 2013, many Palestinian citizens of Israel called on members of their community to boycott the Israeli elections because by participating in elections the Arab population provides a fig leaf for Israeli democracy, which is a democracy only for its Jewish citizens.[2]

In the Palestinian territories these days many people are disillusioned if not furious that their own elected leaders have become corrupt. Some claim that Palestinian politicians benefit personally from their positions but actually work for the Israeli occupation forces. Local politicians may be bribed by wealthy businessmen and, in the global economy more broadly, international corporations hold the power to influence all sorts of policies. They influence elections and decision making far more than any voters anywhere. Ultimately, some people conclude that the contemporary state exists to maintain a labor force and to keep a certain proportion of people out of the labor force through incarceration or repression or the careful management of monetary policy (see Fraser 1998). If states ever were actually the guardians of their own populations, charged with creating the conditions in which the population could live their version of the good life, now this is no longer the case. States seem to labor primarily on behalf of capital, eroding the possibility of democratic rule in the contemporary context of global capital, in which state power is changing, and states seem to be "losing control" (Sassen 1996).

This is one of the reasons some scholar/activists have begun promoting the ideas of anarchy (Bamyeh 2009; Graeber 2002, 2004; Scott 2009, 2012) and looking at the innovative methods some new social movements promote to help people take back control of their lives (Moghadam 2013; Smith 2008). But if the cry of "*libertè, egalitè, fraternitè*" has become the label for a myth, it is precisely the myth we recommend for Palestinians when we continue to press for a sovereign, separate Palestinian state. Nusseibeh does not make his argument in terms of global capital. He remains focused on the local context in which "the Jews could run the country while the Arabs could at last enjoy living in it" (2011:146). Perhaps even more profoundly, this suggestion might be thought of as a fundamental form of Palestinian resistance (*sumud*). Nusseibeh seeks legal residency for Palestinians in all of the greater territory of Israel/Palestine. Remaining in their country with the ability to live and work anywhere might be considered a form of resistance to being removed from their land, or resistance to what Patrick Wolfe (2006) calls the "logic of elimination" that is a central feature of settler-colonial social formations.

But there is something unsettling about Nusseibeh's thought experiment, whether or not one thinks that the right to vote is the path to freedom. The scenario Nusseibeh imagines leaves out so much of the story that it's not really a story at all. A narrative requires a beginning, middle, and end. It needs heroes and villains and, following Hayden White, should lead us to a particular moralizing conclusion. Nusseibeh writes that Palestinians will be granted the right of return, but this extraordinary change appears as a *deus ex machina*. He says that they will be free to speak their own language, commemorate their past, and cultivate their own traditions and culture. But, if Palestinian citizens in Israel today do not experience such freedoms, why should we expect this to change?[3] Nusseibeh is concerned with what matters most in life, and with the suffering and violence surrounding the Palestinian struggle for statehood. He asks that we consider other alternatives. But his thought experiment does not fulfill the requirements of the narrative, and we are left wondering what the moral of his story might be. Recall the words of Ursula Le Guin from Chapter 1.

> "A beginning is that which is not itself necessarily after anything else, and which has naturally something else after it; an end, that which is naturally after something else, either as its necessary or usual consequent, and with nothing else after it; and a middle, that which is by nature after one thing and has also another after it." (Aristotle)
>
> But sequence grows difficult in the ignorance of what comes after the necessary or at least the usual consequent of living, that is, dying,
>
> and also when the soul is confused by not unreasonable doubts of what comes after the next thing that happens, whatever that might be. (Le Guin 1980:192–193)

In Nusseibeh's unfinished tale there is no obvious end, no climax, no triumph, no national liberation, no justice, no conclusion; and if there's no conclusion, then we have not moved, with White (1980), into a new moral era. Instead we have had the foundations of our own moral era unsettled, clouding our vision and obstructing the path forward. Instead of justice and liberation, we are given a further impairment that seems impossible to mend, impossible to continue to resolution. By undoing the full rights of citizens, Nusseibeh becomes a spoiler who expresses primary allegiance not to the nation, but to another cause, in his case the larger cause of ending human suffering.[4] As in the case of the radical religionists, his model undermines the contemporary moral order, and so there is no room for Nusseibeh at the campfire.

ANOTHER ISRAEL

Scholars sometimes imagine possible futures for Israel/Palestine by revisiting the past. In Chapter 3, for example, we saw how a revised vision of the relationship between Arabs and Jews prior to the establishment of the state of Israel could provide an alternative model for living together, an alternative narrative, and an alternative moral imperative. Some scholars suggest looking back to the Ottoman Empire as a model for how minorities could be protected and live together peacefully (Campos 2010), while others suggest that Arabs and Jews use models of living in diaspora to rework their relationships and live as minorities among minorities, rather than one ruling over the other (Boyarin and Boyarin 1993; Rabinowitz 2000), because there already is an "Israeli/Palestinian interculture" (Boyarin 1996:197). Perhaps Nusseibeh is drawing on his personal reflections of how Jews and Arabs lived together in earlier times. He writes about his childhood in Jerusalem in the 1950s and about earlier thoughts on the importance of having equal rights in Israel. Nusseibeh explains that before he advocated a two-state solution, it had seemed clear to him that Arabs and

Jews could live together and that what Palestinians needed was equal rights within a single state.

When reconsidering the possibility of coexistence, maybe Nusseibeh is thinking about all the ways that Israelis and Palestinians already live together and work together. Maybe he imagines the hospital in Be'ersheva or Hadera where Palestinian doctors work alongside Jewish Israeli doctors, together taking care of patients of all sorts of ethnic, racial, and religious backgrounds (cf. Borayin's story of shared assumptions and intimacy [1996:199]). Although these Palestinians may also experience all sorts of discrimination and indignities, nonetheless, like Palestinian members of the Israeli parliament, they work in some of the most prestigious positions.

The model Nusseibeh is suggesting is not something entirely new or unknown in the region, he says. There are already existing situations in which "people voluntarily partake of civil but not political rights" (Nusseibeh 2011:148), including "Palestinian Israelis who support the Islamic movement" and who "on principle" do not participate in the political system (ibid.). He also briefly mentions Arab Jerusalemites, whose status is unusual and complicated.[5] Indeed, there are Jewish Israelis who do not participate in the political system because their religious beliefs prevent their recognition of the legitimacy of the state. Some Orthodox Jews believe that only God can decide when the Jewish people can have sovereignty in the Land of Israel (Rabkin 2006). It is dependent upon the coming of the Messiah, and it was wrong for the political Zionist movement to establish the State of Israel. They do not support the state, vote in elections, participate in the military, or respect national holidays. They live in the space of Israel and benefit from its services and protection but do not recognize the modern state or participate actively in its political system, just like the Palestinians Nusseibeh mentions who support the international Islamic movement. These two sets of people also seem to enact heterotopias within the space of Israel/Palestine.

Or maybe Sari Nusseibeh thinks about a supermarket chain named for its proprietor, Rami Levi. Rami Levi, a relatively new supermarket chain in Israel, boasts the lowest prices in the country. There are Rami Levi supermarkets almost everywhere you go, but one of the most interesting ones is situated in the Gush Etzion settlement bloc, outside Jerusalem in the West Bank. There's nothing remarkable about shopping, of course, but here at Rami Levi one can find religious Jewish settler women working the cash registers and Palestinian Arab men packing the grocery bags. One can see Jewish settler families and Palestinian Arab families wandering through the aisles and making purchases. The supermarket has not been uncontroversial. When it opened in 2010 some rabbis spoke out against the mixed population because they worried that Jewish women might be attracted to Arab men, which might result in mixed marriages.[6] Others feared the mixed population would make the supermarket dangerous and wanted Palestinians to be barred from working or shopping there. But Rami Levi did not cave to these pressures, and the supermarket continues to employ and serve the population of the region.

Of course, Rami Levi, or market forces more generally, do not produce a beautifully idyllic model of equality and coexistence.[7] Mohammed, a Palestinian I met while visiting the West Bank in 2012, lives not far from the supermarket. He clicked his tongue and said, "That's not coexistence! People are just shopping. They don't talk to each other."

Peace, coexistence, justice, and sovereignty are all complicated terms, all holding multiple meanings and promising multiple possibilities. There are organized efforts by high-level diplomats to negotiate, and organized efforts by grassroots-level activists to dialogue, but at the same time life goes on and people live separately, together, working for each other, employed by each other, purchasing from each other, sharing the roads or running each other off them when they are not locked behind walls and fences (Harel 2011).

PEOPLE/TERRITORY/SOVEREIGNTY: THE QUESTION OF TERRITORY

The intense political divisions that mark the space of Israel/ Palestine form people's identities in relation to one another, giving meaning to their lives as they act according to the beliefs that make them who they are, good people who do the right thing, living moral lives that are different from those who behave otherwise. And while we have seen a number of examples that cross these divides, the divisions are often so intense that they seem nearly impossible to bridge. Sometimes the divisions that mark both people and territory are so deeply ingrained that people might not realize the ironies they provoke.

Left-wing Israeli Jews are generally expected to be secular.[8] They are typically sympathetic to the plight of Palestinians and hostile toward Jewish settlers in the Occupied Territories, especially religiously motivated settlers who seem irrational in their beliefs and dangerous in their practices. The expectations these groups have for each other may predetermine their opinions and result in knee-jerk reactions. This was the case one sunny afternoon in 2011 at the University of Tel Aviv.

A demonstration was being held. There was a controversial speaker giving a lecture that had drawn a large crowd, and just outside the lecture hall a group of protesters was holding signs and handing out pamphlets. They claimed that the University had been built on the ruins of the Palestinian village of Kfar Munis; in fact, the faculty club was housed in the home of the village sheikh. The University had benefitted from the destruction of homes and from the displacement of Palestinians. The University, the protestors exclaimed, was a settlement, just like the settlements in the West Bank.

This seems like just the sort of demonstration that left-wing students would organize. They are forever concerned about injustice and especially interested in the Palestinian cause. Left-wing students demonstrate regularly against the Occupation and against

expanding settlements. They are concerned about the rights of Palestinians and the plight of refugees. They cry out at social, economic,
and political injustices of all sorts.

But this time, the left-wing students did not join the demonstration. Was it because they doubted the claim that the University had
been built on the ruins of Kfar Munis? No; in fact, this was no secret.
But instead of joining the demonstration or calling on the University to make amends for past injustices, the left-wing students organized a counter-demonstration. This might seem counter-intuitive.
Were they not interested in calling attention to the displacement of
Palestinians? Were they not concerned about pointing to the injustice of those who benefit from the suffering of others? What would
cause a group of left-wing student activists to demonstrate *against*
their own cause?

As it turned out, the demonstrators handing out flyers about
the University built on the ruins of Kfar Munis were not anarchists
or anti-Zionists. They were not left-wing radicals or communists.
They were distinguished from most of the students on campus by
their external appearance: young men dressed in long-sleeved,
button-down shirts, their heads covered in either black or cro-
cheted *kippahs*. They were a group of right-wing religious settlers.
The students, always suspicious of the settlers, could not imagine
sharing a political agenda. They found themselves unable to highlight the cause of justice for Palestinians if it meant standing together with religious settlers from the Occupied Territories, whose
project they denounce despite, or perhaps because of, its uncanny
resemblance to the dislocation that took place underneath their
own feet.

Many of the left-wing students failed to see any irony in all of this
because they disagree about the conclusions that ought to be drawn.
The right-wing demonstrators were pointing out the similarity between the University of Tel Aviv and settlements in the West Bank
in order to say, if you think the settlements in the Occupied Territories should be removed, then it follows logically that the University,
and maybe all of Tel Aviv, should be dismantled. Indeed, they were

pointing out the settler nature of the entire Zionist project and re-minding everyone that Israel might be considered in its entirety a set-tler state. Surely the students did not think their university or their entire country should be dismantled. Some of them, although they decried the injustice of displacing Palestinians and destroying their homes, drew a clear distinction between the violence that took place prior to the establishment of the State of Israel and the ongoing vio-lence associated with settlement across the Green Line. They might argue that while such acts might have been necessary in the early years to establish a state, such action was no longer justified. The State of Israel inside its pre-1967 borders was recognized in the interna-tional community. It had a right to exist but did not need to continue to expand at the expense of the Palestinians, making the possibility of an independent Palestinian state increasingly difficult to imagine. The growth of settlements and the unequal distribution of water and land are made possible by a military occupation that deprives Pales-tinians of rights and resources so that settlers can roam freely.

And yet, some of the Palestinians who live in these areas have been reaching out to some of those settlers, and some of those set-tlers have been reaching out to Palestinians. Eretz Shalom, or Land of Peace, is a new social movement that celebrated its official inau-guration with a public event in Tel Aviv about two years ago. Eretz Shalom describes itself as

> a social movement that works toward the advancement of peace and dialogue between the Jewish and Arab inhabitants of Judea and Samaria, the occupied West Bank. The movement is mostly made up of sons of Abraham, Jews and Arabs who are interested in living in their homeland in mutual respect and co-operation with their neighbors.[9]

This organization is unusual because Jewish settlers and Palestin-ians are supposed to hate and fear each other. More conventional peace organizations tend to be composed of left-wing and secular Jewish Israelis who often agree with Palestinian characterizations of settlers. Some of these organizations, action groups, or social and cultural initiatives are joint Israeli-Palestinian organizations, but they do not include Jewish settlers.

Eretz Shalom, on the other hand, was initiated by religiously motivated Jewish settlers who live in the West Bank. They believe in the right and responsibility of the Jews to live on all the Land of Israel. This makes them appear suspicious to left-wing Israelis and disingenuous to many Palestinians. It also makes them unpopular among many other settlers, who sometimes throw stones at them or taunt their children or vandalize their homes. The Palestinians of Eretz Shalom take even greater risks to be involved. They may be called traitors and could be arrested and even killed for this activity. Yet, they make joint visits to the bereaved families of victims of the conflict. They meet clandestinely in each other's homes, just to share a cup of coffee and get to know each other. They demonstrate against violence, and the settlers in this group will travel to Palestinian towns where other settlers have burned a mosque or uprooted trees. They show up at bereaved settlers' homes and speak out against the violent acts of Palestinians as if to say, "we are not all like that."

At the Tel Aviv University demonstration, one student recognized the irony of these two counter-demonstrations and crossed the line to join the settlers.[10] This student belonged to a new organization called Eretz Yoshveha ("Land of its Inhabitants"). This is another new group still trying to work out its principles and still in the process of launching itself. Its name indicates that it wants to encompass or stand for all the people of Israel/Palestine, not just citizens or people identified as belonging to one national group or another. But the name also recalls a line from the Bible, *eretz ochel yoshveha*, a land that devours its inhabitants, which perhaps is a way of suggesting the seriousness and urgency of finding another way.

Like Eretz Shalom, this group attempts to contest and invert social, political, and religious relations that have been mapped onto the Land. They do this by crossing Israel's pre-1967 border, the Green Line, which for many has come to be the dividing line between legitimate and illegitimate Israeli communities, between moral and immoral settlements and ways of life. This group begins by suggesting that such divisions are a fallacy. If Eretz Shalom tries to bridge the hateful divide between Jewish settlers and Palestinians, Eretz Yoshveha tries to bridge another deep divide—that between left-wing Israeli Jews and religious settlers in the Occupied Territories. I recently published a book (Dalsheim 2011) that details the complexities that are often either ignored or conflated when we think of the Left and Right in Israel, the secular and religious, and those opposed to occupation versus those in favor of expanding the state of Israel. Eretz Yoshveha denies these stark oppositions, partly because of the complex position of Mizrahim living in the occupied territories, who may be characterized as religious settlers, but also as victims of the Zionist project (Dalsheim 2008).

Some of the Jewish Israelis who live in the Occupied Territories are Jews of Middle Eastern and North African descent, as we saw in Chapter 4. While these Mizrahim tend to practice a traditional form of Judaism, they are rarely ideologically committed to settlement. In many cases, they live in settlements because the housing is less expensive and settlements provide an opportunity to move out of neighborhoods with high unemployment and crime. Left-wing Israelis are sympathetic to the plight of the Mizrahim, who have been discriminated against in Israel (Khazzoom 2005). So if harboring disdain for settlers means animosity even toward the Mizrahi Jews who were able to provide better homes and lives for themselves and their families by moving to the Occupied Territories, some members of Eretz Yoshveha find this problematic. They support programs to improve the lives of Mizrahim, who like Palestinians have suffered from state policies.

The prominent French intellectual Jacques Derrida was both an Arab and a Jew. Recognizing both his Jewishness and his Algerian roots, he found within himself the contradictions of enemy entities, even existential enemies (Anidjar 2003). How can one person be both an Arab and a Jew? How can one person contain enemies within his own identity?

This was the question raised by Ella Shohat (1988) when she wrote about the terrible predicament of Jews of Middle Eastern and North African origin. Arab Jews in Israel—the Mizrahim—had to deny the Arabness of their identities and be Israeli. Their very existence as Arab Jews was a political impossibility: one had to either be on the side of Israelis (Jewish) or be among the enemies of the Jewish state.

This complicated ambiguity of Arab Jewishness (Shenhav 2003) is not only a question of identity. It is also a matter of economics and politics. Just for a moment, I will leave this complexity and speak in terms of ideal types to highlight what seems extraordinary about the members of Eretz Yoshveha. Whereas religiously motivated settlers often speak of the space of Israel/Palestine as a sacred place imbued with ancient history, where Jews are destined to fulfill the promise God made to them, the secular members of this group tend to emphasize the worldly nature of Israel/Palestine. That secular understanding has led many on the Left to recommend dividing the land, trading land for peace, and establishing separate states of Israel and Palestine. They consider religious settlers as ideologically motivated fanatics, expansionists, and land thieves who are the cause of violent clashes and have become the greatest obstacle to peace with Palestinians. And yet the founding members of Eretz Yoshveha, who are secular Israeli Jews, have declared that there is a problem with the idea of dividing the land. It is not because they think the land is sacred, but because they are convinced that the injustices of settlement did not begin in 1967, but rather in 1948; not when Israel gained control over the West Bank, Gaza, and other areas, but with the establishment of the State of Israel itself, which Israelis celebrate as their national independence and Palestinians mourn as their national disaster.[11] In other words, they agree with those demonstrators who came to the University of Tel Aviv to say that it was built on the ruins of a Palestinian village.

Israel must recognize the injustice of the *Nakbah*, Eretz Yoshveha says. They also say that Israel must allow for the return of Palestinian refugees, an idea the right-wing religious demonstrators would strongly oppose. Many Israelis think that granting the right of return to Palestinian refugees would mean the end of the Jewish state, the end of a Jewish majority. But members of Eretz Yoshveha say that Jews must ask the Palestinians for permission to be in Israel/Palestine, and not the other way around.[12] These positions make this group illegitimate in the eyes of many Israeli nationalists who believe their set of principles undermines the right of Israel to exist. But if Eretz Yoshveha seems, at first, to be nothing more than an extension of Palestinian national positions, it is not. In addition to advocating the right of Palestinian return, Eretz Yoshveha also denounces removing settlers from their homes and dismantling settlements in the post-1967 Occupied Territories. They claim that Jewish communities inside the Green Line are also settlements and that they have caused more displacement and injustices than settlements in Judea and Samaria—which, for the most part, were built overlooking, adjacent to, between, and around, but not *on*, the ruins of Palestinian towns.

So, Eretz Yoshveha is unusual for bringing together the left wing of Israel with post-1967 settlers who are considered the right wing of politics. But Eretz Yoshveha is also considered marginal and even esoteric by many in the more mainstream peace organizations. Some think the left-wing motivation is nothing but a ploy to establish a single state for all its citizens that would be the end of the Jewish state. Others think the settlers who are involved also want a single state in all the territory, but they expect it to be a Jewish state with a Palestinian second-class minority, reminiscent of some elements of Sari Nusseibeh's thought experiment. The founding members of the organization disagree with these evaluations and say they are considering many possible models of political organization, but first and foremost they want an end to all forms of injustice including displacement, which they contend cannot be accomplished by starting with the 1967 borders. This group crosses sociopolitical borders and geographical borders of morality, but they hold on to collective identity and do not deconstruct categories of religious or national difference. Nor do they recommend dividing up the territory between these groups; instead, like the "crazy" Rabbi and Sari Nusseibeh, they seek more creative forms of sovereignty.

DERRIDA AGAIN

Given this scenario, thinking with Derrida might cause us to reconsider which elements of identity, belonging, and sovereignty to deconstruct. Rather than focus on national, ethnic, or religious identity, we might consider the political divisions between left and right, secular and religious, and the idea that settlers are only those living beyond the Green Line. Or, we might think about the concept of sovereignty in some of the same ways Derrida has thought about the concept of hospitality.

Derrida wrote that there can never be true hospitality. The guest is necessarily a transgressor, and the position of host, which requires mastery of the house, ultimately undermines the possibility of hospitality (Derrida 2000). His essay "Step of Hospitality/ No Hospitality," begins with the act of an invited guest crossing the threshold. "What does it mean," Derrida asks, "if, for the invited guest as much as for the visitor, the crossing of the threshold always remains a transgressive step?" (Derrida 2000:75). He suggests:

> [It] is as though hospitality were the impossible: as though the law of hospitality defined this very impossibility, as if it were only possible to transgress it, as though the law of absolute, unconditional . . . hospitality . . . the categorical imperative of hospitality commanded that we transgress all the laws of hospitality, namely, the conditions, the norms, the rights and the duties that are imposed on hosts and hostesses, on the men or women who give a welcome as well as the men or women who receive it. (p. 77)

And this is the case because "unlimited hospitality" or an unconditional sort of welcome would mean being prepared to give a guest all of one's home and all of one's self without expecting anything in return. That would be true hospitality, but that, Derrida says, is impossible because the conditions of hospitality are also the conditions of its impossibility. That is, while none of us actually expects to give a guest everything we have, Derrida insists that the whole idea of hospitality depends on such altruism. This becomes increasingly complicated when we realize that a host is also the master of his house (Derrida 2000:5), because to offer hospitality, one must first have the power to host. But, at the same time, to offer hospitality means to give up something of the mastery of the house, to open it to the guest, relinquishing the mastery that makes the act of offering possible to begin with. ("We should treat them well . . . but not give them our house, not even our porch!")

This reflection on hospitality is about much more than accepting guests into one's home. The house might be a country and the guest a foreigner. Derrida uses this metaphor or microcosm to reflect on much broader political issues. The question of hospitality or its impossibility, then, speaks to questions of immigrants, or minority populations, or any people considered "foreigners" or guests, like guest workers, for example. Consider border fences and checkpoints or even gated communities in terms of Derrida's invocation of the idea of trespass. "The foreigner," Derrida writes, "had to begin by contesting the authority of the chief, the father, the master of the house" (2000:5), revealing the power relations inherent in the very notion of hospitality.

The host, in fact, is the sovereign.[13] In Nusseibeh's account, that host allows the "guest" to stay but does not share sovereignty with him. Perhaps this is more realistic than some of the romantic idealizations of hospitality associated with the Middle East. It might be more realistic than idealized notions of popular sovereignty more generally. In these cases deconstruction is not applied to collective identity, to tradition or culture. Instead, it is applied to the notion of popular sovereignty as the means to justice, liberation, and peace. Here, thinking with Derrida (and with Hannah Arendt) we might further suggest that there is no popular sovereignty because rule is never truly shared among all citizens.[14] There are majority and minority groups, more and less powerful people and all sorts of social and economic interests that interfere. If there is no truly shared popular sovereignty, then rethinking sovereignty is at least as reasonable as rethinking identity, and at least as difficult.

ANOTHER STORY?

> I could think of another Abraham for myself . . . *Perhaps*, perhaps then, there would be more than one Abraham . . . *Perhaps*.
> —Derrida (2008:311, quoting Kafka, referring to Kirkegaard)

How can we account for all the stories and be accountable for them? What would it mean to be responsible for the stories recounted in this book and for the countless tales yet untold? One way to be accountable would simply be to pay attention to them—to have the courage to look past the blinding, comforting light of the campfire—and recognize their importance.

Derrida, recalling Kafka's parable, asks us to consider the possibility of another story of the biblical patriarch Abraham. He says, quoting Kafka, that he could "think for himself another Abraham." But rather than focus on the imperfections and daily challenges of ordinary men, Derrida is interested in something else. When he "thinks for himself another Abraham," he thinks of one called Ibrahim. In so doing, he works his tools of deconstruction on the collective identities of those directly involved in the daily struggles of Israel/Palestine. His work moves beyond Arabs and Jews, locating both within a single subject, the figure of Abraham. Such a move should deconstruct enemy categories, or in the very least reveal their constructedness. But as we have seen, Israelis and Palestinians are not interested for the most part in deconstructing their national identities.

If we ask, with Derrida, which stories to tell, how to account for them and how to be accountable for them, we might also ask why he tells this story of deconstruction rather than so many other stories that might be told. And we might ask why this book is telling the stories of spoilers. Derrida's question is a deeply ethical one. If we concede, with Hayden White, that narrativizing is necessarily moralizing, we recall the urgency of these questions. If we tell the hegemonic Israeli story, a tale of two peoples fighting for sovereignty over the same troubled, tiny swath of land, our moralizing conclusion may be that the only possible solution is to continue to fight for that land. Or we might conclude that the only solution is to divide that land between the parties. If we tell a tale of a people whose land has been conquered by foreigners who dominate the land, our moralizing conclusion may be that those conquerors must be defeated and removed from the land so that justice can prevail. This is the story most Palestinians tell. If we tell Derrida's tale, then the conquered and conquerors are the same people, whose suffering might be traced to a different source. That source is Europe in the bridging narrative that scholars like Mohammed Bamyeh have offered. This story suggests that the conflict in Palestine is the outcome of the removal of Jews from Europe, in which their tragedy resulted in a new one for the Palestinians. Zionism, Palestinian nationalism, and the *Nakbah* are all part of a single history that includes European anti-Semitism, European nationalism, European colonialism, and the Nazi genocide.

The first two stories are nationalist in nature. Each presumes the right of "a people" to sovereignty in their homeland, for their right to have the impossible power of the host. The third one questions the existence of "the people" in the first place by deconstructing national identity. But the stories in this book suggest that those directly involved in the conflict in Israel/Palestine are deeply committed to their collective identities. In the case of Sari Nusseibeh, some of them are willing to think about sacrificing sovereignty to maintain that identity. Identity, then, trumps sovereignty. Such an idea seems nearly incomprehensible when told around the blinding flames of the campfire of liberal peace, in the global order of nation-states, in the secular age that defines them both. But if we are to account for the stories and be accountable for them, then we should also look beyond the campfire. There we find the stories of "spoilers," those whose tales undermine some unspoken norm or taken-for-granted assumption about peace, peacemaking, and order in the world. There we find stories that point to different moral orders where popular sovereignty takes a back seat to other pressing concerns. There we find people who want to live on the land that is their land, speak their language, practice their traditions, and uphold the promises of their faiths. We might find these stories unsettling because they challenge the episteme that gives rise to our normative moral and political order.

They unsettle the triumvirate of people/territory/sovereignty on which liberal peace depends. And they unsettle because they point to alternative sovereignties that have yet to be worked out. These are stories of spoilers who spoil liberal peace not necessarily through acts of violence that disrupt rational negotiation processes but by undermining its conceptual foundations. They point to something else and "think themselves beyond the nation," in Appadurai's terms. But they do so without surrendering their collective identity. Nusseibeh gives up citizens' rights and suggests living as resident aliens (or resident natives? or guests?) in an Israeli state. The Rabbi also suggests giving up full citizens' rights because staying on the Holy Land is more important than ruling it. But contemporary peacemaking depends on democratic citizenship and not other sorts of subjects.

To be accountable, then, would mean to take seriously rather than marginalizing and delegitimizing those stories that disrupt the categories through which we generally understand our world. If we pay attention, we begin to notice that there is a pattern emerging in all these stories. They all tell of ordinary people who are thinking and acting in different ways beyond categories of enmity and conflict in Israel/Palestine. They point to sets of actions that suggest something other than two states, two nations divided by a border. And yet they don't quite point to a one-state solution in the sense that we might expect. This is neither two states for two peoples nor one democratic secular state for all its citizens. It includes a range of activities and possibilities that might point to different sets of arrangements to accommodate different sets of needs. And yet those needs seem to result in some remarkably similar ideas and actions. People want to live in peace. They want to work and support their families. They want to be able to move around and to live in their homeland.

What is most remarkable, I think, is the similarity—the mirror imaging—between the ideas expressed by the "crazy" Rabbi and those expressed by the "crazy" Palestinian intellectual. And now, as this book goes to press, these sorts of "crazy" ideas seem to be moving into more conventional circles. Most recently, we've heard the issue of settlers remaining in the territory that would become a Palestinian state discussed in the news. Israeli Prime Minister Benjamin Netanyahu suggested such a possibility. Not surprisingly, his statement has been denounced by a right-wing Israeli politician, by the Palestinian president, and has been labeled as nothing more than a political ploy: a provocation rather than a solution, a notion so wild it must have been designed to fail. And yet, a long-time peace activist, Gershon Baskin, has taken up the question in a recent op-ed in the *Jerusalem Post*.[15] These ideas, taken together with some of the everyday practices recalled in this and the previous two chapters, demonstrate how people on the ground sometimes think and act not so much "beyond the nation" but beyond the nation-state. Scholars, having analyzed and criticized the nation-state for its inherent exclusionary nature and its violence, have tried to move beyond it by deconstructing national identity as an "imagined community." But people on the ground in Israel/Palestine hold on to their collective identities, their languages, their religions, and the traditions that bring so much meaning to their lives in a broad range of ways, only some of which have been explored in this book. They also hold on to their relationship to the land, the landscape, their homes, and their homeland, whether or not scholars can prove such connections to be imagined or socially and historically produced. What the Israelis and Palestinians in these stories seem to be moving beyond are the boundaries of contemporary models of sovereignty. Some act in everyday ways that define those boundaries, while others are struggling for creative ways to defy them. Each story, taken on its own, seems strange, defiant, or crazy. Each story breaks some taken-for-granted norm or falls beyond what is generally acceptable. But if we connect the dots between them, we might find a pattern that reveals subtle changes in everyday practices that point toward other ways of living together, beyond the seemingly intractable conflict that characterizes Israel/Palestine today. That's what lies beyond the campfire.

NOTES

Chapter 1

1. This term is sometimes transliterated as *bobe-mayse*, and its original meaning was quite different and has nothing to do with grandmothers. For more on this term see Weinreich (1980:273, 616).
2. In her book about the Mzeini Bedouin in the Sinai, Smadar Lavie wrote about a "madwoman" who similarly marks the boundaries of a moral order. In that case the madwoman was able to cross boundaries between men and women and defy acceptable gender roles. Her madness could also be read as a kind of freedom—through exception—from gendered constraints (Lavie 1990, Chapter 4).
3. Talal Asad (2011) suggests that a separation takes place between the ethos of democracy and its practice in the political formation of nation-states. That political formation, which depends on a limited demos in the form of the nation, may contain a set of contradictions that necessarily makes democracy itself a fiction. This is a question I take up in greater detail later. See Chapter 7 for a discussion of popular sovereignty.
4. See Wendy Brown (2006) for a critique of "liberal tolerance."
5. While not speaking specifically to the work of peacemakers, in his 1996 book, Jonathan Boyarin details some of the everyday work involved in reinscribing enemy groups in Israel/Palestine as well as how the seemingly mutually exclusive identities "Israelis" and "Palestinians" are regularly thrown into question (Boyarin 1996:200).

6. This is a fluid collective without clear or consistent boundaries. It is a collective that might be described as Western, modern, liberal humanist, peace-seeking, or liberationist, keeping in mind that all of these terms have multiple definitions and that all could and should be thought of as social and historical constructs in much the same way as the idea of national collective identities. I have chosen to use the pronoun "we" at times throughout the book to describe this fluid collective as an indication that, along with the reader, I too might be included in this group. This moral collective is produced, reproduced, and negotiated through processes of differentiation that include the kinds of processes under consideration here.

7. Anidjar's project of deconstructing the idea of an enemy divide between Jews and Arabs reveals historically changing European imaginings of these highly politically charged categories. His work demonstrates how the idea of Europe emerges through the production of these "enemies." Reminding us of the term "Semites," he also makes a compelling argument about how religion can disguise race as well as how race and religion can be conflated (Anidjar 2008). If Anidjar and a number of other scholars including Ella Shohat, Amnon Raz-Krakotzkin, Ammiel Alcalay, and Yehuda Shenhav have been concerned with undoing the division between Arab and Jew as distinct and enemy categories, my project here is somewhat broader. Drawing on these notions of the constructedness of categories of identity and difference, my aim here is both to consider how enemies continue to be produced through powerful discourses and practices, and also to consider the usefulness and limits of such deconstructions in practical politics and peacemaking.

8. This seems to be the case despite the arguments between modernists and primordialists. See Uri Ram (1995) on this point.

9. What "thinking" might mean and what exactly is entailed in the process of thinking is not immediately obvious. For Hannah Arendt thinking is an inherently moral practice, connected to the human faculty for judgment (Arendt 1971, 1994; Beiner 1992/1982:94–101). Like Arendt, Theodor Adorno (1998) was very concerned about the practice of thinking and wrote about the imperative of teaching critical thinking to prevent horrors like Auschwitz. But according to Elizabeth Povinelli (2012), critical thinking of the sort that leads to the kinds of moral judgments that may not be popular at a given historical moment requires a kind of self that can endure the exhaustion of such thinking. Tanya Luhrmann (2013) recently wrote about the work involved in cultivating a self who can practice a kind of sustained meditation, particularly among Evangelical Christians who want to

experience God. This kind of self-discipline might be likened to what Povinelli describes as the will to endurance, except perhaps for the absence of community.

10. Peace scholars distinguish between peacemaking and peacebuilding. The latter term refers to a holistic approach that "transforms" conflict situations by taking into account long-term effects and structural inequities that are considered core causes of conflict. For a useful review of this literature see Omer (2013). It is not clear to me that peacebuilding is necessarily any less "liberal" than peacemaking.

11. The Oslo peace process began in the early 1990s and consisted of a set of agreements between the Israeli government and the PLO. In 1993, President Bill Clinton hosted then Prime Minister Yitzhak Rabin and Chairman Yasser Arafat, who signed the agreement that set the parameters for making peace. The Oslo accords provided for temporary measures, like the establishment of the Palestinian National Authority that would administer the territory under its control. These accords were expected to lead to a final status agreement, which has not happened.

12. See Lustick (1988); Pedahzur and Perlinger (2011); and Zertal and Eldar (2007).

13. This is not to suggest that these groups are not violent or dangerous; they are. But legitimate state institutions can also be violent and dangerous, and we might think about why one type of violent action is considered acceptable in political life and another is not (see Asad 2007).

14. Controlling the borders means not just that Israel regulates the flow of people in and out of Gaza, but that it also restricts nearly everything that might be legally imported or exported from the area, meaning that Palestinians cannot develop their agricultural or industrial economy as Israel does. This has helped to lock Gaza into a permanent state of economic crisis, which has arguably sharpened the radical tone of its internal and external politics.

15. See Mullin (2010), who argues that an ontological threat is the reason that Hamas has been marginalized and removed from the peace process in Israel/Palestine. Her goal is to de-exoticize Islamists like Hamas so that a place can be made for them at the negotiating table in order that a two-state solution can be achieved. Thus, in some sense, despite her critical analysis, she remains within the parameters of liberal peacemaking.

16. Mahmoud Abbas is currently the Palestinian president. But what exactly does that mean? He was elected by the Palestinian people and is in charge of the Palestinian National Authority in parts of the West Bank. One might say he is the president of Palestine. But where is that

place? The Palestinians have gained recognition as an "observer state" by the UN, but the territory of that state is disputed and the president has limited power.

Chapter 2

1. From the Israeli Ministry of Foreign Affairs website: http://www.mfa. gov.il/MFA/Peace+Process/Guide+to+the+Peace+Process/Declaration+ of+Establishment+of+State+of+Israel.htm.
2. *Journal of Palestine Studies* 18(2):213 (Winter 1989).
3. In J. L. Austin's terms, "*conditions* of felicity."
4. Israel Ministry of Foreign Affairs website.
5. http://www.trumanlibrary.org/whistlestop/study_collections/israel/ large/index.php.
6. As Edward Said (1986) explains, for Palestinians recognition of Israeli rights in fact denotes a denial of their own rights. For if Israel has a right to sovereignty in Palestine, then Palestinians necessarily cede their rights to the same.
7. Edward Said was, in many ways, the voice of Palestinians in the West. A prominent Palestinian intellectual and political activist, he was Professor of English Literature at Columbia University, an advisor to Yasser Arafat, and an outspoken defender of Palestinian rights.
8. This might be thought of as liberation from occupation without "freedom" in the sense that Arendt distinguished between these two terms.
9. Retrieved from the CNN archives July 5, 2011 (http://archives.cnn. com/2000/ALLPOLITICS/stories/09/27/mideast.congress.reu/).
10. For a useful discussion on the idea of sovereignty, formal and informal sovereignty, and the nature of sovereign power, see Hansen and Stepputat (2006).
11. Of course, the broader Israeli-Arab conflict, of which this is a part, includes additional players.
12. A number of scholars have suggested that such agreements made between political leaders are potentially unstable because they fail to establish the cultural foundations for shared sets of goals and values among the people involved in the conflict. See Bar-Tal and Bennink (2004) for an example that suggests that arriving at sustained peace requires a longer process of reconciliation aimed more broadly than negotiations between leaders. But even this suggestion remains within the limited notion of two parties to the conflict. In her recent book, Atalia Omer (2013) suggests something more encompassing.

13. Bekerman writes that educational interventions in the form of inter-group encounters that seek to move toward peace through the "recognition of cultural differences" have been widely and for the most part "uncritically acclaimed" (2007:24).

14. In 1986 Edward Said gave a talk at the annual meeting of the International Society of Political Psychology in which he engaged directly with these questions of "recognition" as raised by Herbert Kelman. Said takes issue with Kelman not because of the conflation of nationhood with humanity, but because of the asymmetry between Israelis and Palestinians that is hidden in the idea that these two parties are locked in what is called "the Israeli-Palestinian conflict," which he says creates the appearance of equal footing that in fact "reduces the claims of one by elevating the claims of the other" (Said 1986:31).

15. State-administered schools in Israel include both secular (*mamlachti*) and religious (*mamlachti dati*) public schools in the Jewish sector.

16. The wording of this sentence is purposeful, although I am aware that some readers will take exception to the straightforward declarative phrase, "that God promised the Land to the Jews" or, a few paragraphs later, the use of the word "forgets." Indeed, a reader of an earlier version of this work suggested such wording would unfortunately not be acceptable in a secular academic journal. While in anthropology generally it has not only become acceptable but is considered more ethical to represent the community one studies from their own point of view, this case seems to be an exception. If I were writing about a particular Native American group, for example, and represented their ideas without qualifying that this is "their point of view" or "their interpretation," this would probably not be of particular concern to readers; in fact, I might be admonished for adding those phrases. It seems that the politics in this case makes such "good" anthropology seem problematic. The term "forget" has been used by scholars (probably beginning with Renan) to critique the ways in which nationalist histories, especially that of Israel, make selective use of the past. For example, Joel Beinin (2005) argues that even revisionist histories can carry a kind of forgetfulness, leaving out some people's stories, their truths about the past. Beinin argues that "the so-called 'new' Israeli historiography" continues to exclude Arab voices and sources of evidence, particularly in the work of Benny Morris. In this way, he says, it perpetuates Zionist categories of knowledge and can therefore not be considered revolutionary at all. Although readers might find the "truth" of these biblical tales objectionable (they are myths, not history!) and even despicable in relation to religiously motivated settlers and their project, I submit that the moral impetus to recognize people

and their different ways of being and believing cannot discount these truths. All of this, of course, returns us to a discussion raised by Susan Harding (1991) about the problems of representing what she called the "repugnant cultural other." I have written about representing settlers elsewhere (Dalsheim and Harel 2009), but it seems there is more to be said about this problem. While it is worth considering for the questions it raises about anthropology and politics in general, such a discussion is beyond the scope of this book.

17. Consider the Bedouin and Druze, who have different sets of beliefs, practices, places of origin, dialects, and appearances, as well as the resulting hierarchy of difference.

18. Consider this in relation to the idea of a culture of nationalism, in which, as Gelvin explains, "there is a difference between a 'culture of nationalism' and the nationalist movements that spawn in that culture. 'Culture of nationalism' refers to a social imaginary inhabited by populations who view the assumptions associated with nationalism as self-evident and part of the natural order. Those assumptions are that all humanity is naturally divided into unified societies (nations), each of which has a discrete identity; a nation can be identified by certain characteristics (religion, language, common history) which all of its members share; only national sovereignty can ensure that the interests of the nation and its citizens are protected; nations enjoy a special relationship with a particular territory that is the repository for that nation's history and memory; and nations retain their essential characteristics as they travel through time" (Gelvin 2009:11).

19. See Note 14.

20. Ultra-Orthodox Jews live in Israel but do not necessarily accept the modern political state because it was created by human actors and only God can decide when the People of Israel will once again be given sovereignty in the Holy Land. See Rabkin (2006). On the Neturei Karta and their alliances with Palestinians, see their website: http://www.nkusa.org/.

21. Loren Lybarger (2007) writes about the variation of complex identities among Palestinians, particularly political identities that are often reduced to an oversimplified binary of secular nationalists and Islamists. He gives a detailed analysis of current Islamist activists in a town in the West Bank and in Gaza. See especially his case study in Chapter 4.

22. See Anidjar (2003, 2008) on how the Arab and the Jew as enemies have been constituted as the outside of Europe. See also Ammiel Alcalay (1993) and Jonathan Boyarin (1996).

23. See Benjamin (1968/1940), Lowenthal (1985), and White (1980) for theorizing on the selective, partial and useable pasts of historical narratives. See Whitelam (1996) and Abu El-Haj (1998) on the uses of archeology for Israeli nationalist purposes. On curricula, teaching history, and Israeli national identity, see Ram (1995), Raz-Krakotzkin (2001), and Dalsheim (2003, 2007). See Zerubavel (1995) on the social construction of Israeli collective memory.

24. Here issues of morality enter critical scholarship, which calls for precisely the kinds of thinking that can move outside the constraints that comparisons like the one I have just set up would require. Such moves are found in the work of Ashis Nandy, Judith Butler, William Connolly, and many others, and might be traced to Walter Benjamin and Hannah Arendt as well. Butler (2008) speaks about this in her article about immigration to the Netherlands, and in her recent book (Butler 2012). I will say more about how the idea of power relations is used in critical scholarship to differentiate between population groups for analytical purposes in the next chapter as part of a discussion of the term "subaltern."

25. Taylor's notion of a secular age sometimes seems interchangeable with what others refer to as liberalism, liberal humanism, or liberal multiculturalism—or sometimes, Western modernity. I retain the term "secular" here to refer to the moral order in which sets of beliefs are to be recognized, tolerated, or valued as different than one's own, not necessarily to be accepted as truths, but to be lived alongside of and as one among possible choices. In particular, choices about belief or unbelief in God are especially important to the argument here, as will become clearer later.

26. The qualification is important here, as Bekerman explains that in many instances both Israeli Jews and Palestinians would be threatened by the idea of deconstructing their national identities.

27. In making this claim, I am drawing on personal experiences in political activism, peace work, and conflict resolution, and in educational efforts aimed at consciousness-raising in Israel/Palestine from 1987 to 2005 as well as ongoing conversations with peace activists and scholars.

28. See the introduction to Eley and Suny's *Becoming National* (1996) for a succinct overview of the literature deconstructing national belonging as primordial.

29. See Ernest Gellner's (1983) ground-laying work on the role of public education in nationalism.

30. Although Bekerman does not mention the horrors that have been carried out in the name of nationalism, others certainly have pointed to fascism and Nazism in Europe, for example Chatterjee (1986).

31. Bekerman refers to the "goals of liberal peace-searching" (2007:28), which he describes as strengthening recognition and coexistence.

32. I have chosen to use Bekerman's case as an example because his work reveals a deep commitment to peace and social justice, because his critical evaluation of intergroup encounters is very compelling, and because of the central importance of the dilemma he describes. This analysis is offered in the spirit of Bekerman's own critical work.

33. I should like to be clear that Bekerman himself is well aware of the ways in which the structure of intergroup encounters remains within an essentialist approach to identity (2007:25). It is precisely because of his critique of the role of nationalism and nation-states in the constitution of these essentialized identities, which can be reproduced through encounter groups, that his work is so important for the argument in this book.

34. Walter Benjamin warned us against this belief in progress. I will say a great deal more about Benjamin and temporality in Chapter 4, where I discuss the question of anachronisms and moralities in quests for peace and social justice.

35. For example, consider the intellectuals designing the Palestinian curriculum in Brown's (2007) study. See also the collection of essays written by Palestinian-Israeli academic women (Kanaaneh and Nussair 2010). For these young Palestinian feminists, "Palestinian identity-politics is at one and the same time a constitutive frame of mind and something they feel confident enough to move beyond" (Sa'ar 2011). See also a recent interview with Sari Nusseibeh, the president of Al-Quds University and a prominent public intellectual (Watzman 2011).

36. Harold Saunders was U.S. Assistant Secretary of State in the Carter Administration and a negotiator of the Camp David Accords (Saunders 1999:113).

37. See Poletta (2003) on the usefulness and limits of storytelling to form political alliances in social movements.

38. In making this claim, I am drawing on personal experiences in educational consciousness-raising, political activism, peace work, and conflict resolution in Israel/Palestine. I was trained in intercultural communication in education at the University of Pennsylvania, worked as an Intern for Peace among Jewish and Palestinian citizens of Israel, and taught at the Adam Institute for Democracy and Peace in Israel. One might consider parallels to recent research on the problematic outcomes of humanitarian aid work (see Gourevitch 2010).

39. There have been long debates about both the liberating potential and the exclusionary nature of nationalism and about the differences between European (or Imperial) and postcolonial (or Third World) nationalisms. For useful overviews of this literature on nationalism see Dalsheim (2003, introduction), Eriksen (2010:117–146), and Loomba (2005:155–192).
40. http://www.pjvoice.com/v18/18003transfer.aspx.
41. I realize this is an oversimplification and that those who support Boycott Divestment and Sanctions (BDS) have given a great deal of consideration to its potential for ending the Occupation. For recent debates on BDS see the American Association of University Professors' *Journal of Academic Freedom*, volume 4 (http://www.aaup.org/reports-publications/journal-academic-freedom/volume-4). It should be clear that my comments are meant neither to endorse nor condemn this political tactic.
42. These past injustices include what is known as the Stolen Generation, when Aboriginal children were forcibly removed from their parents as part of the state policy of cultural assimilation between 1910 and 1970. It also includes the concept of *terra nullius* that provided Australian settlers with land that had presumably "belonged to no one" before they arrived. The doctrine of *terra nullius* was officially overturned in 1992 by the Australian High Court in the *Mabo* decision.
43. When native Australians went to court to claim their rights to their ancestral lands they were called upon to prove themselves to be "authentic" Aborigines who still acknowledge and observe Aboriginal traditions, despite the fact that many of these traditions have been criminalized for more than a century, meaning that people could be punished for practicing the traditions they must claim to abide by in order to make successful land claims.
44. Oren Yiftachel (2006) predicts a "gradual binationalism" in which he argues for a single state as the only possible way of achieving democracy in Israel/Palestine. Yiftachel argues that a temporary stage of two states would have to precede this eventual democratic social formation, primarily because Israel would not accept a one-state solution because it feels vulnerable and threatened. Note here, too, the presumption of particular stages of evolutionary progress necessary to achieve peace.
45. Povinelli (2002:4) differentiates between postcolonial and multicultural forms of domination within liberal discourse. Franz Fanon and scholars of the school of Subaltern Studies have suggested that colonial domination worked by inspiring colonized subjects to identify

with their colonizers. In the case of Australia, Povinelli suggests that multicultural domination works by inspiring minority and subaltern subjects to identify with the impossible object of an authentic self-identity. The extent to which this distinction applies to the case of Israel/Palestine is a question that remains to be investigated.

Chapter 3

1. White distinguishes between narrating and narrativizing. According to White, historians can narrate an account of the past without imposing upon it the form of a story (White 1980:6).
2. This has also been a critique leveled against postmodernism in the field of history precisely because of the problem of adjudicating competing claims. See Eric Hobsbawm's essay "Identity History Is Not Enough" (1997:266–277).
3. Ross explains that there is little chance of mediating a conflict without showing "each side" that "a third party understands why it feels as it does" (2004:15). This is a form of recognition that is central to liberal secularism. This recognition of people's feelings is comparable to a liberal recognition of people's beliefs, which only means the fact that they have such beliefs and feelings is recognized, not the truth of those beliefs or feelings.
4. Subjective here in the sense of having a particular take on things because of one's background and experiences. This is quite ironic, of course, since the peacemaker can express her position, but only if she does so according to a set of preconceived, and very powerful, categories.
5. Althusser recognized that hailing does not always work, although he contended that it did in the overwhelming majority of cases, as in the case of the Palestinians in Bekerman's example who resisted the deconstruction of their national identity.
6. This work, of course, includes the groundbreaking scholarship of the Subaltern Studies Group, like that of Ranajit Guha, Amitav Ghosh, Veena Das, Partha Chatterjee, Dipesh Chakrabarty, and Gayatri Spivak, among many others. However, recognizing subaltern pasts is not limited to this work; Edward Said's *Orientalism* is seminal to such work on the Middle East and to postcolonial studies more generally. Although there is some controversy over how the term "subaltern" should be used, it sometimes refers to any oppressed or marginalized group and sometimes is used more narrowly to indicate those who have no access to hegemonic forms of cultural expression and who

cannot tell their own story in their own voice. This is what Dipesh Chakrabarty discussed even in the work of some scholars in the Subaltern Studies Group whose goal it is to represent subaltern pasts. In some sense, the entire *Journal of Palestine Studies* (or *History and Memory* or *Radical History Review*) might be called such a voice. And histories "from below" of marginalized, oppressed, or colonized peoples continue to be written about Native Americans, Latin Americans, African Americans, the African Diaspora, Aboriginal Australians, women, the working class, and so on. See, for example, the work of bell hooks and Gloria Anzaldua on women, gender, sexuality, race, and ethnicity. See Stuart Hall and Paul Gilroy on race and racism and the African diaspora and the writings of Ella Shohat, Yehuda Shenhav, Amnon Raz-Kratkotzkin, and Smadar Lavie on Jews of the Middle East and North Africa.

7. See Brow (1990) and Brow and Swedenburg (1990) for useful discussions on hegemony and using the past in the production of collective identity.

8. As Saba Mahmood (2005:39) wrote, I ask that "we – my readers and myself – embark upon an inquiry in which we do not assume that the political positions we uphold will necessarily be vindicated . . . but instead hold open the possibility that we may come to ask . . . a whole series of questions that seemed settled when we first embarked upon the inquiry."

9. The website of the Jewish community in Hebron includes links to a number of books and articles about the place, its history and to current events there. This is the link to Auerbach's book: http://www.hebron.com/english/article.php?id=580. The website of the Palestinian city of Hebron also displays articles and current events related to the city and has links to information for residents. It also contains sections explaining the agreements reached to redeploy Israeli troops in Hebron and provides maps: http://www.hebron-city.ps/.

10. "Hebron is the city of his grandfathers," she writes, "as well as a place holy to both Muslims and Jews" (Campos 2007:41). Haim Hanegbi grew up in Jerusalem and is a peace activist who recently left the Gush Shalom movement, which calls for a two-state solution, to work toward the establishment of one democratic state for all citizens. See his article explaining his political position based on his memory of good neighborly relations with Palestinian Arabs in his childhood on the website for One Democratic State in Israel/Palestine: http://odspi.org/articles/shavit-hanegbi-benvenisti.html.

11. Indeed, in an article by Auerbach on the Hebron website, he explains that not only is the tomb of the matriarchs and patriarchs (the

Machpelah) significant for people of other faiths, but that "over the centuries, Christians and Muslims attempted to make Hebron exclusively theirs. Beginning in the mid-thirteenth century, Muslim rulers prohibited Jews (and other 'infidels') from entering the Machpelah to pray at the tombs, permitting them to ascend no higher than the seventh step outside the enclosure" (http://www.hebron.com/english/article.php?id=580). Thus, remaining in Hebron is critical to ensure that Jews will have access to their holy sites.

12. The slang term "Kushi" is derived from Kush, which refers to the son of Ham and brother of Canaan (Genesis 10:6) and the country of the supposed descendants of Cush (ancient Ethiopia), comprising approximately Nubia and the modern Sudan, and the territory of southern (or Upper) Egypt.

13. There are also other narratives of Jews of Middle Eastern and North African descent that do not represent such a harmonious past between Jews and Arabs in the region. Campos's representation of the past resonates with those found in the writings of Yehuda Shenhav and Ella Shohat, and are found in the film *Forget Baghdad*. But there is also a film produced by the David Project called *Forgotten Refugees* that laments the way Jews were treated in Arab countries prior to the establishment of the state of Israel.

14. Many secular Zionists (the majority of Israeli Jews are more secular or traditional than orthodox in their religious practices) do not necessarily feel a particular connection to Hebron or to Jerusalem because of the sacred quality of these places. These Israelis express their emotional connection to the places where they grew up, or where their friends and family live. This is a much newer, more personal, and also specifically secular memory.

15. This doesn't mean, for example, that secular Israelis have more political power in the Knesset; it means that "the secular," as Talal Asad (2003) uses the term, comprises a hegemonic cultural milieu, disciplining the public sphere in Israel/Palestine, and in particular around the campfire of conventional or liberal peacemaking.

16. See Charles Taylor's (2002) description of modern "social imaginaries."

17. Clearly there are multiple ways of understanding this claim. One is to take it literally, as an assertion that there were specific other individuals or groups who perpetrated the violence. The other is as a guilty Freudian expulsion of violent impulses from the self onto others who become one's demonic alter ego, and who can bear the blame for actions that are socially disapproved.

18. Assaf Harel (personal communication).

19. Hillel Cohen (personal communication).

Chapter 4

1. See Bamyeh (2009).
2. See Dalsheim (2013) on the different ways the idea of anachronism is applied to Jewish settlers and to Palestinians. I suggest that both perceptions of anachronism frame history as a kind of progress in which peoples or groups might be ranked according to their levels of civilizational attainment. This is an idea that scholars abandoned long ago as an analytical tool, but seem to have retained as a matter of practical political sympathy and judgment. See Connolly (1999:79) on John Stuart Mill and the progress of civilization. Ethno-nationalism is considered inherently violent with roots in fear and hatred of the "other," and affinities with exclusionary practices and racism. David Scott writes of postcolonial nationalism as a social formation whose quests for postcolonial liberation ultimately led to "acute paralysis of will . . . rampant corruption and vicious authoritarianism"(2004:2).
3. The idea of producing moral selves by differentiating through time is hardly new. Perhaps Johannes Fabian (1983, 2006) is best known for bringing these issues to the attention of anthropologists, demonstrating how we differentiate ourselves from the subjects of our analysis.
4. See Ricouer (1980) on Heidegger (*Being and Time*) on "ordinary time" as that of discrete events on a timeline requiring a storyline or plot to hold them together. For a useful overview of anthropological work on the assumptions that underlie "Western" ideas about time, see Barbara Adam (1994).
5. This is not to suggest that anachronism is the only way or even the predominant way in which people differentiate in this case, nor am I suggesting that religiously motivated settlers are the only group who are conceptualized as belonging to the past. However, I think it is worthwhile concentrating on the particularities of this mode of differentiation first because of the racializing implications associated with a linear progressive temporality that measures peoples in terms of civilizational attainment, especially in the context of colonization (for example, see Uday Mehta, 1990). Second, because of how such temporal thinking produces a moral community among those making the assessment, while potentially undermining their goals of achieving social justice and human liberation. An anonymous reviewer of an earlier version of this chapter wrote: "the author simply refuses to acknowledge that the settlers appropriate land from others." The reviewer seemed to think I was missing the point. He or she wrote: "Maybe it has nothing to do with . . . anachronisms and all to do with the fact that the settlers are land thieves!!?" However, my point is

precisely that the notion of anachronism is deployed in such situations in order to differentiate, and that such differentiation works to produce a particular moral community. I am not suggesting that either Palestinians or settlers are anachronistic, nor do I take sides for or against either community. Instead, I am concerned with how such categories of belonging and differentiation are constituted and how this limits the possibilities of recognizing our own and others' humanity, which ultimately undermines the goal of achieving human liberation in the contemporary context in which recognition matters so much. On this last point, see Taylor (1994).

6. Certain kinds of religious beliefs and practices are often imagined as holding society back from advancement or turning it backwards, limiting personal freedoms that are the signs of an open, modern society where individuals can pursue their own paths and fulfill their own desires. As discussed in Chapter 1, these ideas are part of what Charles Taylor (2002, 2007) has called a "modern social imaginary," based on the idea that human beings are "rational, sociable agents who are meant to collaborate in peace to their mutual benefit. This underlying theory provides an idea of moral order, of how to live together in society" (Taylor 2002:92). For example, consider the story Peter van der Veer (2006) tells about the Netherlands and Dutch reactions to pious Muslim immigrants. The Dutch, he explains, understand their national past as moving ever forward to increased human liberation, happiness, and enjoyment that is contrasted to an earlier time when the role of the church was much greater. The piety of Muslim immigrants, he explains, feels like a threat to that forward movement, to the increasingly free society the Dutch have achieved and to their personal freedoms and happiness. See also Judith Butler (2008) on powerful temporal ideas and Muslim migrants in the Netherlands.

7. This analysis might be extended to other radical religionists in Israel/Palestine, such as members of Hamas or Islamic Jihad, but these groups are marginalized in different ways from religiously motivated Jewish settlers. One might begin to consider, for example, Muslim concepts like *dhimmi*, a non-Muslim governed by Muslim law, or the notion of millet and the organization of confessional communities employed during the Ottoman Empire. These ideas could equally be seen as marginalized non-nationalist ideas emanating from religious concepts, ideas that cannot be easily reconciled with the limited imaginings of territorial nationalism. However, a detailed comparison of the deployment of anachronism marginalizing Muslim and Jewish ideas is beyond the scope of this chapter. The point of this chapter

is not to redeem settlers, to prove their moral worth, or to support their actions. It is simply to say that when we do not interrogate our responses to them, we miss what is being accomplished through those responses, and how such oversights might lead us to undermine our own goals.

8. Walter Benjamin's concerns about messianic thinking and its dangers are reflected in a recent debate between Talal Asad and George Shulman (in Scott and Hirschkind 2006). Asad (2006:237) warns against the danger of ideas of redemption and messianic thought when such thought is transposed from the spiritual to the political: "The idea of political redemption is grotesquely out of place in the secular world, a danger to politics and a parody of spirituality." Benjamin is critical of messianic thinking, on the one hand, yet was also interested in new messianic possibilities that could subvert predominant ones. In this sense, Benjamin complicates the separation of spiritual from political that Asad invokes.

9. This is the idea of an alternative history, which I discussed at length in Chapter 3 and considered not only alternative histories but also alternatives *to* history based on Ashis Nandy's ideas about rethinking the past and the problems of historicism.

10. See Auerbach (2009) and Campos (2007) for an example of the conflict over this history.

11. Roxanne Euben (1999) writes similarly about Muslims whose beliefs are disbelieved and considered instrumental. In a very different way, Elizabeth Povinelli (2002) shows cases in which the liberal state through the courts in Australia does not believe the beliefs represented by some Aboriginals about their relationship to the land.

12. This notion of "diametrically opposed to true Jewish values" resonates with an argument J. Boyarin (1996: Chapter 2) puts forth when he intervenes in a conversation between Edward Said and Michael Walzer. One ought not "read Exodus into history" unless one remains true to the text, Boyarin argues. Admittedly Boyarin is having a scholarly debate with other scholars, but he still seems to be suggesting that there is a true version of what the text of Exodus means. We might conclude therefore that although Boyarin values the ambiguity of Talmudic interpretation, he also seems to insist that certain interpretations are legitimate while others are not.

13. Part of the inauthenticity attributed to the current Jewish community in Hebron derives from their representing themselves as the continuation of an earlier Jewish community in Hebron. As we saw in Chapter 3, Michelle Campos (2007) writes against this representation.

14. See Taylor (2002, 2007) on modern social imaginaries.

15. For a powerful (and controversial) argument on the ways in which modern narratives are contained by linear conceptions of temporality, see Hayden White (1987). Max Weinreich (1980) offers an explanation of a particular Jewish way of being that conceives of all of Jewish history as one indivisible whole; exact periodization is not attempted, and events in the ancient past can be understood through the lens of the present, just as the present can be understood as motivated by the ancient past. Just as Jacob is Israel, identified with the people of Israel, Esau is Edom and Haman descended from him. Edom is also Christian Europe, and its opposition, and Jews and Muslims are prefigured in Isaac and Ishmael. What is taken by modern linear thought to be problematic or anachronistic is a different sense of temporality that Weinreich calls "panchronism" (1980:208). See Ian Lustick's description of how acts of violence such as that perpetrated by Baruch Goldstein are often taken out of their religious context and interpreted as "deeds of madmen" (Lustick 1994).

16. See Karl Popper (1959) for an early critique of this kind of prediction as a social scientific method.

17. There also seems to be a limit to possible interpretations because of the context and the meanings a text has had, its history and previous interpretations—because of intertextuality. This is one reason it is difficult to rewrite history curricula. Uri Ram (1995) makes this point, and Jonathan Boyarin (1996:40–67) illustrates this as he disciplines other scholars for their readings of biblical text.

18. Dipesh Chakrabarty (2000) demonstrates the impossibility of representing certain subaltern voices within Western historiography because of the reliance on a particular linear narrative. Judith Butler (2008) argues that linear progressive understandings of modernity create particular divisions that preclude potential alliances between groups, thus interfering with some people's freedoms for the benefit of others. For a critique of Butler, see Dalsheim (2010).

19. It should be noted that there are also self-identified members of the (Jewish) Israeli Left who consider themselves the radical, anti- or non-Zionist Left who would not agree that settler practices were necessary in the past. A well-known scholar/activist representing this position is Uri Davis, who recently gave up his Israeli citizenship to become Palestinian. The Alternative Information Center (www.alternativenews.org/) is a good source for those who want to read more opinions including those from the radical Left. For example, see the recent book by the director of that website: Michael Warschawski's *On the Border* (2005). Another good source is Ephraim Nimni's book, *The Challenge of Post-Zionism* (2003).

20. For an in-depth analysis of the similarity of these depictions and the fury generated among left-wing Israelis see Dalsheim (2005). See also Dalsheim and Harel (2009).

21. I am indebted to Assaf Harel (personal communication) for this idea. Here the messianic temporality of secular nationalism disrupts a neat spiritual/political divide.

22. Gopin (2004) writes that religious traditions can "play a crucial role in the reconstruction of broken human relationships." However, he also insists that this will require "courage by religious people to extricate themselves from the shackles of violent or bigoted interpreters of their traditions."

23. The moral community being created by these judgments is a fragile one, in part because it ignores the deeply entangled nature of economic systems. If it is wrong to make purchases that support the post-1967 settlement project, then it must also be wrong to pay taxes in Israel and wrong to purchase products in Tel Aviv and, if we really want to trace the sources of funding, it would ultimately be unacceptable to work and pay taxes in the United States, which provides economic, material, military, and political support for Israeli settlement policies. Is it then also wrong for Palestinians themselves to work in the settlements in agriculture and in construction? Such complications, of course, are problematic for practical political mobilization and unsettling to the constitution of moral selves among progressive Israelis and left-wing activists and scholars in the international community.

24. On settler colonialism as a structure rather than an event, see Wolfe (1999).

25. Personal communication with former prisoners in Belfast, summer 2012.

26. On "flexible citizenship", see Aihwa Ong (1993, 2006). For additional discussion of this concept in relation to Israel/Palestine see Dalsheim (2013).

27. Some ways of approaching solutions in terms of the power relations of those involved require thinking in terms of "who" rather than "what" the problem is that needs to be solved. Another way to narrate the Israeli-Palestinian conflict would be to say that looking to history to find the true story and the true culprits helps maintain enmity, which ultimately benefits the arms industry more than anyone else (see Laura Nader 2003).

28. The word "monsters" comes from Sartre's famous introduction to Fanon's *Wretched of the Earth*.

29. See Don Handelman (2004:13) on the rhetoric of "no choice" among Israelis as an example of the practices of colonizers who refuse. See

also Talal Asad (2007) on such rhetorical justifications for U.S. military interventions that maintain a moral high ground for interventionist policy.

Chapter 5

1. Rudoren (2012). And, Meeting Sheikh Jabari: The Hebron Fund, AFSI, and Hebron residents. Nov. 20, 2011, in Jabari tent near the Zif Junction, on the outskirts of Hebron (http://www.youtube.com/watch?v=VQjdj8OPz78).
2. Carolyn Nordstrom (2000) writes about a much larger scale of international shadow economies that flourish in war zones. See Parnell and Kane's edited volume (2003) on the implications of crime as a constructed category. See also Charles Tilly (1985) on war making and state making as organized crime. "War makes states," Tilly argues, and "banditry, piracy, gangland rivalry, policing, and war making all belong on the same continuum" (p. 170).
3. "The question of genocide," Patrick Wolfe (2006:387) writes, "is never far from discussions of settler colonialism. Land is life—or, at least, land is necessary for life. Thus contests for land can be—indeed, often are—contests for life." Sari Hanafi (2012) calls this process "spacio-cide."
4. A report by Lourdes Garcia-Navarro on National Public Radio quotes one Palestinian who recently participated in a protest against his leaders as saying: "I think they are trying to silence people because Abbas and his regime have not been able to secure a Palestinian state, they have not been able to help the economy," he says. "And his security agencies are dealing with the people with a police-state mentality" (http://www.npr.org/2012/07/26/157417277/latest-target-for-palestinians-protest-their-leader). In 2008, it was reported that the Palestinian Authority (PA) was blocking certain news sites that were reporting on corruption within the PA (http://electronicintifada.net/content/ramallah-palestinian-authority-blocks-website-reporting-corruption/7814). "The Café on Al Jazeera," broadcast from Ramallah on Aug. 18, 2012, provides an example of a range of views found among Palestinians. Some participants on the show express dissatisfaction with the Palestinian Authority. One woman says it is corrupt and is working for the Israelis, making Occupation easier for them. Another says it has not done enough to promote Palestinian rights and freedoms (http://www.aljazeera.com/programmes/thecafe/2012/08/2012817115155794165.html).

5. See Lavie (1990), and Cohen (2008) for similar situations.

6. Of course, such work going on behind the scenes or in the shadows is not necessarily weak; see Nordstrom and Robben (1995).

7. I have taken the term "scattered hegemonies" to think through an additional set of problems. I chose the word "scattered" rather than "intersectional" because I think it more accurately represents the case at hand. "Intersectionality" (Crenshaw 1989, 1991) is a term that was formulated to refer to the multidimensional lives of marginalized subjects, in particular the lives of black women in the United States. For a review of the usefulness and limits of intersectionality as a tool for feminist and antiracist work, see Nash (2008).

8. See Lori Allen (2013) on cynicism among Palestinians.

9. http://www.bdsmovement.net/2013/report-fourth-national-bds-conference-11080.

10. http://www.bdsmovement.net/2013/electronic-intifada-coverage-of-fourth-national-bds-conference-11038#sthash.SghD8b2o.dpuf.

11. See Talal Asad's (2003) discussion on thinking the secular through questions of agency, pain, cruelty, and torture in Chapters 2 and 3 of *Formations of the Secular.*

12. This, of course, is an oversimplification of life during Ottoman rule. One might argue that Muslims were sovereign, and since that excluded Jews, the Arabs—except perhaps Christians—were not minorities among minorities.

13. In a similar vein, Clifford Geertz wrote, "Cultural analysis is intrinsically incomplete. And, worse than that, the more deeply it goes the less complete it is" (1973:29). And Jonathan Boyarin's (1996) book demonstrated how anthropology and ethics are ongoing, never-finished conversations.

Chapter 6

1. The outrage at Nusseibeh's book led one of my Palestinian colleagues to try to dissuade me from even mentioning him in my work. That colleague was concerned that any association with Nusseibeh might discredit me and prevent some people from engaging with my work.

2. Schmitt's work has been cited over 1500 times by scholars from a number of disciplines. Much of the work on political sovereignty is found in the political science and international relations literature. For a recent example, see Sassen (1996). From the field of anthropology, see Appadurai (1993), Aretxaga (2003), Kapferer (2004), and Ong (2006).

3. Of course, numerous scholars have taken up an in-depth interrogation of the concept of sovereignty. For a useful overview of the history of the theory and concept see F. H. Hinsley (1986/1966). On some of sovereignty's fascinating historical iterations and imaginings see Benton (2010). For a recent review of the anthropological literature, see Hansen and Stepputat (2006).

4. According Charles Taylor (2007, 2010), choice, a particular kind of choice, is a defining feature of the secular age. For Taylor what is important is that belief in God or in the transcendent is contested. Such belief, then, becomes a matter of choice. For Talal Asad, thinking about agency and its relationship to pain is one way of thinking about the secular because "the secular depends on particular conceptions of action and passion." And because secular agency is thought to be aimed toward eliminating human suffering (Asad 2003:67). Asad raises all sorts of questions about what "agency" means and has meant, but suggests that its connotation within the secular is largely directed at empowerment and history-making (73).

5. This theorizing, of course, also presumes certain meanings for what will count as rational and what one ought to consider in one's own best interests.

6. In addition, liberal jurisprudence hinges on intentionality: it is not only what we choose to do, but why. Intentionality is key, for example, to the difference between murder and manslaughter. Here we have both the chosen act and our desired outcomes.

7. Writing about Israeli nationalism, Nadav Shelef (2010) makes the case for what he calls evolutionary change in politics. He offers this theory as "a corrective to the assumption that change must be intentional . . . Just as the story of biological evolution claims that there does not have to be a guiding intelligence behind biological change (not that there cannot be one), so, in the political realm, the evolutionary dynamic implies that fundamental transformations in nationalist ideology do not have to be intentional (not that they cannot be)" (p. 193).

8. See Chapter 7 on how other scholars and activists are seeking alternatives in local efforts and in social movements. For example, see Bamyeh (2009), Graeber (2002, 2004), Moghadam (2013), Scott (2009, 2012), and Smith (2008).

9. This is not to suggest that all forms of collective identity are the same, or that all forms of nationalism are the same, or that all forms of collective identity or of nationalism are based on primordialism. For example, Ammiel Alcalay differentiates between forms of Jewish collective identities. He writes of the long historical process

of transformation in Jewish history: "the gradual exchange of the legal, communal and cultural basis of Jewish existence for the racial the ethnic and the national . . . [which] assumed a final physical form in the Levant" (1993:221). And, as noted in Chapter 1, Rashid Khalidi (1997) writes about Palestinian collective identity that is formed at checkpoints, in interactions with Israeli soldiers. He does not emphasize a common cultural, religious, or linguistic basis of Palestinian identity.

10. See the imaginary map by Julien Bousac (2013) for a striking image (http://www.imaginaryatlas.com/2013/03/14/the-palestine-archipelago/).

Chapter 7

1. See J. Boyarin (1996: Chapter 4) for a detailed account of the outrage that can result from telling certain kinds of stories about Israel/Palestine and the importance of insisting on telling those stories despite the outrage. One might think of this insistence as an example of what Elizabeth Povinelli (2012) calls "the effort of endurance" involved in "thinking." Boyarin's book, in the same vein as earlier work by Ammiel Alcalay (1993), aimed to undermine the dichotomy Arab/Jew that effaces an "entire colonial/cosmopolitan past" (Boyarin 1996:203).

2. "Israeli Arabs, who comprise a fifth of Israel's total population, are descendants of residents who stayed on after the 1948 war of Israel's founding, in which hundreds of thousands of fellow Palestinians fled or were forced to leave their homes. More than half live below the poverty line, compared with a national average of 20%, according to official figures, while some 30% are unemployed, five times the national figure, a Tel Aviv University study estimates." "Arabs are undecided on the merits of their political participation and, given the current facts, whether their votes make a difference," Tel Aviv University lecturer Amal Jamal told Reuters. See "The majority are thinking: 'What's the point?'" (Reuters, Jan. 15, 2013 (http://uk.reuters.com/article/2013/01/15/uk-israel-election-arabs-idUKBRE90E0N520130115)).

3. We might imagine that without the right to vote, these new Palestinian residents of Israel would not pose a demographic threat. With the threat removed, perhaps more freedoms would follow. But this seems far from certain. Of course, there are Israelis who are residents, living in Israel for decades while maintaining citizenship elsewhere, who do not serve in the army or have the right to vote. They may have their

cultural rights protected if they are Jewish, and they may feel quite happy and comfortable living this way. But for Palestinians things might be very different. What if the Palestinians from the West Bank married current Israeli citizens? Would they gain full citizenship and the right to vote through marriage? What would happen to their children? Would those Palestinians who are already citizens have their right to vote revoked? Nusseibeh never says.

4. According to Asad (2003) this larger concern with alleviating all human suffering is a mark of the secular and one of its goals to be accomplished through the exercise of agency.

5. Palestinian residents of East Jerusalem generally hold identity papers as permanent residents rather than as Israeli citizens. For more information and the history of this arrangement see the explanation provided by the Israeli human rights organization, B'Tselem (http://www.btselem.org/jerusalem/legal_status).

6. See http://www.israelnationalnews.com/News/Flash.aspx/189339#.UAac7XDrjwg.

7. See R. Stein (2008) on peace and the tourism industry in the 1990s (http://www.merip.org/mer/mer196/itineraries-peace).

8. There are certainly explicitly religious organizations that are also concerned with the plight of the Palestinians and that are associated with the left wing of Israeli politics; of course this raises questions about what "secular" means and what "left wing" refers to. Rabbis for Human Rights (http://rhr.org.il/eng/) might be one example of a group that considers itself both left wing and religious. The Neturei Karta (http://www.nkusa.org/) are probably not considered "left wing," although they express solidarity with Palestinians. Being ultra-Orthodox Jews, the Neturei Karta are socially conservative, but also anti-Zionist and supporters of Palestinian rights.

9. http://www.eretzshalom.org/?page_id=17. See Assaf Harel (forthcoming).

10. Yehuda Shenhav and Ben Marmali (personal communication). See the website http://www.sos-israel.com/58514.html for more on the group who called themselves "solidarity Sheik Munis" (Hebrew).

11. Eretz Yoshveha was largely inspired by Yehuda Shenhav's (2010) book, *In the Trap of the Green Line*. For an extended discussion of this position see Shenahav (2010 and 2012).

12. There are also disagreements among participants in Eretz Yoshveha over some of these issues.

13. Derrida actually leaves us more room than this reading might suggest because his work also intimates the impossibility of a simple division between the host and the guest, the self and the stranger.

14. Derrida does not explicitly make this move, probably because his concern is with the problematic distinctions between guest and host in the first place. However, Hannah Arendt (2003/1948) deals with such issues in her consideration of citizenship and belonging.

15. According to HaAretz reporter Barak Ravid, Israeli Prime Minister Benjamin Netanyahu reportedly told the World Economic Forum in Davos that "'he has no intention of uprooting a single settlement' and suggested settlers could remain outside Israel's borders under a peace agreement with the Palestinians" (http://www.haaretz.com/news/diplomacy-defense/1.570418). However, when a member of his own cabinet then spoke out against the Prime Minister, the cabinet member, Naftali Bennett, was reprimanded by a spokesperson from the Prime Minister's Office. The Prime Minister's Office reportedly said that Bennett's remarks undermined the Prime Minister. This was not because of the disagreement between them, but because Netanyahu's remarks were intended to elicit a response from the Palestinians that would "expose the real face of the Palestinian Authority" (http://www.haaretz.com/news/diplomacy-defense/1.570754). In other words, it was all a political ploy. But Gershon Baskin, who is the founding Co-Chairman of the Israel Palestine Center for Research and Information (www.ipcri.org) and writes a regular blog called Encountering Peace for the *Jerusalem Post*, took the idea seriously. In a recent piece, Baskin explored the question of settlers remaining in a Palestinian state. In discussions with his Palestinian contacts, he came to understand a more nuanced meaning behind Palestinian rejection of such an idea. As it turned out, Palestinians were reacting to the term "settler," which they associate with certain kinds of behaviors including land theft and acts of violence. However, Baskin reports that Palestinians would not object to "Jews" remaining in Palestine (http://www.jpost.com/Opinion/Columnists/Encountering-Peace-Our-Palestinians-their-Jews-339811).

REFERENCES

Abramson, Larry. 2009. What Does Landscape Want? A Walk in W. J. T. Mitchell's Holy Landscape. *Culture, Theory and Critique* 50(2–3): 275–288.

Abu El-Haj, Nadia. 1998. Translating Truths: Nationalism, the Practice of Archaeology, and the Remaking of the Past and Present in Contemporary Jerusalem. *American Ethnologist* 25(2): 166–188.

Abu-Nimer, Mohammed. 2003. *Nonviolence and Peace Building in Islam: Theory and Practice.* Gainesville: University Press of Florida.

Adam, Barbara. 1994. Perceptions of Time. In *Companion Encyclopedia of Anthropology.* T. Ingold, ed. Pp. 503–526. London and New York: Routledge.

Adorno, Theodor. 1998. Education after Auschwitz. In *Critical Models: Interventions and Catchwords.* New York: Columbia University Press.

Agamben, Georgio. 2005. *State of Exception.* K. Attell, transl. Chicago and London: University of Chicago Press.

Alcalay, Ammiel. 1993. *After Jews and Arabs: Remaking Levantine Culture.* Minneapolis: University of Minnesota Press.

Allen, Lori. 2013. *The Rise and Fall of Human Rights: Cynicism and Politics in Occupied Palestine.* Stanford, CA: Stanford University Press.

Althusser, Louis. 1971. Ideology and Ideological State Apparatuses (Notes Towards an Investigation). In *Lenin and Philosophy and Other Essays.* Pp. 127–186. New York and London: Monthly Review Press.

Anderson, Benedict. 1983. *Imagined Communities: Reflections on the Origin and Spread of Nationalism.* London: Verso.

Anidjar, Gil. 2002. Introduction: Once More, Once More: Derrida, the Arab, the Jew. In *Acts of Religion, Jacques Derrida.* G. Anidjar, ed. Pp. 1–39. New York and London: Routledge.

Anidjar, Gil. 2003. *The Jew, The Arab: A History of the Enemy*. Stanford, CA: Stanford University Press.

Anidjar, Gil. 2008. *Semites: Race, Religion, Literature*. Stanford, CA: Stanford University Press.

Appadurai, Arjun. 1993. Patriotism and Its Futures. *Public Culture* 5: 411–429.

Appadurai, Arjun. 2006. *Fear of Small Numbers: An Essay on the Geography of Anger*. Durham, NC and London: Duke University Press.

Appleby, R. Scott. 2001/1996. Religion as an Agent of Conflict Transformation and Peacebuidling. In *Turbulent Peace: The Challenges of Managing International Conflict*. C. A. Crocker, F. O. Hampson, and P. Aall, eds. Pp. 821–840. Washington, DC: United States Institute of Peace Press.

Aran, Gideon. 1991. Jewish Zionist Fundamentalism: The Bloc of the Faithful in Israel (Gush Emunim). In *Fundamentalisms Observed*. M. E. Marty and R. S. Appleby, eds. Pp. 265–344. Chicago and London: University of Chicago Press.

Arendt, Hannah. 1971. *The Life of the Mind*. Volume 1: *Thinking*. New York and London: Harcourt Brace Jovanovich.

Arendt, Hannah. 1989. *Lectures on Kant's Political Philosophy*. Chicago: University of Chicago Press.

Arendt, Hannah. 1994. Understanding and Politics (The Difficulties of Understanding). In *Arendt: Essays in Understanding, 1930–1954*. J. Kohn, ed. Pp. 307–327. New York: Harcourt Brace.

Arendt, Hannah. 2003/1948. The Perplexities of the Rights of Man, from The Origins of Totalitarianism. In *The Portable Hannah Arendt*. P. Baehr, ed. Pp. 31–45. New York: Penguin.

Arendt, Hannah. 2013/1970. "Thoughts on Politics and Revolution: A Commentary," Interview by Adelbert Reif, *Crisis of the Republic* (Summer 1970). Denver Lindley, transl. In *Hannah Arendt: The Last Interview and Other Conservations*. New York and London: Melville House.

Aretxaga, Begoña. 2003. Maddening States. *Annual Review of Anthropology* 32:393–410.

Asad, Talal. 2003. *Formations of the Secular: Christianity, Islam, Modernity*. Stanford, CA: Stanford University Press.

Asad, Talal. 2006. Responses. In *Powers of the Secular Modern: Talal Asad and His Interlocutors* (Cultural Memory in the Present). D. Scott and C. Hirschkind, eds. Pp. 206–243. Stanford, CA: Stanford University Press.

Asad, Talal. 2007. *On Suicide Bombing*. New York: Columbia University Press.

Asad, Talal. 2011. Thinking about Religious Beliefs and Politics. In *The Cambridge Companion to Religious Studies*. R. Orsi, ed. Pp. 36–57. New York: Cambridge University Press.

Auerbach, Jerold. 2009. *Hebron Jews: Memory and Conflict in the Land of Israel*. Lanham, MD: Rowman and Littlefield.

Austin, J. L. 1962. *How to Do Things with Words*. London: Oxford University Press.

Austin, Jonathan, Benjamin Hoffman, Beatrice Goddard, and Hannah Gray. 2011. *Hamas and the Peace Process: Resistance, Rejectionism, Reconciliation*. St. Andrews, Scotland: University of St. Andrews, Center for Peace and Conflict Studies.

Bakhtin, Mikhail M. 1981. *The Dialogic Imagination*. Caryl E. and M. Holquist, transl. Austin: University of Texas Press.

Bamyeh, Mohammed. 2003. Palestine: Listening to the Inaudible. *South Atlantic Quarterly* 102(4): 825–849.

Bamyeh, Mohammed. 2009. *Anarchy as Order: The History and Future of Civic Humanity*. Lanham, MD: Rowman and Littlefield.

Bamyeh, Mohammed. 2010. On Humanizing Abstractions: The Path Beyond Fanon. *Theory, Culture & Society* 27(7–8): 52–65.

Bar-Tal, D., and G. H. Bennink. 2004. The Nature of Reconciliation as an Outcome and as a Process. In *From Conflict Resolution to Reconciliation*. Y. Bar-Siman-Tov, ed. Pp. 11–38. Oxford: Oxford University Press.

Beiner, Ronald. 1992/1982. Hannah Arendt on Judging. In *Lectures on Kant's Political Philosophy*. R. Beiner, ed. Pp. 89–156. Chicago: University of Chicago Press.

Beinin, Joel. 2005. Forgetfulness for Memory: The Limits of the New Israeli History. *Journal of Palestine Studies* 34(2): 6–23.

Bekerman, Zvi. 2007. Rethinking Intergroup Encounters: Rescuing Praxis from Theory, Activity from Education, and Peace/Co-existence from Identity and Culture. *Journal of Peace Education* 4(1): 21–37.

Bekerman, Zvi. 2009. Identity Versus Peace: Identity Wins. *Harvard Educational Review* 79(1): 74–83.

Benjamin, Walter. 1968/1940. Theses on the Philosophy of History. In *Illuminations*. H. Arendt, ed. Pp. 253–264. New York: Schocken Books.

Ben-Porat, Guy. 2006. *Global Liberalism, Local Populism: Peace and Conflict in Israel and Palestine and Northern Ireland*. Syracuse, NY: Syracuse University Press.

Benton, Lauren. 2010. *A Search for Sovereignty: Law and Geography in European Empires, 1400–1900*. Cambridge: Cambridge University Press.

Bhabha, Homi K. 1994. Of Mimicry and Man: The Ambivalence of Colonial Discourse. In *The Location of Culture*. Pp. 85–92. London and New York: Routledge.

Boyarin, Daniel, and Jonathan Boyarin. 2003/1993. Diaspora: Generation and the Ground of Jewish Diaspora. In *Theorizing Diaspora*. J. E. Braziel and A. Mannur, eds. Pp. 85–118. Malden, MA: Blackwell.

Boyarin, Daniel, and Jonathan Boyarin. 1993. Diaspora: Generation and the Ground of Jewish Identity. *Critical Inquiry* 19(4): 693–725.

Boyarin, Jonathan. 1996. *Palestine and Jewish History: Criticism at the Borders of Ethnography*. Minneapolis and London: University of Minnesota Press.

Brow, James. 1990. Notes on Community, Hegemony, and the Uses of the Past. *Anthropological Quarterly* 63(1): 1–6.

Brow, James, and Ted Swedenburg, eds. 1990. Tendentious Revisions of the Past in the Construction of Community. *Anthropological Quarterly* 63(1): 1–62.

Brown, Nathan. 2007. The Palestinian National Authority: The Politics of Writing and Interpreting Curricula. In *Teaching Islam: Textbooks and Religion in the Middle East*. E. A. Doumato and G. Starrett, eds. Pp. 125–138. Boulder, CO and London: Lynne Rienner.

Brown, Wendy. 2006. *Regulating Aversion: Tolerance in the Age of Identity and Empire*. Princeton, NJ and Oxford: Princeton University Press.

Butler, Judith. 2008. Sexual Politics, Torture, and Secular Time. *British Journal of Sociology* 59(1): 1–23.

Butler, Judith. 2012. *Parting Ways: Jewishness and the Critique of Zionism*. New York: Columbia University Press.

Callan, Brian. 2013. Something's Wrong Here: Transnational Dissent and the Unimagined Community. *Contemporary Social Science* [forthcoming].

Campos, Michelle. 2007. Remembering Jewish–Arab Contact and Conflict. In *Reapproaching Borders: New Perspectives on the Study of Israel–Palestine*. S. Sufian and M. LeVine, eds. Pp. 41–65. Lanham, MD: Rowman and Littlefield.

Campos, Michelle. 2010. *Ottoman Brothers: Muslims, Christians, and Jews in Early Twentieth-Century Palestine*. Stanford, CA: Stanford University Press.

Chakrabarty, Dipesh. 2000. *Provincializing Europe: Postcolonial Thought and Historical Difference*. Princeton, NJ: Princeton University Press.

Charbonneau, Louis, and Michelle Nicholas. 2012. Palestinians Win de facto U.N. Recognition of Sovereign State. Reuters, November 30.

Chatterjee, Partha. 1986. *Nationalist Thought in the Colonial World: A Derivative Discourse?* Minneapolis: University of Minnesota Press.

Cohen, Hillel. 2008. *Army of Shadows: Palestinian Collaboration with Zionism, 1917–1948*. Berkeley and Los Angeles: University of California Press.

Collins, John. 2011. *Global Palestine*. New York: Columbia University Press.

Connolly, William E. 1999. *Why I Am Not a Secularist*. Minneapolis and London: University of Minnesota Press.

Cooper, Frederick, and Ann L. Stoler. 1997. *Tensions of Empire: Colonial Cultures in a Bourgeois World*. Berkeley and Los Angeles: University of California Press.

Coward, Harold, and Gordon S. Smith. 2004. *Religion and Peacebuilding.* Albany: State University of New York Press.

Crenshaw, Kimberle. 1989. Demarginalizing the Intersection of Race and Sex: A Black Feminist Critique of Antidiscrimination Doctrine, Feminist Theory and Antiracist Politics. *The University of Chicago Legal Forum*: 139–167.

Crenshaw, Kimberle. 1991. Mapping the Margins: Intersectionality, Identity Politics, and Violence Against Women of Color. *Stanford Law Review* 43(6): 1241–1299.

Dalsheim, Joyce. 2003. Uncertain Past, Uncertain Selves? Israeli History and National Identity in Question. PhD diss., Graduate Faculty of Political and Social Sciences of the New School for Social Research.

Dalsheim, Joyce. 2005. Antagonizing Settlers in the Colonial Present of Israel–Palestine. *Social Analysis* 49(2): 122–143.

Dalsheim, Joyce. 2007. Deconstructing National Myths, Reconstituting Morality: Modernity, Hegemony and the Israeli National Past. *Journal of Historical Sociology* 20(4): 521–554.

Dalsheim, Joyce. 2008. Twice Removed: Mizrahim in Gush Katif. *Social Identities* 14(5): 535–551.

Dalsheim, Joyce. 2010. On Demonized Muslims and Vilified Jews: Between Theory and Politics. *Comparative Studies in Society and History* 52(3): 581–603.

Dalsheim, Joyce. 2011. *Unsettling Gaza: Secular Liberalism, Radical Religion, and the Israeli Settlement Project.* New York: Oxford University Press.

Dalsheim, Joyce. 2013. Theory for Praxis: Peacemaking, Cunning Recognition, and the Constitution of Enmity. *Social Analysis* 57(2): 59–80.

Dalsheim, Joyce, and Assaf Harel. 2009. Representing Settlers. *Review of Middle East Studies* 43(2): 219–238.

Dehaene, Michiel, and Lieven De Cauter. 2008. *Heterotopia and the City: Public Space in a Postcivil Society.* London and New York: Routledge.

Derrida, Jacques. 2000. *Of Hospitality: Anne Dufourmantelle Invites Jacques Derrida to Respond.* R. Bowlby, transl. Stanford, CA: Stanford University Press.

Derrida, Jacques. 2008. Abraham, the Other. In *Religion: Beyond a Concept*. H. de Vries, ed. Pp. 311–338. New York: Fordham University Press.

Dudai, Ron, and Hillel Cohen. 2007. Triangle of Betrayal: Collaborators and Transitional Justice in the Israeli-Palestinian Conflict. *Journal of Human Rights* 6:37–58.

Durkheim, Emile. 1997/1933. *The Division of Labor in Society.* New York: The Free Press.

Eley, Geoff, and Ronald Grigor Suny. 1996. *Becoming National.* New York and Oxford: Oxford University Press.

Eriksen, Thomas Hylland. 2010. *Ethnicity and Nationalism: Anthropological Perspectives*. London: Pluto Press.

Ettinger, Yair, and Ilan Lior. 2011. Menahem Froman, the Rabbi of Tekoa, Formally Establishes Eretz Shalom. Haaretz.co.il (February 27).

Euben, Roxanne. 1999. *Enemy in the Mirror: Islamic Fundamentalism and the Limits of Modern Rationalism*. Princeton, NJ: Princeton University Press.

Fabian, Johannes. 1983. *Time and the Other: How Anthropology Makes Its Object*. New York: Columbia University Press.

Fabian, Johannes. 2006. The Other Revisited. *Anthropological Theory* 6(2): 139–152.

Falah, Ghazi-Walid. 2003. Dynamics and Patterns of the Shrinking Arab Lands in Palestine. *Political Geography* 22(2): 179–209.

Fanon, Franz. 1963/1961. *The Wretched of the Earth*. C. Farrington, transl. New York: Grove Press.

Fanon, Franz. 1967. *Black Skins, White Masks*. C. L. Markmann, transl. New York: Grove Press.

Faubion, James D. 2008. Heterotopia: An Ecology. In *Heterotopia and the City: Public Space in a Postcivil Society*. M. Dehaene and L. De Cauter, eds. Pp. 31–40. New York and London: Routledge.

Feige, Michael. 2009. *Settling in the Hearts: Jewish Fundamentalism in the Occupied Territories*. Detroit: Wayne State University Press.

Foucault, Michel. 1984. Different Spaces. In *Essential Works of Foucault, 1954–1984*. Volume 2: *Aesthetics, Epistemology, Methodology*. 1988. J. D. Faubion, ed. New York: The New Press.

Foucault, Michel. 2008/1967. Of Other Spaces. In *Heterotopia and the City: Public Space in a Postcivil Society*. M. Dehaene and L. De Cauter, eds. Pp. 13–30. London and New York: Routledge.

Fraser, Nancy. 1998. From Redistribution to Recognition? Dilemmas of Justice in a Post–Socialist Age. In *Theorizing Multiculturalism: A Guide to the Current Debate*. C. Willett, ed. Pp. 21–49. Oxford: Blackwell.

Geertz, Clifford. 1973. Thick Description. In *The Interpretation of Cultures*. Pp. 3–32. New York: Basic Books.

Gellner, Ernest. 1981. Nationalism. *Theory and Society* 10(6): 753–776.

Gellner, Ernest. 1983. *Nations and Nationalism*. Oxford: Blackwell.

Gelvin, James. 2009. Arab Nationalism: Has a New Framework Emerged? *International Journal of Middle East Studies* 41(1): 10–12.

Gilroy, Paul. 2005. Between Camps. In *Nations and Nationalism: A Reader*. P. Spencer and H. Wollman, eds. Pp. 149–162. New Brunswick, NJ: Rutgers University Press.

Gopin, Marc. 2002. *Holy War, Holy Peace: How Religion Can Bring Peace to the Middle East*. New York: Oxford University Press.

Gopin, Marc. 2004. The Context of Middle Eastern Conflict. http://law. hamline.edu/files/Judaism%20and%20Peacebuilding.pdf.

Gordon, Neve. 2008. *Israel's Occupation*. Berkeley and Los Angeles: University of California Press.

Gorenberg, Gershom. 2000. *The End of Days: Fundamentalism and the Struggle for the Temple Mount*. New York: The Free Press.

Gourevitch, Phillip. 2010. Alms Dealers: Can You Provide Humanitarian Aid Without Facilitating Conflicts? *The New Yorker*, October 11, pp. 102–109.

Graeber, David. 2002. The New Anarchists. *New Left Review* 13:61–73.

Graeber, David. 2004. *Fragments of an Anarchist Anthropology*. Chicago: Prickly Paradigm Press.

Gramsci, Antonio. 1971. *Selections from the Prison Notebooks of Antonio Gramsci*. Q. Hoare and G. N. Smith, eds. New York: International Publishers.

Grewal, Inderpal, and Caren Kaplan. 1994. *Scattered Hegemonies: Postmodernity and Transnational Feminist Practices*. Minneapolis and London: University of Minnesota Press.

Guha, Ranajit. 1994/1983. The Prose of Counter-Insurgency. In *Culture/Power/History: A Reader in Contemporary Social Theory*. N. B. Dirks, G. Eley, and S. B. Ortner, eds. Pp. 336–371. Princeton, NJ: Princeton University Press.

Halevi, Ilan. 1987. *A History of the Jews: Ancient and Modern*. London: Zed.

Hanafi, Sari. 2012. Explaining Spacio-cide in the Palestinian Territory: Colonization, Separation, and the State of Exception. *Current Sociology* 61(2): 1–16.

Handelman, Don 2004. *Nationalism and the Israeli State: Bureaucratic Logic in Public Events*. Oxford and New York: Berg.

Hansen, Thoman Blom, and Finn Stepputat. 2006. Sovereignty Revisited. *Annual Review of Anthropology* 35:295–315.

Harding, Susan. 1991. Representing Fundamentalism: The Problem of the Repugnant Cultural Other. *Social Research* 58(2): 373–393.

Harel, Assaf. 2011. Highway 60 Visited: Part 1. *Anthropology Now*, March 4, 2011 (http://anthronow.com/online-articles/highway-60-visited).

Harel, Assaf. 2012. The People! Demand! Social Justice! About Social Change in Israel and Palestine. *Journal of Contemporary Anthropology* 3(1): 80–85.

Harel, Assaf. (Forthcoming). The Eternal Nation Does Not Fear a Long Road: Time among Jewish Settlers. PhD diss., Rutgers University.

Hasan, Manar. 1993. Growing Up Female and Palestinian in Israel. In *Calling the Equality Bluff: Women in Israel*. B. Swirsky and M. Safir, eds. New York: Teachers College Press.

Hawley, Charles. 2012. European Right Wing Stirs up Middle East Peace Process. *Spiegel Online*, July 7, 2012.

Helman, Sara. 2002. Monologic Results of Dialogue: Jewish-Palestinian Encounter Groups as Sites of Essentialization. *Identities: Global Studies in Culture and Power* 9:327–354.

Hinsley, F. H. 1986/1966. *Sovereignty*. Cambridge: Cambridge University Press.

Hobsbawm, Eric. 1997. *On History*. New York: The New Press.

Kanaaneh, Rhoda Ann, and Isis Nussair. 2010. *Displaced at Home: Ethnicity and Gender Among Palestinians in Israel*. Albany: State University of New York Press.

Kant, Immanuel. 1903/1795. *Perpetual Peace: A Philosophical Essay*. London: George Allen and Unwin Ltd.

Kapferer, Bruce. 2004. State, Sovereignty, War and Civil Violence. *Social Analysis* 48(1): 64–73.

Kaplan, Caren. 1994. The Politics of Location as Transnational Feminist Practice. In *Scattered Hegemonies: Postmodernity and Transnational Feminist Practices*. I. Grewal and C. Kaplan, eds. Pp. 137–152. Minneapolis: University of Minnesota Press.

Kelman, Herbert C. 2004. Reconciliation as Identity Change: A Social-Psychological Perspective. In *From Conflict Resolution to Reconciliation*. Y. Bar-Simon-Tov, ed. Pp. 111–124. Oxford: Oxford University Press.

Khalidi, Rashid. 1997. *Palestinian Identity: The Construction of Modern Consciousness*. New York: Columbia University Press.

Khalidi, Walid. 1991. The Palestine Problem: An Overview. *Journal of Palestine Studies* 21(1): 5–16.

Khazzoom, Aziza. 2005. Did the Israeli State Engineer Segregation? On the Placement of Jewish Immigrants in Development Towns in the 1950s. *Social Forces* 84(1): 115–134.

Kipling, Rudyard. 1995/1897. *The Jungle Book*. New York: William Morrow and Company.

Lavie, Smadar. 1990. *The Poetics of Military Occupation: Mzeina Allegories of Bedouin Identity Under Israeli and Egyptian Rule*. Berkeley: University of California Press.

Lazaroff, Tovah. 2012. A Sheikh, Settlers and MPs Meet in Hebron Hills Tent. *The Jerusalem Post*, July 7, 2012.

Le Guin, Ursula. 1980. It Was a Dark and Stormy Night; or, Why Are We Huddling About the Campfire. In *On Narrative*. W. J. T. Mitchell, ed. Pp. 187–196. Chicago and London: University of Chicago Press.

Lentin, Ronit. 2008. *Thinking Palestine*. London and New York: Zed Books.

Little, David, and R. Scott Appleby. 2004. A Moment of Opportunity? The Promise of Religion in Peacebuilding. In *Religion and Peacebuilding*.

H. Coward and G. S. Smith, eds. Pp. 1–26. Albany: State University of New York Press.

Loomba, Ania. 2005. *Colonialism/Postcolonialism*. London and New York: Routledge.

Low, Setha. 2008. The Gated Community as Heterotopia. In *Heterotopia and the City: Public Space in a Postcivil Society*. M. Dehaene and L. De Cauter, eds. Pp. 153–163. London and New York: Routledge.

Lowenthal, David. 1985. *The Past Is a Foreign Country*. New York: Cambridge University Press.

Luhrmann, Tanya. 2013. Conjuring Up Our Own Gods. *New York Times*, October 14, 2013.

Lustick, Ian. 1988. *For the Land and the Lord: Jewish Fundamentalism in Israel*. New York: Council on Foreign Relations.

Lustick, Ian. 1994. Preface to the 1994 Edition. In *For the Land and the Lord: Jewish Fundamentalism in Israel*. New York: Council on Foreign Relations Books.

Lybarger, Loren D. 2007. *Identity and Religion in Palestine: The Struggle Between Islamism and Secularism in the Occupied Territories*. Princeton, NJ: Princeton University Press.

Mahmood, S. 2005. *Politics of Piety: The Islamic Revival and the Feminist Subject*. Princeton, NJ and Oxford: Princeton University Press.

Marx, Karl. 1978/1852. The Eighteenth Brumaire of Louis Bonaparte. In *The Marx-Engels Reader*. R. C. Tucker, ed. Pp. 594–617. New York: W.W. Norton and Company.

Mehta, Uday. 1990. Liberal Strategies of Exclusion. *Politics and Society* 18:427–454.

Memmi, Albert. 1967. *The Colonizer and the Colonized*. Boston: Beacon Press.

Moghadam, Valentine M. 2013. *Globalization and Social Movements: Islamism, Feminism, and the Global Justice Movement*. Lanham, MD: Rowman and Littlefield.

Mullin, Corinna. 2010. Islamist Challenges to the Liberal Peace Discourse: The Case of Hamas and the Israel–Palestine Peace Process. *Millennium—Journal of International Studies* 39(2): 525–546.

Nader, Laura. 2001. Crime as a Category. *The Windsor Yearbook of Access to Justice* 19:326–340.

Nader, Laura. 2003. Departures from Violence: Love Is Not Enough. *Public Culture* 15(1): 195–197.

Nandy, Ashis. 1983. *The Intimate Enemy: Loss and Recovery of Self Under Colonialism*. Delhi: Oxford University Press.

Nandy, Ashis. 1995. History's Forgotten Doubles. *History and Theory* 34(2): 44–66.

Nash, Jennifer C. 2008. Re-Thinking Intersectionality. *Feminist Review* 89:1–15.

Nathansohn, Regev. 2010. Imagining Interventions: Coexistence from Below and the Ethnographic Project. *Collaborative Anthropologies* 3:93–101.

Neslen, Arthur. 2011. *In Your Eyes a Sandstorm: Ways of Being Palestinian*. Berkeley: University of California Press.

Newman, Edward, Roland Paris, and Oliver Richmond. 2009. Introduction. In *New Perspectives on Liberal Peacebuilding*. E. Newman, R. Paris, and O. Richmond, eds. Pp. 3–25. New York: United Nations University Press.

Nimni, Ephraim. 2003. *The Challenge of Post-Zionism: Alternatives to Israeli Fundamentalist Politics*. London: Zed.

Nordstrom, Carolyn. 2000. Shadows and Sovereigns. *Theory, Culture & Society* 17(4): 35–54.

Nordstrom, Carolyn, and Antonius C. G. M. Robben. 1995. *Fieldwork Under Fire: Contemporary Studies of Violence and Survival*. Berkeley: University of California Press.

Nusseibeh, Sari. 2011. *What Is a Palestinian State Worth?* Cambridge, MA and London: Harvard University Press.

Ochs, Juliana. 2011. *Security and Suspicion: An Ethnography of Everyday Life in Israel*. Philadelphia: University of Pennsylvania Press.

Omer, Atalia. 2013. *When Peace Is Not Enough: How the Israeli Peace Camp Thinks About Religion, Nationalism, and Justice*. Chicago: University of Chicago Press.

Ong, Aihwa. 1993. On the Edge of Empires: Flexible Citizenship Among Chinese in Diaspora. *Positions* 11(3): 745–778.

Ong, Aihwa. 2006. *Neoliberalism as Exception: Mutations in Citizenship and Sovereignty*. Durham, NC and London: Duke University Press.

Pappe, Ilan. 2000. The Construction of a Bridging Narrative in the Israeli-Palestinian Conflict. Association for Israel Studies 16th Annual Meetings: Multiple Perspectives on Israel, Tel Aviv University.

Paris, Roland. 2010. Saving Liberal Peacebuilding. *Review of International Studies* 36:337–365.

Parnell, Phillip C., and Stephanie C. Kane. 2003. *Crime's Power: Anthropologists and the Ethnography of Crime*. New York: Palgrave Macmillan.

PeaceNow. 2012. Settlement Watch. http://peacenow.org.il/eng/content/reports.

Pedahzur, Ami, and Arie Perlinger. 2011. *Jewish Terrorism in Israel*. New York: Columbia University Press.

Podeh, Elie. 2000. The Portrayal of the Arab-Israeli Conflict in History Textbooks (1948–2000). *History and Memory* 12(1): 65–100.

Poletta, Francesca. 2003. *It Was Like a Fever: Storytelling in Protest and Politics*. Chicago: University of Chicago Press.

Popper, Karl R. 1959. Prediction and Prophecy in the Social Sciences. In *Theories of History*. P. Gardiner, ed. Pp. 276–285. New York: The Free Press.

Povinelli, Elizabeth. 2002. *The Cunning of Recognition: Indigenous Alterities and the Making of Australian Multiculturalism*. Durham, NC and London: Duke University Press.

Povinelli, Elizabeth. 2012. The Will to Be Otherwise/The Effort of Endurance. *South Atlantic Quarterly* 111(3): 453–475.

Rabinowitz, Dan. 2000. Postnational Palestine and Israel? Globalization, Diaspora, Transnationalism, and the Israeli-Palestinian Conflict. *Critical Inquiry* 26(4): 757–772.

Rabkin, Yakov M. 2006. *A Threat from Within: A Century of Jewish Opposition to Zionism*. F. A. Reed, transl. London: Zed.

Ram, Uri. 1995. Zionist Historiography and the Invention of Modern Jewish Nationhood: The Case of Ben Zion Dinur. *History and Memory* 7(1):91–124.

Rawls, John. 1971. *A Theory of Justice*. Cambridge, MA: Belknap Press of Harvard University Press.

Raz-Krakotzkin, Amnon. 2001. History Textbooks and the Limits of Israeli Consciousness. *Journal of Israeli History* 20(2/3): 155–172.

Renan, Ernest. 1990/1882. What Is a Nation? In *Nation and Narration*. H. Bhabha, ed. Pp. 8–22. London: Routledge.

Ricouer, Paul. 1980. Narrative Time. In *On Narrative*. W. J. T. Mitchell, ed. Pp. 165–186. Chicago and London: University of Chicago Press.

Ross, Dennis. 2004. *The Missing Peace: The Inside Story of the Fight for Middle East Peace*. New York: Farrar, Straus and Giroux.

Rudoren, Jodi. 2012. Barefoot in a Tent, Neighbors Trading Vows of Mideast Peace. *New York Times*, July 6.

Sa'ar, Amalia. 2011. Review of Kanaaneh and Nusair, eds., Displaced at Home: Ethnicity and Gender among Palestinians in Israel. *Review of Middle East Studies* 45(1): 113–115.

Said, Edward. 1978. *Orientalism*. New York: Random House.

Said, Edward. 1992/1979. *The Question of Palestine*. New York: Vintage Books.

Said, Edward. 1986. The Burdens of Interpretation and the Question of Palestine. *Journal of Palestine Studies* 16(1): 29–37.

Sassen, Saskia. 1996. *Losing Control? Sovereignty in an Age of Globalization*. New York: Columbia University Press.

Saunders, Harold H. 1999. *A Public Peace Process: Sustained Dialogue to Transform Racial and Ethnic Conflicts*. New York: St. Martins Press.

Schmitt, Carl. 1985/1922. *Political Theology: Four Chapters on the Concept of Sovereignty*. Chicago: University of Chicago Press.

Scott, David. 2004. *Conscripts of Modernity: The Tragedy of Colonial Enlightenment*. Durham, NC and London: Duke University Press.

Scott, David, and Charles Hirschkind, eds. 2006. *Powers of the Secular Modern: Talal Asad and His Interlocutors*. Stanford, CA: Stanford University Press.

Scott, James. 1985. *Weapons of the Weak: Everyday Forms of Peasant Resistance*. New Haven and London: Yale University Press.

Scott, James C. 2009. *The Art of Not Being Governed: An Anarchist History of Upland Southeast Asia*. New Haven and London: Yale University Press.

Scott, James C. 2012. *Two Cheers for Anarchism: Six Easy Pieces on Autonomy, Dignity, and Meaningful Work and Play*. Princeton and Oxford: Princeton University Press.

Shafir, Gershon. 1989. *Land, Labor and the Origins of the Israeli-Palestinian Conflict, 1882–1914*. New York: Cambridge University Press.

Shelef, Nadav G. 2010. *Evolving Nationalism: Homeland, Identity, and Religion in Israel, 1925–2005*. Ithaca and London: Cornell University Press.

Shenhav, Yehouda. 2003. *The Arab Jews: Nationalism, Religion, Ethnicity*. Tel Aiv: Am Oved.

Shenhav, Yehouda. 2010. *In the Trap of the Green Line [bemalkodet hakav hayarok]: A Jewish Political Essay*. Tel Aviv: Am Oved. (Hebrew)

Shenhav, Yehouda. 2012. *Beyond the Two-State Solution: A Jewish Political Essay*. Cambridge: Polity Press.

Shohat, Ella. 1988. Sephardim in Israel: Zionism from the Standpoint of its Jewish Victims. *Social Text* 19(20): 1–35.

Silberstein, Laurence J. 1993. *Jewish Fundamentalism in Comparative Perspective: Religion, Ideology, and the Crisis of Modernity*. New Perspectives on Jewish Studies. New York and London: New York University Press.

Sivan, Emmanuel. 1995. The Enclave Culture. In *Fundamentalisms Comprehended*. M. E. Marty and R. S. Appleby, eds. Pp. 11–68. Chicago and London: University of Chicago Press.

Smith, Jackie. 2008. *Social Movements for Global Democracy*. Baltimore, MD: Johns Hopkins University Press.

Spivak, Gayatri. 1988. Can the Subaltern Speak? In *Marxism and the Interpretation of Culture*. C. Nelson and L. Grossberg, eds. Pp. 271–313. Basingstoke: Macmillan Education.

Sprinzak, Ehud. 1999. *Brother Against Brother: Violence and Extremism in Israeli Politics from Altalena to the Rabin Assassination*. New York: Free Press.

Starrett, Gregory. 2003. Violence and the Rhetoric of Images. *Cultural Anthropology* 18(3): 398–428.

Stein, Rebecca. 2008. *Itineraries in Conflict: Israelis, Palestinians, and the Political Lives of Tourism*. Durham, NC: Duke University Press.

Taylor, Charles. 1994. The Politics of Recognition. In *Multiculturalism: Examining the Politics of Recognition*. A. Gutman, ed. Pp. 25–74. Princeton, NJ: Princeton University Press.

Taylor, Charles. 2002. Modern Social Imaginaries. *Public Culture* 14(1): 91–124.

Taylor, Charles. 2007. *A Secular Age*. Cambridge, MA and London: Belknap Press of Harvard University Press.

Taylor, Charles. 2010. Afterword: Apologia pro Libro suo. In *Varieties of Secularism in a Secular Age*. M. Warner, J. VanAntwerpen, and C. Calhoun, eds. Pp. 300–324. Cambridge, MA and London: Harvard University Press.

Telhami, Shibley. 2004. Between Faith and Ethics. In *Liberty and Power: A Dialogue on Religion and U.S. Foreign Policy in an Unjust World*. Pp. 71–94. Washington, DC: Brookings Institute Press.

Tilly, Charles. 1985. War Making and State Making as Organized Crime. In *Bringing the State Back*. D. R. Peter Evans and Theda Skocpol, eds. Pp. 169–191. Cambridge: Cambridge University Press.

van der Veer, Peter. 2006. Pim Fortuyn, Theo van Gogh, and the Politics of Tolerance in the Netherlands. In *Political Theologies: Public Religions in a Post-Secular World*. H. de Vries and L. E. Sullivan, eds. Pp. 527–538. New York: Fordham University Press.

Warschawski, Michel. 2005. *On the Border*. L. Laub, transl. Cambridge, MA: South End Press.

Watzman, Haim. 2011. The Mideast Maverick: Sari Nusseibeh Proposes an Interim Route to Peace in the Middle East. In *The Chronicle of Higher Education* [online].

Weber, Eugen. 1976. *Peasants into Frenchmen: The Modernization of Rural France, 1870–1914*. Stanford: Stanford University Press.

Weinreich, Max. 1980. *History of the Yiddish Language*. S. Noble, transl. Chicago and London: University of Chicago Press.

White, Hayden. 1980. The Value of Narrativity. *Critical Inquiry* 7(1): 5–27. Reprinted 1980 as The Value of Narrativity in the Representation of Reality. In *On Narrative*. W. J. T. Mitchell, ed. Pp. 1–24. Chicago and London: University of Chicago Press. (Citations refer to the *Critical Inquiry* edition.)

White, Hayden. 1987. *The Content of the Form: Narrative Discourse and Historical Representation*. Baltimore, MD: Johns Hopkins University Press.

Whitelam, Keith W. 1996. *The Invention of Ancient Israel: The Silencing of Palestinian History*. London: Routledge.

Wilder, David. 2011. A 'Shekhi' Chaye Sarah in Hebron. In *Blessings from Hebron*: Arutz 7, November 22.

Wolfe, Patrick. 1999. *Settler Colonialism and the Transformation of Anthropology: The Politics and Poetics of an Ethnographic Event*. London: Cassell.

Wolfe, Patrick. 2006. Settler Colonialism and the Elimination of the Native. *Journal of Genocide Research* 8(4): 387–409.

Yiftachel, Oren. 2006. *Ethnocracy: Land and Identity Politics in Israel and Palestine*. Philadelphia: University of Pennsylvania Press.

Zertal, Idit, and Akiva Eldar. 2007. *Lords of the Land: The War for Israel's Settlement in the Occupied Territories, 1967–2007*. New York: Nation Books.

Zerubavel, Yael. 1995. *Recovered Roots: Collective Memory and the Making of Israeli National Tradition*. Chicago and London: University of Chicago Press.

INDEX

Note: Locators followed by 'n' refer to notes.